Research on the Couch

Is psychoanalysis knowledge? Is psychoanalysis a science, or is it hermeneutics? Can clinical material be considered research data?

Psychoanalysis is ambiguous about whether it is about meaning or about truth, and the relations between these two compelling experiences. Psycho-analysts often think of their work as closer to the humanities than to medical and natural science. The wider the gap between science and psychoanalysis appears, the more psychoanalysts feel pulled to something that respects subjectivity, the humanity of their patients themselves, and so move away from the procedures of natural science.

Research on the Couch is a relevant and timely contribution to the current debate about both the nature and validity of psychoanalysis and its body of knowledge. Freud always regarded his clinical material as his research data. In this book, R.D. Hinshelwood aims to explore that view and defend Freud's claim while acknowledging the criticisms of single-case studies and the inevitable problems for research into human subjectivity and personal experience. To this end the book reviews Freud's own methods of dissemin-ating his discoveries, discusses the problem of evaluating different claims to psychoanalytic knowledge, and presents a cogent logical model for testing psychoanalytic theories clinically.

This book develops a model for the generation and justification of psychoanalytic knowledge, a 'parascience' just as rigorous as natural science, and one that addresses the subjectivity of meaning. *Research on the Couch* will be of interest to psychoanalysts of all schools, academics, clinicians, students and those keen to further their knowledge of psychoanalytic studies.

R.D. Hinshelwood is Professor in the Centre for Psychoanalytic Studies, University of Essex. He is a Fellow of the British Psychoanalytical Society, and a Fellow of the Royal College of Psychiatrists. He has authored numerous books and articles on Kleinian psychoanalysis. *Observing Organisations* (2000) was edited with Wilhelm Skogstad and is among a number of texts he has written on psychoanalytic methodologies.

The New Library of Psychoanalysis
General Editor: Alessandra Lemma

The New Library of Psychoanalysis was launched in 1987 in association with the Institute of Psychoanalysis, London. It took over from the International Psychoanalytical Library, which published many of the early translations of the works of Freud and the writings of most of the leading British and Continental psychoanalysts.

The purpose of the New Library of Psychoanalysis is to facilitate a greater and more widespread appreciation of psychoanalysis, and to provide a forum for increasing mutual understanding between psychoanalysts and those working in other disciplines such as the social sciences, medicine, philosophy, history, linguistics, literature and the arts. It aims to represent different trends both in British psychoanalysis and in psychoanalysis generally. The New Library of Psychoanalysis is well placed to make available to the English-speaking world psychoanalytic writings from other European countries and to increase the interchange of ideas between British and American psycho-analysts. Through the Teaching series, the New Library of Psychoanalysis now also publishes books that provide comprehensive, yet accessible, overviews of selected subject areas aimed at those studying psychoanalysis and related fields such as the social sciences, philosophy, literature and the arts.

The Institute, together with the British Psychoanalytical Society, runs a low-fee psychoanalytic clinic, organises lectures and scientific events concerned with psychoanalysis and publishes the *International Journal of Psychoanalysis*. It also runs a training course in psychoanalysis that leads to membership of the International Psychoanalytical Association – the body which preserves internationally agreed standards of training, of professional entry, and of professional ethics and practice for psychoanalysis as initiated and developed by Sigmund Freud. Distinguished members of the Institute have included Michael Balint, Wilfred Bion, Ronald Fairbairn, Anna Freud, Ernest Jones, Melanie Klein, John Rickman and Donald Winnicott.

Previous general editors have included David Tuckett, who played a very active role in the establishment of the New Library. He was followed as general editor by Elizabeth Bott Spillius, who was in turn followed by Susan Budd and then by Dana Birksted-Breen.

Current members of the Advisory Board include Liz Allison, Giovanna di Ceglie, Rosemary Davies and Richard Rusbridger.

Previous members of the Advisory Board include Christopher Bollas, Ronald Britton, Catalina Bronstein, Donald Campbell, Sara Flanders, Stephen Grosz, John Keene, Eglé Laufer, Alessandra Lemma, Juliet Mitchell, Michael Parsons, Rosine Jozef Perelberg, Mary Target and David Taylor.

Research on the Couch

Single-case studies, subjectivity
and psychoanalytic knowledge

R.D. Hinshelwood

Routledge
Taylor & Francis Group

LONDON AND NEW YORK

First published 2013
by Routledge
27 Church Road, Hove, East Sussex BN3 2FA

Simultaneously published in the USA and Canada
by Routledge
711 Third Avenue, New York, NY 10017

Routledge is an imprint of the Taylor & Francis Group, an informa business

British Library Cataloguing in Publication Data
A catalogue record for this book is available from the British Library

Library of Congress Cataloging in Publication Data
Hinshelwood, R.D.
  Research on the couch: single case studies, subjectivity, and
  psychoanalytic knowledge/authored by R.D. Hinshelwood. – 1st ed.
  p. cm.
  Includes bibliographical references.
  1. Psychoanalysis – Research.   I. Title.
  RC504.H557 2013
  616.89'17 – dc23
  2012035924

ISBN: 978-0-415-62519-7 (hbk)
ISBN: 978-0-415-62520-3 (pbk)
ISBN: 978-0-203-37455-9 (ebk)

Typeset in Garamond
by Florence Production Ltd, Stoodleigh, Devon

Printed and bound in Great Britain by
TJ International Ltd, Padstow, Cornwall

Contents

Foreword

Charles M.T. Hanly
President of the International Psychoanalytic Association

Contemporary psychoanalysis has two problems. The first is the co-existence of diverse theories, at least some of which appear to be inconsistent with each other, without any reliable means of determining which is the most probable. Exacerbating this situation has been the tendency toward the formation of schools that tend to substitute controversy for enquiry. It is held, by some, that the clinical observations of analysts are conditioned by the theories to which they adhere, so that they can only make observations that confirm their preferred ideas. The second problem confronting psychoanalysis has been uncertainty about the reliability of clinical observations as such, that is, not uncertainty about a particular observational claim (for some definite reason(s)), but about any and every clinical observation. Post-modern epistemological subjectivist claims that clinical experience is irreducibly subjective have nourished this uncertainty. If, in the analyst's experience of the patient, the analyst is unable to differentiate what is owing to the patient from what is owing to the analyst (as though normal subject–object differentiation was suspended (or rendered useless) by the clinical situation), then there can be no such thing as a clinical fact in psychoanalysis. If there are no reliable observations of clinical facts revealing the psychic reality of patients, then there is no basis for a trustworthy enquiry into which of the two inconsistent theories is more probable. Clinical theory, no less than metapsychology, is left in the lurch, floating beyond confirmation or falsification.

Research on the Couch constructively addresses these problems in psycho-analysis today by elaborating a methodology that aims to enable clinicians to test psychoanalytic knowledge claims. In this respect, Hinshelwood's *Research on the Couch* is a return to Freud, but not to Freud's texts or his theories; it is a return to Freud's reliance on clinical psychoanalytic observation in the development and construction of psychoanalytic theory. But perhaps it would be more accurate to say that, in this respect, Hinshelwood, as a Kleinian analyst, is not so much returning to Freud as he is seeking to improve on Freud in an important respect. Freud's use of inductive reasoning depended largely on Mill's method of agreement, which states that if two or more occurrences of a phenomena have only one condition in common, then the condition in which they all agree is the cause (or effect) of the phenomenon under consideration. A limitation of this inductive method is symbolized by the black swan pictured on the cover. Also, the method of agreement is not able to discriminate among two (or more) conditions that accompany the phenomenon under investigation. Nor does the method of agreement prove causality, although there are circumstances under which it can establish a reasonable probability. Hinshelwood's method seeks to prove causality by clarifying and articulating, in Hume's words, an "experimental method of reasoning" for psychoanalysis.

Hinshelwood's method of clinical enquiry aims to be theory neutral. This is a crucial feature because of the diversity, and sometimes inconsistency, of current theories. Any methodology that tests theories clinically cannot depend on any particular one of them to guide its enquiries. Such a method could not establish a corrective against being able to find only self-confirming evidence. Hinshelwood's method offers a way of finding clinical evidence that is inconsistent with a theory. Built into it is the potential for coming upon negative instances. Thus, Hinshelwood's method provides the basis for a "willing suspension of belief" in order to test whether or not an idea for an interpretation enables us to uncover a clinical fact or is merely being used to confirm a preferred, preconceived notion; as Hinshelwood states it, "it is that independence of the test from the theoretical allegiances of the tester" that we seek. The method of clinical enquiry proposed in this book is a method for proponents of any and all schools.

At the heart of Hinshelwood's method, there is an integration of two otherwise frequently antagonistic views in current thinking about the nature of psychoanalytic knowledge. One view is that psychoanalysis is an empirical natural science seeking causal explanations of the structure and dynamics of psychic life. The other view sees psychoanalysis as a hermeneutical science that interprets the meaning of the formative experiences in a life. The profound links, even identities, between interpretations, meaning and causality at work in the individual life do seem to be evident, both philosophically and psychoanalytically. In interpreting the meaning of parapraxes, dreams, neurotic symptoms, associations and transferences, their meanings are found in the wishes they seek to satisfy, in the repressed memories the wishes invest, and in the anxieties the wishes arouse. The meanings of these clinical phenomena are found in the motives of desire and defence that cause them. Hinshelwood has integrated this identity of meaning and causality in the methodology he has developed for psychoanalytic clinical enquiry.

Whatever reservations, criticisms or modifications of Hinshelwood's clinical methodology *Research on the Couch* may stimulate, the fundamental thrust of his work is of great significance for psychoanalysis. Clinical psychoanalysis has been, and remains, the primary source and testing ground of psychoanalytic knowledge. The reliability of clinical observation has long been questioned from without by some prominent philosophers of science and, more recently, from within by analyst advocates of epistemological subjectivism and theoretical relativism. One promising response to these criticisms has been the development of methodologies for group enquiries, which include analysts of differing theoretical persuasions, directed at studying clinical reports of analytic process. The most important aim of these methodologies has been to enhance the reliability of clinical observations. This search for reliable clinical evidence has led to the formation of various Working Parties and IPA Work Groups, in which analysts explore the possibility of consensus about clinical facts independently of theoretical investments. Hinshelwood's contribution to this undertaking is of great importance because it seeks to provide a methodology that can heighten the reliability of the clinical observations of individual practitioners in their daily clinical work by more objectively testing the interpretations they make and the theories they hold. This openness to the evidence of what happens in the clinical process when interpretations are made should also result in better clinical results. An important element of this openness is the inclusion in Hinshelwood's method of a search for negative instances, as well as for confirmations. It is an analytic attitude that allows the unexpected to be and encourages the acceptance and correction of error with equanimity. The direction of Hinshelwood's proposals in *Research on the Couch* is a return to Freud that promises to lead psychoanalysis toward a stronger future.

Foreword

Marianne Leuzinger-Bohleber
Professor, Sigmund Freud Institut, Frankfurt

R.D. Hinshelwood devotes his book to central topics of contemporary psychoanalysis: What kind of a science is psychoanalysis really? What did Freud mean when he defined psychoanalysis as a special "science of the unconscious"?

We know that as a young man, Freud was very interested in philosophy and the humanities before turning with remarkable passion to the natural sciences. In the laboratory of Ernst Brücke's Institute of Physiology, he became acquainted with a strictly positivistic understanding of science that attracted him throughout his entire life. As we know, Freud later, however, turned away from the neurology of his time since he recognized the methodological limitations of research of the psyche in this discipline. He defined his *Interpretation of Dreams*, the founding work of psychoanalysis, as "pure psychology". Moreover, he understood himself as a physician whose observations were as exact as a natural scientist. His wish for a precise and "empirical" examination of his hypotheses and theories protected Freud, as Joel Whitebook (2010) notes, from his predilection for wild speculation. Thus, Freud as a "philosophical physician" could establish a new "science of the unconscious". Hinshelwood strongly agrees with Whitebook: making a plea to rediscover a basic, methodologically-improved, scientific stance for the clinician, in order first to counteract one of the main dangers today: a drift from the theoretical plurality of psychoanalysis into an attitude of "anything goes"; and, second, to regain the self-confidence of the psychoanalyst as a "clinical researcher."

In his understanding of psychoanalysis, Freud created a unique relationship between the natural sciences and the humanities. His conceptualization of psychosexuality, for instance, was a new approach to considering the dialectics between biology and psychology, the mind and the body. At the same time, Freud's thinking was always stimulated by literature and art, and inspired by the rich knowledge on the *conditio humana*, the basic conflicts of human beings rooted in their infantile phantasies and the first object relations, which become lifelong unconscious sources of thoughts, feelings and behavior.

It has been one of Freud's great achievements that he embraced a wide range of psychoanalytic research and defended its independence as a specific scientific discipline. He resisted the danger of integrating psychoanalysis either into the world of medicine, the humanities, or the cultural sciences. Hinshelwood, expert in the history and philosophy of science, agrees with my statement made in my research lecture given at the IPA centenary celebration in London, 2010, that the conflicting dangers of being either "swallowed up" by a certain academic discipline, or of being marginalized as a sect or a "secret religiously structured society", can be observed again and again in the history of psychoanalysis.

These dangers appear prominently in the struggle to understand the "Wissenschaft" ("science") of psychoanalysis. A painful process of de-idealization was indispensible in order to relinquish a "negative narcissism", in which psychoanalysis had blossomed in the 60s and 70s as unique and incomparable, a "science between the sciences", between nomothetical sciences and hermeneutics. Psychoanalysts have since had to mourn the loss of their exclusive position in the scientific world, and find their rather unspectacular place as a psychoanalytic research discipline in the diverse world of contemporary sciences. The differentiation between the natural sciences and the humanities given by Dilthey at the beginning of the 20th century has proven to be far too simple (see Hampe, 2003).

As Hermann von Helmholtz pointed out one hundred years ago, each single researcher is increasingly forced to dedicate himself to more and more *specific* methods with more and more *narrowly defined* questions. For this reason, modern scientists, and – as Hinshelwood elaborates – psychoanalysts as well, are, for the most part, highly specialized experts with a highly specialized knowledge concerning their own discipline and only a limited knowledge about adjacent disciplines. They are, therefore, dependent upon networking at an international, intergenerational and interdisciplinary level.

In connection with this process of differentiation, also the criteria of "science" and "scientific truth" in the respective disciplines have changed and is becoming more specific, not only in the natural sciences but also in the humanities. The concept of a *unified* science, of "science", relying on the experimental design and on the double-blind experiment in classical physics, has proven to be a myth: we live out in these times of the "plurality of science".

Influenced by these societal and scientific developments, psychoanalysis has lost its claim to a meta-position from which to interpret not only clinical but also cultural phenomena. It has thereby lost part of its charisma. If psychoanalysts are capable of mourning this loss of exclusivity, they might find a more modest but adequate acceptance and interest as specific researchers of the unconscious in today's pluralistic world of sciences. As all other disciplines, *psychoanalysis has developed a differentiated, independent method of research for the examination of its specific object of research: of unconscious conflicts and phantasies in the clinical psychoanalytical situation.* It has, like other disciplines, its own criteria of quality and truth which it must represent with transparency and self-confidence in the scientific dialogue, so that, as any science, it may be criticized from outside. Psychoanalysts, thus, have to communicate the quality of their scientifically based, "true" knowledge of the unconscious determinants of individual and collective behavior in public and scientific discourse.

Hinshelwood's book can be seen as an inspiring, innovative attempt to describe the specificity of psychoanalysis, as "research on the couch" which must be characterized as a "science of subjectivity". He compares research within the psychoanalytic situation, with experimental research in a laboratory with similar ambitions, although a different methodology from natural science. He postulates that psychoanalytic theories can be compared and tested in a very rigorous way that allows one to determine the "truth" of a certain psychoanalytic interpretation or a specific meta-psychological position. Hinshelwood makes a plea in this context for single case studies, that he revaluates as scientific instruments:

> Though single case studies are the frequent rule in natural science, such as Eddington's observations of the magnetic pull on light during the eclipse of 1919, not to mention Columbus' geographical 'experiment', it can be just as valid in psychoanalytic research. However, the definitive nature of a single case depends in psychoanalysis on a carefully thought out design just as in science.
>
> (p.179)

Hinshelwood presents a logical model for testing psychoanalytic concept and theories by clinical observations and illustrates his procedure by examples taken from psychoanalytic publications, Freud himself (the Ratman) and from his own clinical material taken from some of his psychoanalyses. He is surprised that we find it not so difficult to put clinical material into a research format *after* its publication. This suggests a usable model, provided certain conditions are met, making predictions, and generating precise research data.

This enquiry into using clinical material for research culminated in a mould, a protocol, comparable to the logical model of natural science, where the logic ensures a degree of certainty which is transparent enough to be critiqued by others. The point of the protocol is to keep the intuitive inspiration, of analyst and patient, focused into one area of the work, whilst giving space for logical testing of that essentially human intuition. Clinical material can surprisingly be sufficiently transparent to other researchers, not present in the setting, despite the usual assumption that the privacy of the psychoanalytic consulting room can be as transparent as the subsequent reporting of a laboratory experiment by a physical scientist. The conclusion is that some such logical model can go some way to reduce the anything-goes Babel state of psychoanalytic theory.

Thus Hinshelwood's book makes an important contribution toward understanding psychoanalysis as a "specific science of the unconscious". His suggested
method sees a combination of "causal-description" and "hermeneutic-
understanding" in clinical research which demands a high level of competence
in the perception and assessment of psychoanalytic processes, and therefore
may be only implemented by especially gifted and experienced psychoanalysts
and clinicians, such as R.D. Hinshelwood himself. The approach could thus
prove more helpful for testing their theories by psychoanalysts themselves.
That meets the dangers of fragmentation within the psychoanalytical
community, a goal it may more easily meet perhaps than to convince the non-
psychoanalytical, evidence-based world of medicine that psychoanalyis is
anchored – through transparency of its specific knowledge base, of its clinical
observation, and concepts – in the world of science by opening it to critiques
from the outside, by a "third party".

The book honours, in a fair and a lucid manner, the psychoanalytical
psychotherapy research dealing with outcomes, which is aimed at preserving
our role in health care systems in these times of evidence-based medicine.
Rightly, he has pointed out the danger of identifying oneself with the aggressor
in psychotherapy research, thus losing the genuine psychoanalytic view of its
research object. Currently, we are conducting, at the Sigmund Freud Institute,
Frankfurt, a large study of chronically depressed patients, comparing psychoanalytic treatment with behavior therapy. We are combining clinical and
extraclinical, qualitative and quantitative, subjective and objective dimensions
of therapeutic change (cf. LAC Study, www.sigmund-frund.institut.de). Such
research projects mediate between the retreat into a psychoanalytic ivory tower
on one hand, and the danger of submitting psychoanalysis to an alien and
inadequate scientific understanding of the unconscious on the other hand.
This field of conflict cannot be dispersed, but can only repeatedly be reflected
upon, using such questions as Hinshelwood's arising from his impressive
summary of the history of science and other epistemological considerations.
For this important reflecting process, this book is a source of stimulation and
inspiration. We would wish that experienced clinicians would implement
Hinshelwood's model, which like the clinical, psychoanalytic research of the
LAC Study, seeks to preserve psychoanalysis as a creative and serious science.

> My own wish is that the development of a model such as this one is a
> contribution to the future of psychoanalysis, however troubling the task
> of comparing our theories with each others' is going to be. And that in
> the long run, both psychoanalysts and the public might have more
> confidence in psychoanalysis being a body of coherent knowledge.
> (p. 202)

Therefore, I wish that this innovative and inspiring book may reach a broad
group of readers within and outside of the psychoanalytic community.

Preface

[This is an] attempt to introduce the experimental method of reasoning into moral subjects.

David Hume, 1748

In 1997 when I moved from the National Health Service to the University of Essex, where a young and innovative Centre for Psychoanalytic Studies was getting off the ground, I was faced with the question: what are psychoanalytic studies? I started up a yearly Master's course in critical methodology, with the central theme being the question: how do we know that psychoanalytic knowledge is valid? The course at the time was connected with the demoralising 'Freud-bashing' during the 1980s and 1990s. My course ran for a decade; I, at least, learned a lot. This book represents one result.

Clinicians cannot afford the 'luxury' of questioning their ideas. They need certainty in practice, not a Socratic scepticism. Like patients who want the certainty that treatment will rescue them, so clinicians need certainty that they have the wherewithal to achieve what is required of them. Conceding with pessimism that clinical material cannot produce valid theories, leaves us with no theory to speak of, because clinical work is the foundry that has wrought virtually all psychoanalytic knowledge.

Chiesa (2009) found that many psychoanalysts are reluctant to accept research as necessary evidence – especially outcome research. A kind of division of labour has grown up, resembling that between pure and applied science. Some do psychoanalytic research which generates knowledge and some apply it in a treatment 'technology'. There is general doubt now about Freud's dictum that 'It was impossible to treat a patient without learning something new; it was impossible to gain fresh insight without perceiving its beneficent results' (Freud 1926, p. 256). One reason for this collapse of confidence in the clinical process is because clinical research has fallen behind the kind of rigour now demanded of scientific conclusions. For instance, Charles Hanley, a recent president of the International Psychoanalytic Association, commented, 'psychoanalysis has a crippling epistemological defect uncharacteristic of other sciences in that its theories are not subject to verification but must rely upon the point of view and basic assumptions of groups of analysts' (Hanly 1983, p. 402). There is increasingly a myth that all the psychoanalytic knowledge we have accumulated and now use is merely a speculative belief. One concerned researcher has pointed to the need to 'take cognisance of the twin facts that there is more than one way to practise psychoanalysis and that it is necessary to avoid "anything goes"' (Tuckett 2005, p. 33). And those from outside look at the psychoanalytic 'movement' as now abandoning a rigorous research base, '[Critics] attempt to characterize and explain the rise of psychoanalysis as a successful social movement, and [are] concerned more with its institutional modes of self-justification and defence than with the validity of its theories as such' (Rustin 1987, p. 103).

It implies, for many people, psychoanalysts and others, that we must go outside the clinic to justify our beliefs in order to claim them as useful, effective knowledge.

In addition, as Hartmann has said, 'It is difficult to describe clearly, in logical terms, what is generally called "clinical research"' (Hartmann 1958, p. 131). Half a century later, there is still not a lot of logical clarity, hence the intentions of this book.

Psychoanalysts sometimes adopt a siege mentality against these problems and we have fallen behind. Criticism of psychoanalysis as non-scientific comes from a change in the character of science itself in the latter half of the twentieth century, and not to any sub-scientific hocus-pocus practised by Freud. Hilary Putnam, the American philosopher of science, argues, 'The method of science in fact changes constantly as the concept of science changes' (1981, p. 17). But our lagging behind leads to a loss of respect from outside the psychoanalytic world. While inside, without a proper consensus-generating method for evaluating theory, engaged debate with each other over what counts as knowledge has withered. As a result, we now have a variety of largely untested and sometimes mutually incompatible concepts, and this increases suspicion of psychoanalytic claims.

I share something of Freud's ambition to defend clinical psychoanalysis as research, although we might refrain from rigidly claiming it to be a science. It may in fact be something parallel to natural science – para-science, as it were. So on the whole, of Shevrin's (1995) trio – Dr Case, Dr Sample and Dr Link – I count myself with Dr Case. I will accept the following summing up: 'Internal validation has to deal with the problems of subjectivity of observations and circularity of reasoning, external validation with the problem of relevance' (Zachrisson and Zachrisson 2005, p. 1353). There is a categorical distinction between external and internal methods of validation. The problems of subjectivity and circularity are absolutely central to the present book.

The aim is to challenge the current pessimism about clinical research and clinical knowledge-generation. We will therefore explore a logical model for psychoanalytic research in order to investigate what validates psychoanalytic knowledge. It will need to discriminate between the values of different theoretical concepts. It is as cogent as I am able to make it, but I have no illusions that this account is flawless. If the model wobbles away from the necessary coherence, it needs repair or replacing. It no doubt bears all my own limitations, but I can hope that it will at least stimulate others with less, to do better. But the project should not be abandoned. Psychoanalysis needs such a method, as well as the patients who might be deprived of the benefit of psychoanalysis if we do not effectively defend the knowledge psychoanalysts have discovered.

There are many people who have indirectly contributed to enabling my thoughts to focus on the issues. Not least are those involved in my own training and formation as a psychoanalyst, who include Stanley Leigh, Isabel Menzies and Sydney Klein, as well as subsequent teachers including most prominently Esther Bick, Betty Joseph and Irma Brenman-Pick; and not least of course the many analytic patients who allowed me to practise upon their tender worlds. Colleagues who have stimulated my curiosity over the years in these profound questions are too numerous to do justice to, as also are students I have taught (though I want to mention Christine Franke whose Ph.D. thesis I make reference to, and also Linda Harvey who offered her photo for the cover of the book). I do need, however, to mention by name two immediate colleagues at Essex who have supported and challenged me: Karl Figlio, the remarkable founder of the Centre for Psychoanalytic Studies, and, for a brief while, Nick Midgely, who has his own path in this methodological territory. My whole academic journey was indelibly marked by the influence of Bob Young, and my membership of the Free Associations group which formed and carried forward his project. Finally, and not least, has been the provision of 'space' and nurture, and the tolerance of my nail-biting, generously given by Gillian Walker.

Finally let me thank my readers and hope that you number among you many of the critics of psychoanalysis broad-minded enough to read a defence of the rigour of psychoanalytic thinking and its knowledge creation.

Part I

Introduction

The centrality of the psychoanalytic method within the psychologies has been increasingly displaced by instrumental (behavioural) approaches of one kind and another that objectify (and often quantify) personal experience. Psychoanalysis is the prime psychology still concerned with human *experience* itself and, as such, it necessarily relinquishes the instrumental approach. Psychoanalysis may claim to discover valid and reliable knowledge. But, our knowledge is also the 'instrument' of change, the change agent. The 'act' of knowing is not the beginning of change – first to know and then to make the change. Knowing something is the beginning and the end. New knowledge is an added element to the state of mind, and re-arranges everything else. This is what is meant by 'insight' – a new vista on the self is a new self. That is a crucial element of working with a mind. Psychoanalysts have been disheartened by the advance of practices based on instrumental action, and we have often avoided engagement with them. This book starts by addressing the core criticisms that have contributed to the decline in confidence in psychoanalysis in the last half-century.

Because of the unique nature of our knowledge and operational methods, doubt has been cast on the possibility of rigorous research that reaches the standard of other medical and scientific disciplines. Without comparable research, uncontested claims can be made for more or less any theory – a situation referred to as 'anything goes' (Tuckett 1994a, p. 865). Much of the predicament of psychoanalysis today is that the core problems of focusing on experience severely restrict the strength of the claim to be scientific. Freud's authoritative opinion won't protect us now. We are living in 'a post-apostolic era' (Arlow 1982, p. 18). Nor is this contemporary scepticism towards our theories helped by the fact that so often we criticise each other within the world of psychoanalysis, often without the empirical and logical rigour of the physical sciences.

There are no doubt multiple reasons of a personal kind that inhibit necessary rigour in our discussions; problems of unresolved transferences, excessive group dynamic loyalties, the effects of uncontained counter-transference, and intersubjective pressures arising within the work itself.

However, the starting point for this book is that there are also significant epistemological reasons why consensus among ourselves is hard to reach. Though the more personal aspects can no doubt exploit the intellectual ones, it is valid to address the key epistemological issues themselves. They are:

- that the material we work with is the subjective experiences of our patients, rather than more objectively observed and measured data;
- that theory-building is uncontrollably and wildly liberated by our inability to test and compare psychoanalytic theories; and
- that the uniquely personal quality of our material makes single-case studies suspect.

Chapter 1 will give an account of how these problems mount to almost insuperable obstacles, and show the scale of the problem to be tackled. Because psychoanalysis is difficult to defend as a science, various reactions can be seen:

- *Outcome studies*: Under financial pressures, research has turned towards measuring outcome and effectiveness of whole treatments (see for instance Richardson, *et al.* 2004).
- *Process research*: Focusing on the clinical setting has addressed many detailed aspects of psychoanalysis itself using quantitative measures and qualitative evaluations (often using audio/video recording) of the psychoanalytic process in treatment (e.g. Luborsky 2001; and Chapter 2).
- *Extra-clinical research*: Another response turns to experimental methods outside the clinical setting (see Rubenstein 1976).
- *Social science methods*: There has been a turn to the methods of social science which Rustin (1989) has strongly advocated, noting the correspondence between clinical observation and naturalistic observation, or fieldwork. Tuckett (1994b) applied grounded theory (Glaser and Strauss 1967) to the psychoanalytic process; and more recently (Tuckett *et al.* 2008) he commenced a project resembling ethnographic fieldwork with groups of psychoanalysts (see Chapter 2).
- *Hermeneutics*: Another strategy admits psychoanalysis is not a natural science, and then immediately re-erects psychoanalysis as something else; as a hermeneutic discipline (Strenger 1991; and Chapter 10).
- *Meanings are causes*: Others (e.g. Davidson 1963; Hopkins 1982), acknowledging that psychoanalysis is about meanings, have tried to argue the epistemological point that meanings effectively function as causes.

Although this book will not take any of these positions, and will seek to defend psychoanalysis as a rigorous and evidenced body of knowledge *in its own right*, we can place the present study in relation to the range of major studies of *process research* which we will turn to in Chapter 2.

Chapter 3 will be a brief resume of the logical model, which will eventually be developed in Part III. The development of this logical model is the main product that attempts to face the numerous issues that we encounter in claiming psychoanalysis as valid knowledge.

After these three introductory chapters, Part II will address the epistemological issues and problems in developing a rigorous approach to human subjectivity. Part III is the nub of the argument, developing a logical model for psychoanalysis without relinquishing the specificity of psychoanalysis, or the unique experience of the subjects we work with every day. Perhaps Chapters 17, 18 and 19 are the crucial core of this book's contribution, and that to which the earlier part of the book leads.

In Part IV we will test examples of published clinical cases fed into the logical model.

Chapter 1

Holding the centre

Criticism of psychoanalysis and psychoanalysts is not new. In the early years, Freud thought that emotionally toned criticisms were inevitable. As a Jew he expected blind dismissal. Kraft-Ebbing viewed Freud's (1896) aetiology of hysteria as 'a scientific fairy-tale in public' (Jones 1953, p. 289); and David Eder, in 1911, rendered a meeting of the British Medical Association totally silent in response to his address on psychoanalysis (Jones 1955). Around the same time, the *British Medical Journal* in 1907 thundered outrage in a leader: '[Psychoanalysis] usurps the confessional . . . [and is] in most cases incorrect, in many hazardous, and in all dispensable' (*BMJ* 1907). Based on a credulous assessment of the alleged comment by the Wolfman that this man is a 'Jewish swindler, he wants to use me from behind and shit on my head' (Freud's letter to Ferenczi, 13 February 1910; Brabant *et al.* 1993, p. 138; see also Obholzer 1982), Fish's (1989) critique confirms the fascination for wild allegations to substitute for calm judgement.

Ad hominem criticism has continued to flourish happily in later years (Masson 1984; Crews 1993, 1998; Fish 1989, and Webster 1995). Cioffi (1970) argued there is no evidence of psychoanalysis as an effective treatment therefore Freud was a liar, an argument based on that of Eysenck and Rachman (1965). Another categorisation is that of Crews, a prominent critic who regarded psychoanalysis as failing on three important counts: (a) psychoanalysis is no use as therapy; (b) it fails as a scientific body of knowledge; and (c) Freud mischievously posed as an intrepid and path-breaking reporter of new discoveries, when he was not. Psychoanalysis appears to be multivalent in attracting criticism from so many different angles, as it is equally multivalent in attracting interest. Though no criticism can be accepted simply at face value, our defensiveness cannot either. Despite being often fervent and emotionally toned, some criticisms may at times be realistic, and should give us pause for thought.

The demand 'physician, heal thyself', appears to be applied to people in the psyche professions much more freely, and harshly, by both the general population and uninformed professionals. High-achieving people are not immune from personal idiosyncrasies, and some are frankly insane, without it invalidating their academic and creative achievements: for example, the 'beautiful mind' of John Forbes Nash who won the Nobel Prize despite suffering from schizophrenia (Nasar, 1998; and see Kay Jamison's (1993) *Touched with Fire*, a psychiatric study of artists and writers (including Byron)). Of course, this is not to recommend an insane psychoanalyst, just that out-of-the-ordinary achievement is not necessarily incompatible with mental disturbance, even psychosis. Nevertheless, it appears that an extreme standard of mental health is often expected of psychoanalysts, and a special suspicion is visited upon us if we are just ordinary. So, the poison pen seems more readily applied when it comes to Freud and psychoanalysis. The myth is that all psychological workers will be honed to psychic perfection, and anyone who is not should expect to be discounted. The extraordinary persistence of personalised argument that sidesteps the normal conventions of scientific and philosophical criticism was remarked on by Forrester: 'The one thing historians of science don't usually do is spend much time in print . . . doubting the trustworthiness of scientists. There are deep and profound reasons why this is so' (Forrester 1997, p. 218).

There is no reason why dishonest scientists should not be exposed (e.g. Cyril Burt;[1] see Joynson 1989), but when it comes to psychoanalysis, such criticism has been inventively promoted.

At the same time, there has been adulation from early on. Leonard and Virginia Woolf, under the influence of the Stracheys, set out to become Freud's publisher in English. And W.H. Auden's poetic eulogy at the time of Freud's death in 1939, told us 'he is no more a person / now but a whole climate of opinion / under whom we conduct our different lives'. Freud was noted by a whole range of different segments of Western intellectual and professional culture (for an account of the diffusion into British culture, see Hinshelwood 1995).

Maybe this intellectual sport is directed towards psychoanalysis because it is the most personal of 'sciences', and in fact the most personal of psychologies. Psychoanalysis, as Sebastian Gardner (1993) has argued, is only an extension of ordinary 'folk psychology'. As human beings, we are all psychologists and we make our own assessment of other people's thoughts, feelings and mental states all the time; 'Not everyone is bold enough to make judgements about physical matters; but everyone – the philosopher and the man in the street alike – has his opinion on psychological questions' (Freud 1938a, pp. 283–4). If psychoanalysis is a science, it also displays intimacy, passion and rhetoric. It may therefore be perfectly understandable that criticism also strays from the rational to the passionate.

Despite this, more thoughtful criticisms have developed since the 1950s, and have engaged the attention of a number of philosophers of science (Stengel 1951; Pumpian-Mindlin 1953; Popper 1959; Hook 1959; Nagel 1959; Grunbaum 1959). Erich Fromm in 1970 started his book, *The Crisis of Psychoanalysis*, by stating that 'Contemporary psychoanalysis is passing through a crisis which superficially manifests itself in a certain decrease in the number of students applying for training in psychoanalytic institutes' (Fromm [1970] 1973, p. 9).

However, the doubts thrown on psychoanalysis have been more substantive than this superficial manifestation, Fromm himself regarded the problem as the mechanistic and scientistic direction ego-psychology had been heading. Perhaps Sydney Hook's symposium in 1958 in New York (Hook 1959) started the serious challenge. Despite the respect for psychoanalysis, that symposium failed to convince of the scientific respectability of psychoanalysis partly because of the laconic performance of the psychoanalysts presenting (notably Hartmann who gave the opening address), as well as the new view of science emerging in the 1950s (see Chapter 7).

The multiple strands of criticism by a very broad spectrum of people do need careful attention. Milton *et al.* (2004, pp. 79–98) classified them according to their core arguments – (a) critics of the truth and knowledge claims of psychoanalysis: Popper, Cioffi and Grunbaum; (b) critics who question Freud's stature and originality (contextualisers): Roazen, Ellenberger and Sulloway; (c) critics from political and ideological perspectives: Millett, Timpanaro, Szasz and Rycroft; (d) patient critics: Sutherland and Sands; and (e) general critics: Webster, Crews and Masson.[2]

This is not the only categorisation. Gomez (2005), taking up only the first of Milton's categories, found exemplars of three different kinds (Grunbaum, Nagel and Habermas), philosophical critiques which, despite their reservations, do retain respect for facets of psychoanalysis. Many other philosophers have taken a look at psychoanalysis, because it promises understanding of the nature of mind. These include Sartre (1943), who believed psychoanalysis dubious for promulgating a bad faith by normalising the inauthentic state of being driven by an unknown self (the unconscious). Wittgenstein ([1942] 1966) also thought Freud was wrong and that apparent unconscious drives were merely those forces concealed in speech acts. Wollheim (1984), on the other hand, as well as some of his students (Gardner 1993, Hopkins 1982), fully supported Freud, though in one of psychoanalysis' derivative forms, Kleinian object-relations. Psychoanalytic theories have dispersed and now fan out with unrestrained abandon into numerous competing varieties and sub-varieties. This state is now termed Babel, 'where: (1) the same words name different concepts; (2) the same concepts are named by different words; (3) there are a number of words only validated within the context of a given frame of reference' (Aslan 1989, p. 13). Others have also used this term, Babel (Tuckett 1994a; Steiner 1994; Gabbard and Williams 2002), and it has led some (for instance, Eagle 1997) to recall Yeats's prophetic poem:

> Things fall apart; the centre cannot hold;
> Mere anarchy is loosed upon the world,
> The blood-dimmed tide is loosed, and everywhere

The ceremony of innocence is drowned;
The best lack all conviction, while the worst
Are full of passionate intensity.

('The Second Coming' 1921)

The 'centre', as Freud might have conceived it, has not held. Because psychoanalysis is a discourse, it can vary under social, cultural and linguistic influences; even national schools of psychoanalysis are noticeable. Moreover, as Sandler (1983) described, psychoanalysts' theories are not always explicit, and so in use they may implicitly evolve and diverge from other theoretical frames, which themselves may be similarly evolving in other directions. That variation then makes it difficult to compare like with like.

From outside, the cacophony of differing views makes psychoanalysis look unconvincing. From within the world of psychoanalysis, these schisms attract bitterness and intransigence. The motivations for the relentlessly diverging spectrum of theories is of interest, and needs attention in its own right. Freud's notion of how differences attract group narcissism and schism came from his ironic notion of neighbours: 'It is always possible to bind together a considerable number of people in love, so long as there are other people left over to receive the manifestations of their aggressiveness . . . I gave this phenomenon the name of "the narcissism of minor differences"' (Freud 1930, p. 114). This can be applied to the world of psychoanalysis as well. Our schisms attract similar bitterness and intransigence. Helmut Thomä commented (see also Werman 1988), 'It is quite likely that the controversies between groups and "schools" of psychoanalysts are motivated by what Freud (1930) calls "the narcissism of minor differences"' (Thomä 1969, p. 688).

Psychoanalytic schools narcissistically guard the group's knowledge and set it against others with a hostility approaching siege mentality. This leads to further retreat into our separate groups, each marked by its conceptual convictions.

Core problems of psychoanalytic research

Psychoanalysis has undoubtedly to meet certain key challenges, which at times it has been loath to do.

> It cannot be denied that there is an increasing tendency not to apply to the data of observation or to the methods of interpretation such scientific controls as are available. The consequence is that a great deal of what passes as attested theory is little more than speculation, varying widely in plausibility.
>
> (Glover 1952, p. 403)

Cogent issues about the nature of psychoanalytic knowledge, and unproductive debate among analysts interact, and require us to respond equally cogently.

Meeting external criticism and dealing with the 'Babel' means we need strategies for defending our better theories against less good ones – and indeed requires some proper understanding of what makes one better than another. I will attempt to trace the roots of a large number of these issues to four core problems:

1   Subjectivity: the field of observation is a subjective one, yielding subjective data. But in addition, the means of gathering the data is via an instrument that is equally subjective, the person of the psychoanalyst. Without the objective data of natural science, Freud's claim that psychoanalysis can 'take its place as a natural science like any other' (Freud 1938b, p. 158) appears to be defeated. It is perhaps a 'science of subjectivity' instead (Heimann 1943; Meissner 1999).
2   Single-case studies: at first sight, the problem of generalisation from unique, single-case studies appears insurmountable, and leaves psychoanalysis way behind most experimental psychology, which depends so expertly on massed and aggregated samples often of very large numbers of subjects.
3   Science as testing: Freud depended heavily on inductive thinking to justify his theories scientifically. The nature of science and of scientific testing of theories, has changed since his claims, and requires both more rigour, and also a different kind of justification. Popper (1959) developed a logical model of science, ruling out inductive thinking, and emphasising the deductive testing of theories (testing to destruction, as it were), to which he claimed psychoanalysis was unable to conform (Popper 1963).
4   Data collection: separate psychoanalytic groups with different theories about what clinical material means, select very different material as evidence of their theories. A circular process occurs in which theories to be tested are used to select the data to test the theory.

The case against psychoanalysis as a natural science, is formidable. It seems to be excluded from being knowledge at all. I propose to resist this apparently irrefutable verdict.

The problems cannot be dismissed. Psychoanalysts have to address what kind of knowledge we possess, even if it is not science in the ordinary sense. We need a strategy for sorting out which are the 'best' theories. That means a differential valuation of schools, which will provoke an obvious reluctance. Difficulties of achieving consensus over which theories to hold, is difficult enough in science because of vested interests of career and of funding, but the natural sciences have a well-developed logical model to evaluate their hypotheses and theories. Such a logical model is not readily available for psychoanalytic schools. If psychoanalysis is not exactly natural science, we still need our own logical model that is as cogent as that of natural science, and in parallel to it.

In the next chapter, I shall briefly review some important work on psychoanalytic concepts at work, as it were, but researched 'off the couch'. There are some limitations to this approach, but I will nevertheless support the conclusion that investigating process rather than progress is still along the right lines. Something is still required in terms of research design and data collection, that will overcome the limitations, and it is the purpose of this book eventually to explore them.

Chapter 2

Research off the couch

Important research projects have been designed and carried out over the last 50 years on psychoanalytic theory – it is now generally known as 'conceptual research' (Sandler *et al.* 1991; Dreher 2000). In this chapter I shall consider a number of research projects that differ from the one developed in this book. As Widlocher clarified: 'it is necessary to clearly oppose a process that considers psychoanalysis as a research tool with one that considers it as an object of research' (Widlocher 2003, p. xx).

There are two research designs of the latter type – the approach that considers psychoanalysis an object of research. These are research projects *on* the analytic process as data, being post hoc, off-the-couch as it were, and undertaken *after* the clinical session. They contrast with the approach that considers the psychoanalytic process itself as the research tool, which will be the concern of the rest of the book, returning to Freud's claims for *within-session* research so that the psychoanalytic process *is* itself the research process. It would seem a truism to observe, 'Formulations of the events of analysis made in the course of analysis must possess value different from that of formulations made extra-sessionally' (Bion 1970, p. 26). That debate is background to the discussions of the following projects.

Because this chapter is *not* about the model to be described in this book, I shall start with a general summary, so that some readers may wish to glean only a brief impression of the contrasting research designs, and go straight on to the main argument of the book, returning to this chapter afterwards if they wish.

General summary

The first section of this chapter concerns what is now called 'process research', mostly inspired by the Menninger Project; while the second section considers the social science approach developed by Tuckett, akin to ethnographic fieldwork, based on a focus group method.

Process research

The massive Menninger Psychotherapy Research Project (PRP) commenced in 1954, at the Menninger Clinic. The Menninger family had been particularly forward-looking following the Second World War (Menninger 1946). The intention of the research project was to find the factors that are responsible for the outcomes, rather than the simple measures of outcome produced by these factors. A number of projects, mostly conducted in the United States over the last 50 years, were inspired by the Menninger Project. The five projects discussed here painstakingly recorded sessions, sometimes the whole of a treatment. The records and recordings have subsequently been sampled and analysed thematically to generate what is objective data and then used to generalise themes – found or supplied – across several psychoanalyses. On occasions the data has been tested statistically to capture themes and regularities. The aim has been to find objective support for generalisations about individual psychoanalyses, and groups of psychoanalyses, or the concepts employed in them. It is a method that resembles and indeed aims to conform to a normal process of *naturalistic observation*, such as the biologist piecing together the components of a natural habitat; or an astronomer observing features of gravitational and electro-magnetic fields during a solar eclipse.

With the exception of the Mount Zion group in San Francisco, the development of evidence is such that support for psychoanalytic theory has been on the basis of logical induction (for an account of inductive versus deductive methods of logic in research, see Chapter 6). Joseph Weiss of the Mount Zion group did initially seek evidence from a more subjective view of the analytic process. To test his novel theory, he found evidence of subsequent release from repression of unconscious contents, following the theory's use. In that one instance, the logic conformed to a test process within a *single case*, and used a deductive logic based on causality – 'if this, then that' (see Chapter 8 for a full application of this logic of the single case in psychoanalytic research).

In general, these research studies aim to do two things:

1   to struggle with the subjectivity and intersubjectivity of the analytic process by rendering it objective; and
2   to accumulate such data to support theories inductively.

The question whether psychoanalytic data should be primarily subjective or objective is not their concern, since these studies tend to assume that research must always use objective data. Nevertheless, there is a sensitivity and almost an apology that the unique subjectivity of a psychoanalytic case must be rendered objective.

Ethnographic research using focus groups

A second and highly original development is David Tuckett's recent extensive work with groups of psychoanalysts to discuss the nature of interventions that were actually made in practice. This work is based on the *implicit* theorising that psychoanalysts do in the immediacy of the interpretive moment during the session. One psychoanalyst presents to the group some sessional material to which the other members of the group respond by attempting clarification of the purpose and strategy of the presenter. This is a reflective form of enquiry using a group in which multiple perspectives can come together to tease out the rationale for the intervention. The interaction between the presenter and the probing group produces a debate which may go on for a number of hours. What analysts actually do in a psychoanalytic session, and why, is then agreed by a consensus within the group. This is a logical process based on an intuitive induction, that is, steadied by the introspective reflection of the presenting psychoanalyst. It resembles the ethnographic or anthropological fieldworker exploring the cultural assumptions of a group or a society. This method is adapted from the well-tried fieldwork enquiry of standard social science.

What is discovered by this method is the range of theories actually used in practice. It is not a method for comparing theories – neither what counts as a standard for the best, nor a method of comparison between two competing ideas. This is not about psychoanalytic knowledge; it is about what individual psychoanalysts *believe* is valid knowledge. Therefore this method stresses the psychoanalytic profession as a self-sustaining culture rather than a group with authority to enquire into the status and value of the knowledge in use.

Critique

There are certain issues about both these kinds of research as viewed from the position taken in the present book:

- Psychoanalysis concerns subjective experience and there is a real issue about how to sustain the subjectivity of the individual patient (and maybe the psychoanalyst).
- Although there is a great deal to be gained from the inductive elaboration of theories from a body of data, this is no longer the hallmark of science which has, over 50 years, systematised methods of testing theories, in addition to simply making generalisations. While human and social sciences may argue they can only generate new ideas, and cannot test knowledge like physical scientists do, it may not be necessary to include psychoanalysis among them.
- Defining the dimensions of the psychoanalytic model seems a really important contribution. Despite the result being a cultural analysis of the in-use conventions about theories, explicit or implicit, psychoanalysts

are indeed interested in the actual variances along these dimensions, and there is some requirement to show, for the sake of patients (and other funders), that psychoanalytic knowledge is more than a set of beliefs and conventions of practice.

I shall proceed to look at these research projects in more detail, and hopefully to justify the above summary and critique. It is just as possible to read this book by going directly to Parts II, III and IV now, and returning to issues in this chapter again afterwards.

Process research

The original paradigm for process research in psychoanalysis has been Breuer's use of hypnosis to relieve Anna O of symptom after symptom. On each occasion the hypnotic catharsis was followed by symptom modification. That sequence

symptom – hypnotic catharsis – symptom modification

inspired Freud and, with some reluctant help from Breuer, they elaborated a rather intricate theory of psychic energy.

Today we require outcome studies of whole treatments rarely now in terms merely of symptom reduction, but more usually personality change and relational maturity. Nevertheless, in practice, psychoanalysts still use an in-session process in their everyday work. After their intervention they expect a response of some kind. They look for a change in the way the patient speaks and relates. However, different schools of psychoanalysis select different aspects of the material to indicate a significant response (Table 2.1).

Many forms of disciplined thinking about psychoanalytic knowledge are possible, and the table below is not intended to be comprehensive. These kinds of observations are rules of thumb, and their variety tends to support the view that clinical work is not systematic enough at present for research. The pressures in the psychoanalytic situation do not always allow careful estimation of the effects of a psychoanalysis.

Table 2.1 A varied sample of process-significant events

Breuer	Symptom reduction
Freud	Coherent symbolic meaning
Anna Freud (resistance analysis)	Emergence of preconscious derivatives
Klein	Less inhibited play
Ezriel's tripartite interpretation	Move to required relationship
Grunbaum's 'tally'	Patient's recovery
Winnicott	Increased exposure of authentic self
Kohut	Increment in empathic security
and so on	

Whatever degree of precision we may thus achieve, at least ideally, in the process of ordinary clinical interpretation, or of short-term prediction, if one accepts their conceptual closeness, seems to diminish distressingly, however, as the time dimension and the element of variability and unspecifiability of the future life situation are introduced.

(Wallerstein 1964, p. 681)

Systematic research

In consequence, a number of more systematic off-couch studies of the analytic material developed, and these tackle:

- problems of objectivity;
- the need for a range of examples, or a sampling strategy; and
- standardisation through questionnaires, blind rating and various other quantitative methods.

The following projects were selected for inclusion here because they (a) focus on process, usually micro-process within the session, and (b) respect the uniqueness of single cases. Despite that, they implicitly defer to medical research and experimental psychology. The concern for objective observation has tended to dominate, and has been enhanced by some form of electronic recording of sessions, in some cases all the sessions of an entire psychoanalysis. Sometimes several, or numerous psychoanalyses, have been amalgamated to develop more general indicators of the clinical psychoanalytic process. These indicators may then be used to generate questionnaires for rating the processes of subsequent treatments on standard dimensions. Often multiple raters of the recorded material are used, sometimes including the conducting analyst, and sometimes not.

What follows is a brief description of the five best-known, large-scale attempts to systematise psychoanalytic process research.

The projects started with the Menninger Psychotherapy Research Project, and the interest in what factors constitute an effective psychoanalytic treatment. This, from the beginning, appeared to be conceived in terms of testing which of the classical concepts were in use in a particular treatment, aiming to provide evidence to validate those concepts. Fairly rapidly, in the late 1950s and the 1960s, criticisms of psychoanalysis as unscientific from various quarters pressed upon the research and almost certainly this was connected to another motive, the justification of the scientificity of psychoanalysis.

The Menninger Project and Robert Wallerstein

The Menninger Psychotherapy Research Project started early from 1954, running until 1982.

Simply put, we wanted to learn more about what changes take place in psychoanalysis . . . (the outcome question in formal research design), we also wanted to learn how those changes come about, through the interaction of what constellation of factors of variables in the patient, in the therapy and the therapist, and the patient's ongoing life situation (the process question).

(Wallerstein 1986, p. 6)

This is the landmark project with which Robert Wallerstein is identified. It has influenced most subsequent process research. Forty-two treatments (22 psychoanalytic and 20 non-specific expressive therapies) were followed in detail.

Wallerstein (1986) discussed the problems of choosing between micro- and macro-process approaches. Despite reservations (see Wallerstein 1986, pp. 47–50), the team eventually chose the longer scale – evaluation at start, termination, and two-year follow-up. As Wallerstein claims, this does not rule out the gaining of knowledge about process on a shorter timescale, but in fact his massive report focused on the enormous amount of data on outcome.

Numbers of predictions were made individually for *each* of the 42 patients. Prediction on the long timescale inevitably depended on gross features of both the patient and of therapeutic theory. Predictions and their confirmation were assessed with the notion of a 'disciplined subjectivity' taken from Erikson (1958). In summary, 'an effort is made at explicit long-term prediction of the course and outcome of psychoanalytic treatment, derived from the comprehensive assessment of the nature of the patient's personality structure and illness and from the postulates of the psychoanalytic theory of therapy' (Wallerstein 1964, p. 691). Thus, they honoured the unique subjectivity in each case by seeking generalities in the person-specific dynamics and their changes, over the course of each individual therapy.

Research features of this project are: (a) long timescale; (b) prediction of outcome was possible; (c) person-specific changes; (d) generalisations across cases; (e) theory testing rather than theory building; and (f) raters outside the clinical session. There is strictly speaking no single-case design, but the project pioneered the attempt to retain the specificity of the individual dynamics. Though the project is, strictly speaking, an outcome study, the outcome is assessed case-by-case, on the basis of specific features of individual treatments.

The project is important in pointing the way towards process study of individual cases, and most later studies have taken off from the Menninger Project, while turning to shorter-term process.

Luborsky and the Penn Psychotherapy Project

Originating in 1967, inspired by the Menninger Project where Lester Luborsky's research interests began, the Penn Project attempted to isolate various measurable parameters in a treatment. For Luborsky and Crits-Christoph (1988), the data we use clinically is only empirical research data if we investigate it using parameters based on principles from outside the clinical setting. They argued that 'we should at least take a peek at what we would find if we looked in the direction of the principles of the psychoanalytic process, as these are implied by empirical studies' (Luborsky 2000, p. 148). Here 'empirical studies' means that research needs to be conducted *on* the process – not at all that the clinical process is the research. Thus they predicted change using parameters that the experimenters, not clinicians (nor the patients), provided on six measurable dimensions:

> the severity of the patient's psychiatric disorder, the therapeutic alliance, the changes in the transference pattern and a new reliable measure of it, the changes in mastery and a new measure of it, the changes in insight, and the preconditions of recurrent symptoms expressed during the course of treatment.
>
> (Luborsky 2000, pp. 153–4)

These measurable changes contrasted with the qualitative impressions that clinicians might have. Changes on the parameters were operationalised to give quantitative assessments to gauge therapeutic change. For instance, it may be predicted that as a treatment progresses the therapeutic alliance tends to strengthen, while the transference relationship reduces.

Eventually, in the course of the project, they homed in on three parameters with specific clinical relevance: (a) the treatment alliance, (b) the transference and (c) the accuracy of interpretation (Luborsky and Crits-Christoph 1988). The effects of the psychoanalytic treatment could then be gathered from the within-treatment process, *but* through these applied quantitative measures. The project evolved methods for evaluating the three key themes:

The treatment alliance: A questionnaire method was developed to administer to the patient (Luborsky 1976).

Transference: An attempt was made to quantify the transference patterns of relating. This was derived from Freud's (1912) notion of the 'transference pattern'. Luborsky (1976) eventually identified the core conflict relationship theme (CCRT) as a practical way of operationalising the concept of transference. This was measured from a series of 'relationship events' and sub-categorised as three components: (a) the patient's wishes/needs towards the other; (b) the responses of that other; and (c) the responses of the self. The CCRT can be assessed on transcripts of single sessions (even on published material, as Luborsky and Crits-Christoph (1988) demonstrated). Multiple judges could be used – there being a reasonable inter-rater reliability. And they showed a reliability over time.

Accuracy of interpretation: With regard to the 'accuracy of interpretation', this was gauged by the congruence between the evaluation of the patient's

CCRT (core conflicts as expressed in the material), and the import of the interpretation. The degree of concordance is then an objective measure of the interpretive accuracy. The project has compiled, for future research, the recording of 17 whole treatments (Luborsky 2001). However, the subjects were treated with psychotherapy (including cognitive behavioural therapy) rather than psychoanalysis.

Results: It was found that (a) where the initial patient experience of therapy is positive there tends to be a better outcome of therapy, and (b) the therapeutic alliance becomes more positive during therapy, implying an inverse relationship between the therapeutic alliance and the transference.

Luborsky and Luborsky (1993) compared their Penn methods with the studies of the Ulm group (see later), with the Mount Zion group (see later), with the Patient Experience of the Relationship with the Therapist (PERT) measure (Gill and Hoffman 1982), with the Dynamic Focus Method (Schact and Binder 1982) and with Horowitz's (1979) Configurational Analysis. Strength was sought in building a consensus among approaches to the dynamic diagnosis of conflict. Interestingly, considering the importance of interpretation and its accuracy in a psychoanalytic treatment, it is surprising that there was less work on 'accuracy of interpretation' for the Penn group to compare with.

Research features: Luborsky's work arises out of the Menninger Project, but has some distinct features: (a) the research parameters were supplied by the researchers rather than the treatments' themes; (b) the method is a questionnaire; (c) objective dimensions are sought; (d) a timescale process during the therapy is used; (e) various therapies are studied, but not usually psychoanalysis; (f) a library of recordings has been accumulated; and (g) inter-project consensus and solidarity has been attempted.

Process research at Ulm

The Ulm Process Research Group's 'aim was to establish ways to describe systematically long-term psychoanalytic processes in various dimensions and to use descriptive data to examine process hypotheses' (Kächele and Thomä 1993, p. 117).

The group commenced in 1963 (Kächele 2009), with Helmut Thomä and Horst Kächele. Kächele (1988) described several variants of a form of thematic analysis conducted over the whole course of completed analyses. Using colleague discussion of session-by-session material, a treatment could be seen as a number of phases. This was refined by systematically taking blocks of five sessions, spaced at regular intervals. In one form, topics from the transcripts of sessions, or audio/video recordings, were counted by non-analysts, drawing on Dahl's (1983) notion of a psychoanalyst's 'topic index'. Topics can be plotted as a graphic expression of the phases of a treatment. Thematic foci can be pinpointed, and then used to identify the phases, each characterised by some constellation of themes/topics. In one form topics and themes are specific for each treatment. In a variant form, general psycho-analytic concepts, such as transference, guilt, insight, and so on were counted, and the blocks discriminated by computer analysis. More extensive use of computer-assisted analysis has been developed (Mergenthaler 1985). The team emphasised a systematic, *prospective* method, to contrast with the customary ad hoc clinical method of reflecting on observations with hindsight.

The Ulm project has 'focused on four psychoanalytic process research cases on which systematic time series of recorded sessions were transcribed and stored' (Kächele and Thomä 1993, p. 115). The authors advocated a four-level approach:

1   clinical case study (mostly the 'novella-like' form of ordinary clinical description);
2   systematic clinical description (using analysis of comprehensive audio or video recording to generate characteristic themes from the various phases of treatment);
3   guided clinical judgement procedures (using general conceptual themes, as indicated above); and
4   computer-assisted text analysis.

Currently, recordings of the treatment sessions of 22 psychoanalytic patients have now been transcribed for these purposes. Four of these have been extensively studied, including Amalia X, who is the focus of their most recent text (Kächele *et al.* 2009).

Like most other process research the timescale is midway between outcome of a whole analysis, and the micro-analysis of momentary interactions provoked by interpretation. The research is by 'objective observers of the analytic process' (Kächele *et al.* 2009, p. 220). Characteristic of most clinical research projects is that they view the clinical process as no more than a novella lived out by two people. Proper investigation of that life together is for those *outside* the clinical setting, albeit the clinician may be an important member of the research team once he is outside the treatment setting.

Results: It proved possible (a) to identify phases in the course of a treatment, but the phases are not organised in an ontogenetic sequence (as suggested by Fürstenau's (1977)) but follow an unconscious process negotiated between the needs and wishes of the patient and the possibilities of handling those of his analyst (see Kächele and Thomä 1993, p. 114), and (b) to show a move from a more passive to a more active voice in the course of the treatment.

Research features: The characteristics of this project to be noted are (a) a shorter timescale is addressed, the phases of a treatment; (b) raters outside the clinical setting are used for 'objectivity'; (c) the intersubjective narrative of the analytic couple was respected; (d) four levels of clinical process were defined by the research team; (e) a library of recorded analyses has been built up; and (f) computerised data analysis was developed.

Jones's modified Q-test

Enrico Jones's project is one of the few process projects that was not directly influenced by, or did not collaborate with, the Menninger Project. Trained raters used a 1–9 scale to sort 100 characteristics for a session. This was adapted from Stephenson's Q-testing (Jones 2000; Ablon and Jones 2005). Items referred to A, the analyst, and P, the patient, and included, for instance, 'When the interaction is difficult A accommodates in an effort to improve relations', 'P is committed to the work of therapy', 'Discussion centers on cognitive themes (ideas or beliefs)', 'A conveys non-judgmental acceptance' (see Jones 2000, for a full list of the 100 items). It was possible to isolate by factor analysis a small number of general aspects of the interaction between the clinical couple which changed over the course of a specific treatment. These items were bundled statistically into 2–3 clusters (factors) unique for each patient and therapy. Thus a specific indicator of change for each therapy was possible, which they called a Psychotherapy Process Q-Sort (PQS).

The material used was taken from the recorded sessions of other projects (those of Luborsky, and of Weiss and Sampson – see later) as well as their own. Only some of the therapies studied were psychoanalytic treatments, others included brief dynamic therapy, and cognitive behavioural therapy. High inter-rater reliability was demonstrated. The analysis for the different forms of therapy produced significantly different factors.

Research features: This project shared some characteristics with the Menninger one: (a) changes on an outcome timescale; (b) person-specific changes; (c) generalisations across individuals, but within therapy categories; (d) a questionnaire method, with statistical factor analysis; (e) raters outside the clinical session; (f) wide comparisons of therapies; and (g) theory testing rather that theory building.

The Mount Zion group (San Francisco) and response to interpretations

The Mount Zion Research Group in San Francisco (later known as the San Francisco Psychotherapy Research Group), established by Joseph Weiss and Harold Sampson (Weiss and Sampson 1986, Sampson 1992), attempted during the 1970s and 1980s to research therapeutic process in the clinic including the use of *clinical* observation of in-session process.

Their research started with a new psychoanalytic theory, and the ensuing attempt to find rigorous clinical evidence that establishes this theory as superior to competing theories. The theory evolved from a chance observation that the unconscious asserts a control of a quasi-voluntaristic kind over the expression of certain prohibited impulses and wishes. The researchers explain:

A distinctive aspect of Weiss's theory is the assumption that patients are highly motivated to solve their problems and that they work actively throughout treatment (by testing the therapist) to obtain experiences and knowledge that will help them do this. Also distinctive is the assumption that the patient works in accord with unconscious plans as to which problems to tackle first, and which ones to defer until later. Patients decide unconsciously how they may work with their therapists to get help. They unconsciously coach their therapists with the aim of guiding them, so that they may provide the experiences, display the capacities, or convey the knowledge that patients need to disconfirm their pathogenic beliefs. Patients unconsciously monitor their therapists' attitudes toward the pathogenic beliefs they are working to change.

(Weiss *et al.* 1995, pp. 13–14)

The new theory (the higher mental functioning hypothesis)[1] is thus:

higher functioning (secondary process) occurs at the unconscious level.

And this is significantly different from traditional, conventional theory (*the automatic functioning hypothesis*):

an unconscious threshold of unpleasure *automatically* triggers repression mechanistically (primary process).

The researchers set out to explore how the two theories could be compared, using serendipitous findings of clinical occurrences. Weiss described Miss P (Weiss and Sampson 1986, pp. 23–6) as a single clinical case who showed the possibility of higher mental functioning operating unconsciously. Miss P made a decision to finish treatment, but it appeared that she imperfectly understood her own decision, which the psychoanalyst pointed out, and he did not agree to the termination. Eventually the patient continued her analysis, paradoxically showing some relief! The new hypothesis can explain the paradox on the grounds that her object, the analyst, was tolerant of her impulsive rejection and did not reject her. The paradox cannot be explained on the basis of the conventional theory. The conclusion is that the new theory is superior, because it explains more than the conventional theory. This principle of superior explanatory power is important in comparative conceptual work (see Edelson 1985; see p. 107 of the present book). (This example of Miss P is considered further in Chapter 14.)

However, in addition, Miss P subsequently produced some direct evidence of her unconscious change by recovering a long-forgotten memory of an incident in childhood which indicated to her that her mother wanted her to die (i.e. recovering the memory was some lifting of repression). The psychoanalyst, Weiss, could then put two and two together – the historical experience of mother rejecting Miss P when young in the most spectacular way by wanting her dead, was put together with the confounding experience that the psychoanalyst wished to keep her and not reject her. Thus the drama of rejection was played out in the transference, in such a way that Miss P must have wished to test whether the analyst would reject her. That he did not was a reassurance against her worst fear (engendered when young) that he, like her mother, would reject her. The fact of the recovery of memory – the repression was relaxed – is hard evidence of the fundamental change process in the unconscious dynamics, the researchers claimed.

Weiss was impressed that the engagement with the analyst in this dramatic testing of how rejecting he was, implied the operation of higher mental functions. Importantly, the formulation and execution of a 'test-plan' implies sophisticated higher functions operating unconsciously, and this goes radically *against* Freud's classical view that the processes occurring in the unconscious only involve displacement, condensation, and the neglect of reality including time and causality. Instead, the patient specifically but unconsciously tested a pathological belief system.

The research thinking stressed the process of memory recall, following the reassurance. Although the intervention was not an interpretation, Weiss recognised later that conscious insight did help, so interpretations do actually do something (Weiss 1992). But what do they do? This led to further research into the outcome of individual interpretations (see Hoffman 1983). The San Francisco group took segments of free association before an interpretation and after an interpretation (Weiss 1988) and subjected them to evaluation by independent judges (blind to other judges). They assessed the change in the patient's level of experiencing as measured by the Experiencing Scale (M.H. Klein *et al.* 1969), or by the change it produced in the patient's level of insight as measured by the Morgan Patient Insight Scale (unreferenced in Weiss's account).

This project started by understanding the research potential of the clinical occurrences as they processed in sequence. There is a hint here of what is done in actual clinical work, although the researchers moved on to more systematic and 'objectifying research' *on* the clinical process. Thus intuitive, clinical research within the session subsequently provoked systematic research.

Results: The results of this second phase of research on the response to interpretation confirmed (a) a positive change in the patient's experience and insight, and (b) that most change between before and after, occurred when an interpretation dwelt most closely with a test-plan the patient was believed to be addressing.

Research features: There are important characteristics similar to the Ulm clinical-cum-systematic research: (a) crucially the design sets up two theories in such a way that one gets knocked down (theory-testing); (b) unconscious functioning can be logically inferred from clinical process; (c) within-session *process* was asserted above clinical features and themes; (d) a single case could decide between two theories; (e) interpretation was (eventually) granted central place in the process; and (f) objectivity was pursued by the use of (blind) raters.

Summary

These five projects show a wide array of characteristics:

- length of timescale
- objectivity
- recorded library
- predictions
- person-specific
- multiple therapies
- theory-testing
- inter-project consensus
- levels of process
- inference from clinical material
- single case
- interpretation central to clinical process.

Mostly these systematic strategies are concerned with longer timescales of process, and with developing greater objectivity through recording, questionnaires, researcher-introduced variables, and external raters of material. There is a considerable effort to employ *prediction* in an experimental way, while attempting to retain the person-specific quality of a psychoanalysis. Externalisation strategies like computer-assisted thematic analysis are attempted in the effort to establish the reputation of the research design. Even when the San Francisco group (Weiss and Sampson) started out with research based on clinical inference, interpretive process and a decisive single case, they moved subsequently towards a more consensually agreed research strategy emphasising methods of objectification.

Some other process research developments

Associated with the University of Illinois, Merton Gill pioneered a scheme for distinguishing transference aspects of the therapeutic relationship from the non-transference aspects (Gill and Hoffman 1982; Hoffman and Gill 1988b). Detailed research analysis on the audio-recorded sessions of nine full treatments made it possible to develop a coding scheme for the use by 'judges' to allot communications by the patient into three categories: *Category 1*: not about the transference; *Category 2*: implicitly or indirectly about the transference; and *Category 3*: directly about the transference. This coding scheme has come to be known as the Patient's Experience of the Relationship with the Therapist (PERT). Gill and his co-workers compared this post-session form of research with that of Luborsky (Hoffman and Gill 1988b), and with that of Weiss and Sampson of the San Francisco group (Hoffman and Gill 1988a). Luborsky, in turn, reviewed a compendium of 15 research projects using the idea of a central relationship pattern (Luborsky and Luborsky 1993) – alongside their own Core Conflict Relationship Theme (CCRT).

The research group in Boston (following Luborsky and Spence 1971) developed scales for generalised concepts which can be applied to individual patients. Measurements of several features – painful emotion, impairment of defensive manoeuvres and activation of threatening conflictual fantasies – were developed from the analysis of transcripts of sessions (Knapp et al. 1975). They claim that the movement on the quantitative scales followed closely the variations in qualitative assessments of patients' states.

This clutch of research projects aim on the whole at the same target, a specific pattern of relations revealed in the psychoanalytic setting, variously called the transference, the core conflict, the patient's experience. Two conferences were held by the NIMH in 1982 and 1983 to establish research projects in psychotherapy (Schlesinger 1984), and an international conference was convened by the Ulm group in 1985 which brought together many of these projects and assisted in creating some consensus on psychoanalytic process research (Dahl et al. 1988). Shapiro and Emde edited a special supplement to the *Journal of the American Psychoanalytic Association* in 1993. The consensus appears to be around 'repetitive structures' in clinical data (Teller and Dahl 1993, p. 45). Teller and Dahl (1993), noting this consensus, cite the convergence of Luborsky's CCRT approach (Luborsky and Crits-Cristoph 1988), Horowitz's configurational analysis, (Horowitz 1979) Strupp's cyclical maladaptive patterns (Strupp et al. 1988), Weiss and Sampson's Higher Mental Functioning hypothesis (Weiss and Sampson 1986), Gill and Hoffman's PERT (Gill and Hoffman 1982), and Dahl's Fundamental Repetitive and Maladaptive Emotion Structures (Dahl 1983). Rubovits-Seitz (1995) points out that the consensus refers to a recurring pattern for individual patients, in the manner of Freud's (1914) notion of the repetition-compulsion.

Wallerstein (2001) described the consensus as formed around descriptions at three points in the clinical process – problem, treatment and outcome. The various projects hold that those three descriptions should converge (Strupp et al. 1988). And there has been considerable inter-project collaboration around that consensus. It has inevitably tended to increase the solidarity, but in more recent years, that consensus has tended to restrict research to the development of rating scales of themes processed in the consensually agreed way. All this has been made possible, according to Wallerstein (2006), by the 'development and deployment of suitable technology, namely the possibilities for audio recording and of computerization with high speed computer word or situation searches' (Wallerstein 2006, p. 319). This has enabled the development of micro-process analysis for determining structural change in the ego (Bucci and Maskit 2007), and thus to bring a closer correspondence between outcome studies and process studies.

Of course, descriptive coherence along the process timeline is essential, but the collaborating groups have also come to see psychoanalytic research in a particular way. Therefore, research on the clinical process is now seen as that which takes place *from outside* the process even though it reaches inside the setting for its research data. This has come to be known as 'empirical research', or sometimes 'formal research' in psychoanalysis, and despite differences within the various projects, as demonstrated above, 'empirical research' is often taken to be psychoanalytic research in general. As Boesky (2002) has complained this has left so-called 'clinical research' high and dry as if it is no longer relevant. By clinical research he meant the generation of 'evidence' directly from the clinical process, as opposed to evidence *about* it. Clinical research in that sense is the classical method from which Freud and all the early pioneers gained their theories – and, for that matter, *our* theories.

There is an endeavour to restrict research on clinical material and clinical process to observation which is as objective as possible and, if practicable, measurable. Simple exercises such as giving the same transcripts of sessions to several analysts, as reported for instance by Hansell (2000), or Scharff (2001) and others, fade out of serious attention, because no formal means of making comparisons is used, and merely swapping clinical impressions is exactly what the major projects dissociate themselves from.

Conclusions on process research

Despite the beginnings of an integration of micro-process research with long-term progress and outcome, the process versus outcome distinction still stands, as there is a difference of purpose. Outcome studies are intended to provide evidence of effectiveness. The shorter timescale process, especially the within-session process, is aimed at conceptual analysis of what goes on in the process that produces the outcome. Concepts inform and invigorate interpretations and, in fact, outcome studies of effectiveness are themselves ineffective and confusing unless there is a precise knowledge of what exactly the outcome stems from. Different schools of psychoanalysis use different concepts, and thus make different interpretations and interventions, which achieve different outcomes. Without a clarity about the interpretive (or other) interventions based on specific theories, the estimates of outcome are crude at best. For instance, the notion that the outcome at termination and follow-up can be linked to micro-change in ego structure (as, for instance, the Menninger study assumed) already makes a presumption about the metapsychology, since micro-change may also be conceived in alternative terms, those, for instance, of changed object-relations, or the intersubjective mutual penetrations between the partners.

This research started out with an interest in providing validation of classical psychoanalytic concepts, and probably the justification of psychoanalysis as a science. However, from the 1970s, as the pluralistic nature of psychoanalytic ideas became evident, the need for effective comparisons of concepts (and practices) increased, and the validation of concepts within only one tradition of psychoanalysis appears rather limited, even parochial. And one sympathetic philosopher remarked, some time ago, 'If you were allowed (methodologically speaking) to interpret responses by means of any theory at all, then every response would confirm the one being tested' (Wisdom 1967, p. 46).

Without a sturdy method of making such comparisons between schools of thought, we now have a wide variety of competing concepts, terminologies and practices gathered into schools of psychoanalysis, and psychoanalysts have become unsure of the nature of their own subject: 'Psychoanalysis is passing through a difficult period in its history (Wallerstein, 1988). It is still unclear whether there will emerge further splintering, further dilution, or a gradual re-unification and re-integration' (Hanly 1990, p. 375).

The tribal nature of psychoanalytic schools comes from personal pressures on psychoanalysts (e.g. Eisold 1994), as well as quite valid professional pressures. The later has been discussed by Sandler (1983), showing how concepts and terminologies become stretched, compressed and remoulded by new uses.

As a result the field of psychoanalytic ideas has not been brought into coherence by the process research described. And the undisciplined pluralism has led to new concerns about the research most necessary for psychoanalysis today. One major research initiative is that of Tuckett, directly addressing the morass of differing ideas used in clinical work.

Tuckett's ethnographic method

In the process research just considered, the findings are produced by a method that appears independent of the clinicians involved in the psychoanalyses. However, Tuckett starts with the view that the conceptual resources of the psychoanalyst need to be much more precisely defined, taking as his starting point: 'Research should be directed towards making explicit the implicit concepts of practising psychoanalysis, and it is suggested that this process will result in the accelerated development of psychoanalytic theory' (Sandler 1983, p. 43).

So, the clinicians, their subjectivity, and their influential professional context needs meticulous exposure. Instead of trying to bypass it, as it were, in the interests of objectivity, we might ask if there is a value to investigating the concepts and practices by which the clinicians come to their interventions? This is problematic, of course. As David Tuckett pointed out, pluralism is probably only effective if there is a system for giving order to the variance. The field of psychoanalysis has now become too divergent to achieve that ordering easily; 'once pluralism was finally accepted – as it needed to be – the place of "pluralistic" tolerance of new and varied approaches would accelerate. Nothing really exists to contain or displace them' (Tuckett 2008a, p. 9).

Moreover, with the constant remoulding of concepts, there is a blight on clear discussion and debate. As Tuckett had accurately diagnosed, 'the tendency to fit facts to theories, when supported by a method of reporting that was opaque, may have damaged the capacity of this tradition to engage in robust debate and to transmit ideas successfully and credibly to neophytes' (Tuckett 2000, p. 245). Tuckett set out to explore this field of observation.

The problem of reaching agreement and consensus between psycho-analysts is not a new one. In his role as editor of the *International Journal of Psychoanalysis*, Tuckett published a large symposium on the nature of a psychoanalytic fact (see Chapter 15). His somewhat despairing editorial introduction (Tuckett 1994a) regarded the achievement as something of a Tower of Babel. Clearly his curiosity was piqued as to what kind of a discipline psychoanalysis is. So, his subsequent project began with the concern whether a core model of a psychoanalytic treatment still exists. Given that there is no longer a consensus on what psychoanalysis entails, Tuckett asked:

- How do we know when what is happening between two people should be called psychoanalysis?
- What is a psychoanalytic process?
- How do we know when one is taking place?

This starting point is predicated on the view that the actual ideas used by a clinician in practice are those that are mobilised because they represent the core of his/her model (Tuckett 2008a).

His research involved a highly original and organisationally elaborate method. From 2002, and under the auspices of the European Psychoanalytic Federation (EPF), he gathered together psychoanalysts from across Europe to form working seminars which had the characteristics of both focus groups and action research.

Because of the personal and emotional ingredients of the current diversity, these working seminars met for as long as 12 hours. To achieve some form of consensus they needed that extended 'space' to cope with the anxieties, rivalries and hostile resistance. Groups met every couple of years at EPF conferences. The core of each group discussion was a detailed presentation of clinical material presented from one of its number. At the start, the discovery of a model of what psychoanalysis is, was likely to produce a variety of conflicting models. And so it turned out. The models to which individual group members worked, and their terminologies, provoked considerable difficulty in communication.

The project was grounded in the *use* of psychoanalytic ideas in practice. In effect, it investigated the clinical culture, the attitudes, beliefs, and inter-vention practices of clinicians, and resembled the way a social anthropologist might set about looking at a different culture from his own, through enquiring into the beliefs and practices that are deemed to constitute the studied society.

In the development of these focus groups, the initial debates disputed the form of discussion (Tuckett 2008a). Being psychoanalysts, they had a tendency to adopt a free association method, which of course brought out the implicit thinking of the free associating member, rather than the presenter. This is typical of clinical seminars when the presenter is subjected to an auxiliary supervision. Tuckett called it 'overvision'. Consequently, a degree of structuring of the discussion became more necessary and accepted. The aim was to be able to open a space for each member to appreciate *both* the presenter's point of view, *and* the group members' own. The members of the groups became familiar with listening not just to the presentation, but to the way of thinking which led to the actual interventions in the practice presented. That is, the audience became familiar with the task of listening to the presenter, to 'know where he was coming from'. With that development, there was then the possibility of understanding where each of the members of the group was coming from, in comparison to the presenter.

Out of the extended discussions of the presentations, various themes became apparent. These could be extracted from transcripts of presentations and discussions, using a grounded theory method (Glaser and Strauss 1967). Interestingly, Tuckett (1994b) had previously explored an analogy between developing an interpretive insight in the clinical work with the social science method of grounded theory.

One result was a set of categories of interventions that a psychoanalyst might make (this account is based on Tuckett 2008b):

- maintaining the basic setting;
- adding an element to facilitate unconscious process;
- questions, clarifications, reformulations, aimed at making matters conscious;
- designating here and now emotional and phantasy meanings of a situation;
- constructions aimed at providing elaborated meaning;
- sudden and apparently glaring reactions not easy to relate to A's normal method.

These were empirically found in the discussions, and approximate to what the practice of psychoanalysis consists of. They are categories, and are not the actual differences of opinion between the seminar group's participants – for instance differences over what the basic setting is that has to be maintained, still exist; or emotional and phantasy meanings may be conceived in very different terms by different psychoanalysts. They constitute a second order of structure – a structure of dimensions along which individual opinions vary. The groups also found a second grid, one that addressed more abstract and theoretical features of the presenters' interventions:

- What is wrong?
- What is heard?

- Furthering the process.
- How does 'What is wrong' change through psychoanalysis?
- What creates the analytic situation?

Again, this is a second order of dimensions, along which variation between concepts and schools may occur. This grid of theoretical dimensions overlaps with another venture of the EPF, also inspired by Tuckett's enterprising research initiative. The other project was to study the generation of theory from practice (Canestri 2006).

Finally, the two grids – of interventions and theories – were then used in later meetings to structure discussions, with suitable ongoing adaptation and evolution of the grids as it became appropriate.

Results: It was confirmed that there is a plethora of psychoanalytic models, characterised by positions on the dimensions that emerged. The models are not all compatible, and there is no clear way of dealing with the discovered variety. Indeed, a resistance stemmed from personal commitment to a school and the rivalry provoked by this kind of enquiry. These resistances needed dealing with. However, it was found that given sufficient time, these insecurities could in fact be managed and the seminars approached an effective working, task-oriented modality.

As to the primary concern – whether we could still claim that a core psychoanalytic model exists – the answer seemed to be that there is indeed a model identifiable as a psychoanalytic one used in practice. However the model was the set of higher-order dimensions along which interventions and theories varied. These multiple dimensions form a structured space which is the contemporary psychoanalytic model, and the contemporary psychoanalytic model is probably completely defined by those dimensions, making it distinct from other possible models in the therapeutic world. The analysis of debate produced a set of superordinate and abstract axes, so that a psychoanalytic model is today defined by dimensions of variation in practice and theory; and not by which specific forms of practice (and theory) are the right ones.

Critique and conclusions: This was an empirical study, like the process research projects above, though the research data it produced is very different. In this instance, it is not 'objective' data. The approach is a social science one, inquiring into those attitudes, beliefs and practices as actually existing. This refrains from any judgement about the attitudes and practices. In line with qualitative social science research, those results are taken as the 'construction' by that social group – the analytic school and individual. Attempts are made to see each group's belief system in its own terms, rather than to evaluate them in some general way, or by some evaluative comparison with each other.

Though this research has provided an important confirmation of the psychoanalytic model, in terms of the abstract, second-order dimensions, it does not dirty its hands, as it were, in getting into evaluative questions that might give greater discipline to the pluralism which dismayed Tuckett. We still need a method that can give us some means of prioritising the various concepts and practices (perhaps in relation to specific jobs which they have to do). In that sense the research did not tackle the problem of uncontrolled pluralism, though it did demonstrate that discussion across the boundaries between schools is, in fact, possible.

Tuckett's EPF project is a response to the conditions we find in the psychoanalytic discipline today, as the process research in Section 1 responded to the issues in the 1950s–80s. He has addressed an issue that is of profound importance to psychoanalysis: is there a truly psychoanalytic model of treatment? And he has come up with an affirmative answer.

Conclusion to Chapter 2

I do not believe I have captured *all* the relevant research initiatives in these two approaches (see Leuzinger-Bohleber *et al.* 2003 for a broader panorama of contemporary research activity). But it is enough to give a general overview of what is being done, and to position the current book in relation to them. The growing hegemony of 'empirical' process research sees the clinical process as the material in the clinic to which research methods can be applied.

The contrasting approach sees the clinical process as *itself* the research process. The latter gives back to the clinician the possibility of once more joining up the ordinary work with a research perspective – Freud's *junktim*. The specific approach in this book is to support that junction. It is something more modest, and more everyday, than mounting a specific research programme. The dedication of money and specific teams of people to research projects is not necessary if it were accepted that clinical work *is* research work.

However, in another sense this book offers something more ambitious. By relocating research in the actual treatment process, there are advantages beyond the simple economy of time and money. These will include the crucial issues of:

- the variety and volume of material available in the already published literature; and, above all,
- the need for cross-school comparisons.

However, the need to overcome the problems requires careful thought, a need to understand how science achieves its convincing rigour, and how psychoanalysis may develop that rigour without having to claim a pseudo-objectivity in place of its truly subjective nature. If clinical work is indeed to be research it has a number of difficult hurdles to vault. We will need to address the threefold problems – subjectivity, theory testing as well as building, and single-case research design. In addition there is the problem of data selection, which is potentially distorted by the parallel 'need' for data that can provide partisan support for a particular theory.

The projects visited in this chapter are exemplary in establishing a clear starting point for contemporary conceptual research – first, to tackle the need for evidence and validation through the process research described; and, second, to tackle the problems of pluralism as the ethnographic fieldwork does. With the achievements in this field of interest, we could then proceed to an appropriate method for evaluative comparisons.

Comparative evaluation of concepts held by different schools and their differential effects on treatment techniques has to go in a different direction from the research discussed in this chapter, carried out off-couch. This is the project for this volume. It will seek to go beyond accumulating supporting evidence in validation of specific concepts of a single school, and it will do more than test the notion of a psychoanalytic model in all its variance. In fact the design will be a form of *on-couch* process research. It will focus on one only of Tuckett's six types of interventions – the *interpretation*. It is not that this rules out other types of intervention for therapeutic use, just that this interpretive intervention is the most appropriate for comparative research purposes. In the next chapter we will give a preparatory summary of the logical model in anticipation of its development in Part II and beyond.

Chapter 3

Possibilities

Process research (and indeed outcome studies) has gained a name for being psychoanalytic research. However, Dreher protested:

> Unfortunately empirical researchers – including those in psychoanalytic psychotherapy research – often forget to mention, when testing hypotheses, that their hypothesis should not only be tested empirically, by suitable procedures, but they should also undergo an examination of logical form in order to establish consistency and durability.
>
> (Dreher 2000, p. 14)

It is to that more neglected field that we need to turn: adequate conceptual research that is evaluated by a precise logical model, one which should stand comparison with a scientific model.

I have devoted a considerable space in Part II to examining the core problems for this field of research in psychoanalysis. Only in Part III will we get on to developing an answer to these problems. The answer will be a logical model that aims at addressing the core problems and their consequences in a manner that is comparable in rigour to that of natural science. Because a certain amount of deferred gratification is required of the reader before reaching the account of the logical model, I shall attempt now to pre-empt impatience by giving a very schematic summary of the model.

The research logic: Nothing of the model is actually *explained* here; that will come in Part III. Below are listed merely the steps that form the model:

- one theory may be compared with another, or it may be invalidated on its own;
- if the theory is formulated correctly, one single-case will invalidate it or compare it definitively against an alternative;
- the test is by clinical interpretation;
- the material prior to the interpretation will be understood by the theory under test;

- that interpretation will indicate how, in terms of that theory, certain impulses, wishes, anxieties, functions or other aspects of the ego are unconsciously, repressed, split off, projected, or whatever;
- a prediction is based on applying the clinical theory that interpretation enables some degree of the relevant unconscious elements to emerge consciously in the clinical process;
- the prediction, in all cases, is that following the interpretation there will be a shift in the material towards a greater acknowledgement, ownership, and expression of the supposed unconscious element, which the interpretation points to in the pre-interpretation material;
- the prediction allows no other shift;
- the post-interpretive response will indicate a meaning, using the *same* theory as the understanding of the pre-interpretive meaning (i.e. the same theory that is being tested).

To confirm the validity of an interpretation therefore requires certain precise conditions to be met:

- psychoanalytic theories are of two different kinds, performing two different functions – *clinical* theories and *metapsychological* theories;
- clinical theories apply to the understanding of the process sequence – from pre-interpretive material to post-interpretive material;
- metapsychological theories are those from which interpretations are formulated (of the pre- and post-interpretive material), and which the model puts up for test;
- the two sets of material pre- and post-interpretation must acquire meaning via a *single* metapsychological theory;
- the shift post-interpretively must be precisely as predicted, towards the emergence of that which is unconscious according to the theory, and no other shift, however promising;
- the selection of the sets of material, before and after the interpretation, have to be exactly identified by a protocol which should preferably conform to the method of a triangulation.

All these terms, methods of identifying data, and so on will be developed, examined and explained in Part III. The result is intended to move towards a procedural method that tends to be neutral to different theoretical schools. The purpose is the resolution of rivalries, competition and conceptual incompatibilities. In short we can:

- forget the suspicion of single-case studies which can prove to be more definitive than large sample testing, given the right conditions;
- acknowledge the subjectivity of the field of investigation without being apologetic about it, since it is the unique contribution of psychoanalysis;

- retain causality and the possibility of prediction, while simultaneously keeping subjective meaning and narrative to the fore; and
- face the challenge of developing facts that are not biased to one or another psychoanalytic school.

The rest of this book is one way towards these ambitious aims.

Part II

Basics: what is belief, what is science?

Justifying psychoanalytic knowledge within the current vortex of doubt and criticism may appear daunting. As much as anyone, psychoanalysts like to believe in what they know; as David Hume exclaimed, 'No weakness of human nature is more universal and conspicuous than what we commonly call CREDULITY, or a too easy faith in the testimony of others' (Hume [1748] 1999, p. 112).

Since the Hixon Lectures in 1950 on psychoanalysis as science (given by Hilgard, Kubie and Pumpian-Mindlin; edited by Pumpian-Mindlin 1953), there has been unease about the scientificity of psychoanalysis – 'its discontents', as Flugel (1954, p. 71) styled the published report. The large interest in whether psychoanalysis is a science can be confirmed by the numbers of papers published in the psychoanalytic literature (as attested by the PEPWeb database) after Popper's (1963) *Conjectures and Refutations*, and after Grunbaum's (1984) *The Foundations of Psychoanalysis*. Were the answer that psychoanalysis is not a science, then it is as if the whole psychoanalytic venture might be invalidated.

This part of the book covers much of the ground that Dreher (2000) also examined, though with a slightly different purpose, and has been impelled by Kächele's urgency: 'The case for psychoanalytic research is not academic, it is imperative' (Kächele *et al.* 2009, p. 1).

The chapters of Part II will consider background issues that come into the judgement of what psychoanalysis is. These include the criticisms, the strategies of conviction and some of the relevant aspects of epistemology, as well as an account of the hermeneutic and post-modernist strategies. These epistemological issues are not comprehensive and touch only on those aspects of the philosophy of knowledge which seem relevant to the specific features of, and conditions for, psychoanalytic research.

Chapter 4 opens this section by considering the various ways, good and bad, by which people can become convinced that some belief or opinion is true knowledge. It is important that as psychoanalysts we address our own convictions. Our understanding as psychoanalysts makes us especially primed to be sensitive to the resistances and illusions of the invalid forms of feeling convinced.

Chapters 5 and 6 will give some idea of the conceptual ingredients for testing knowledge, and how they relate to psychoanalytic knowledge. Chapters 7 and 8 will then focus on how those ingredients are deployed in science, and their relevance for psychoanalysis. Freud, in fact (Chapter 9), employed various methods to convince people. Chapters 10 and 11 will be concerned with alternative strategies to evade the dominant criticism of psychoanalysis: if psychoanalysis is *not* science, what else might it be?

Chapter 4

Feeling convinced

Feeling convinced, like all affective states, arises from internal factors, external factors, social ones and unconscious ones. Conviction is a very definite experience, but not necessarily reliable:

> Descartes took everything he could clearly and distinctly conceive to be true. Such clarity of conception is found, however, in many who are manifestly insane. This was pointed out by Locke, who mentions the same defect in connection with enthusiasts.
>
> (Wisdom 1949, p. 6)

Psychoanalysts surely know the pitfalls of a belief in one's own convictions. The problem is that whatever the origins, the effect of conviction feels the same. If we map out the methods of instilling conviction, we can assess the effectiveness and acceptability of each variety. I will look in turn at seven sources of conviction:

1   experimental science
2   inductive generalisation
3   patterns and narratives
4   personal authority
5   social support and coercion
6   personal defensiveness and
7   psychotic delusion.

They are not all comparable in their degree of acceptability, and they have varying degrees of logical rationality.

Experimental science

In the contemporary world, the experiments of material science pretty much lead the market as the means of convincing the listening audience. The method discussed in Chapter 6 relies on Popper's hypothetico-deductive method, involving an answerable question and empirical data to answer it.

Conviction comes from exploiting the compelling logic of deduction by setting up the experiment in such a way that it confirms or dis-confirms a prediction. The certainty of logical deduction may be harnessed to empirical evidence by the hypothetico-deductive research design; but its cost is the determinism and causality which appears to negate human agency and experience. Because of public expectations of research, and its claimed certainties, this logical approach has seemed the obvious choice for clinical psychoanalytic research, although it appears to allow no place for wishes, intentions and decisions in human experiencing.

Inductive generalisation

The experimental method (as argued in Chapter 6), is only one aspect of science, since people have traditionally used inductive approaches to empirical observation as the means of generating and evidencing ideas, hypotheses and theories. When Newton, noticing an apple fall, connected this with the general observation that most things with weight, if unsupported, are drawn downwards to the ground with a constant force, he was generalising certain occurrences into a general theory – the law of gravity. Darwin's discovery of a common influence (the demands of the ecological niche) when studying the natural variation of finches in the Galápagos Islands involved a similar process. That process, moving from the particular to the general, is induction, but it does not possess a logical inevitability (see Chapter 6). Human knowledge has always rested on induction including verification. Because of its intuitive rather than logical base, the inductive process is more open to debate and opposition, than deductive logic, even though both kinds of argument may feel just as convincing.

Patterns and narratives

Like repetitions, patterns of perception (visual or other) that conform to recognisable shapes carry a palpable sense of conviction. The pattern is *felt* as something with meaning. In a London street a four-legged animal with fur which barks, accompanying a person, is likely to be recognised as a dog. A 'dogginess' is composed of a set of characteristics that make it recognisable. It could possibly be some other kind of animal, but the mind of a Londoner is primed to recognise the conjunction, and associated characteristics, in the specific context as a dog – not a wolf, for instance. Pattern recognition became the basis of gestalt psychology – the psychology of forms. It is like the child's game of joining dots to complete a drawn outline of some object. The sense of significance, of successfully completing the recognition of a pattern, is an important source of the experience of conviction – we *know* that the animal in the street is a dog. However, finding patterns in the external world are not necessarily evidence of *actual* regularities, and we may note how astrology finds patterns in the sky which automatically carry a sense of significance.

It may be the propensity for finding gestalt patterns which led Plato to postulate his theory of ideal forms. Jung's notion of archetypes would also seem to derive from such gestalts. Equally, Clive Bell's notion of 'significant form' in aesthetics seems to have had a similar derivation.

Similar to intuitive generalisation, pattern recognition can carry intense conviction in many areas of life, though it would seem to require additional checking of a justifying kind (i.e. testing) to link the conviction to the actual existing reality.

Personal authority of experts

Conviction arising from faith induced by teachers and priests is another means of creating conviction, and uncomfortably prevalent among psycho-analytic schools,

An analyst, let us say, of established prestige and seniority, produces a paper advocating some new point of view or alleged discovery in the theoretical or clinical area. Given sufficient enthusiasm and persuasiveness, or even just plain dogmatism on the part of the author, the chances are that without any check, this view or alleged discovery will gain currency, will be quoted and requoted until it attains the status of an accepted conclusion (Glover 1952, p. 403).

It is less reliable than the preceding methods, since faith in authorities is more open to extraneous influences. A political leader exerts a strong emotional power over his followers. This is understood all too well by psychoanalysts who know of that influence as the transference. The effect of an authority on personal conviction is also the acknowledged culprit for much of the tribal conflicts among the schools of psychoanalysis. As Hacking (1999) has noted, however, the potential abuse possible by those regarded as authorities in recent history, has led to greater and greater weight being placed on the authority of evidence, rather than of persons.

At the same time, it is not necessarily emotional and irrational. Accepting the authority of someone with extensive experience might be reasonable, because they do have more experience and training. Each person does not have to start from square one on everything. Thus, feeling a conviction on the basis of the words of an authority is somewhat mixed. Some good sense can be interfered with by such emotional bonds, but it can also be efficient. And clearly the development of human knowledge through this kind of social accumulation rises from the capacity for individuals to pass on their experience to each other and to later generations.

Social support and coercion

Alongside the influence of an authority there is also peer group pressure which can be extremely influential. Early experimental social psychology (Asch 1952; Milgram 1963; Sherif and Sherif 1956) showed the power of a group of peers to influence an individual's personal judgement of the most basic kind – including, in the case of Asch's experiments, to question one's own physical perceptions, like the length of a line. The development of belief systems is therefore particularly strong in groups, and for that reason particularly suspect. The evidence is that much of our perception of social forms, and of other people, is highly influenced by a process of 'social construction' (Berger and Luckman 1967), which shows how our impressions, perceptions and recollections are shaped by implicit assumptions held in common. The members of a social group 'belong' to the group by virtue of their allegiance to the assumptions of that group.

This view of group dynamics and membership is compatible with Freud's (1921) view of the group ideal as the unconscious libidinal cathexis that unites the members (see also Hinshelwood 2009). Rustin (1989) also makes this connection between sociological (ethnographic) observation and psychoanalytic observation, but there are differences as well. Implicit social theories are more accessible, potentially, than the individual's repressed ones; for instance, questioning this social field of discourse can raise the implicit group assumptions and attitudes to awareness, but individual repressed assumptions and attitudes are much more resistant to exposure.

If one person sees in the position of the stars the shape of a hunter, he may consider it of special significance. If he finds someone else who shares his view of the constellation, then the strength of the conviction is doubled in each – or even more than doubled. The serendipitous arrangements of the constellation of stars is hardly significant on its own, but supported by the shared significance of others, the capacity for pseudo-conviction increases exponentially with the numbers of people involved.

One of the many forms of social conviction is ordinary superstition instilled and sustained by the cultural group. This form of conviction-creation is particularly unreliable, but strongly determines behaviour. One variant is the pressure arising in power relations, when one person or group may coerce another with methods of physical or psychological pain. Such methods are effective at generating conviction and have been known as 'brainwashing' since the Korean War in the 1950s. Increasingly, in recent years, the hidden pressures in language and other semiotic systems have been under investigation and radical exposure. The insidious and coercive quality of social attitudes, distortions and prejudices in the very means of expression and communication behoves us to vigilance. Kuhn has shown that in effect science itself is influenced by these interpersonal, group processes arising from peer support (and expert authority) to support enduring 'paradigms', conservatively clung to for as long as possible.

Social pressures towards conviction is a not-to-be ignored reality which, however, has mixed benefits, and is therefore to be subjected to a vigilant caution.

Personal defensiveness

Some people cling to ideas and beliefs as a means of protecting themselves from the pain of doubt and uncertainty. Britton and Steiner (1994) called these 'overvalued ideas', and because they are emotionally protective, it costs a lot to give them up, or to allow them even to be questioned. These are states of conviction which are held for 'internal' reasons, and if they are beliefs about the external world they can be seriously maladaptive.

Indeed many symptoms could be considered to be 'overvalued ideas'. For instance, agoraphobia is a compelling conviction about the dangerousness of going out of the home. Such deeply personal conviction and pseudo-certainty is well known and contributes to suspicions about the way subjectivity can cause distortions, a topic of great importance here. On the whole, such convictions can only be used with a psychoanalytic sensitivity to the understanding of unconscious enactments which we will discuss later (Chapter 14).

Psychotic delusion

Finally, at the most maladaptive end of the spectrum, are psychotic belief systems. Schreber's delusions about repopulating the world were tenaciously held. Freud (1911) described this as a delusional reconstruction of a world that Schreber believed had suffered a previous catastrophe. Despite Schreber's intelligence and culture, and his ability to live in some circumstances quite normally, his delusional conviction was never far away, and could appear very easily to intrude upon his mind, and take hold of him. This is a tenacious form of conviction that we must avoid, though the infectiousness even of psychotic conviction can create the alarming phenomenon of a *folie à deux*.

If psychoanalysis is not scientific knowledge . . .

These various forms of feeling convinced must lead us to be careful about how we intend to influence the convictions of others. Conviction resting on the first three forms needs to be prioritised, although social pressure (the fifth form) is a very important influence which needs to be used cautiously.

Strong support for the view that experimental science is the method of choice has led to some spirited defence of clinical psychoanalytic research as science (notably Edelson 1983, 1984). However, many psychoanalysts consider that scientific evidence may not be reliably available in the psychoanalytic clinic and needs to be sought elsewhere. That view can be exemplified by Fonagy's scepticism:

> Certainly, analysts of different theoretical orientations all claim to have observed similar confirmatory responses to their interpretations although

these were derived from mutually exclusive theoretical frameworks and thus must, in principle, have at times been at least partially, wrong. In view of these objections data from the 'interpretive laboratory' should be treated with great caution.

(Fonagy 1982, p. 128)

The ironic term 'the interpretive laboratory' (borrowed from Rahman 1977) expresses Fonagy's extreme caution about clinical research of this kind. Such psychoanalysts then turn to various other kinds of rigorous support, including outcome studies, process studies, neuroscience (Solms and Turnbull 2002; see also the severe critiques of neuroscience by Blass and Carmeli 2007, and Talvitie and Ihanus 2011) and experimental infant psychology (Gergely and Watson 1996; Trevarthen 1977; Mahler *et al.* 1975; Stern 1985).

The problem is whether the 'interpretive laboratory' can be given a new life and new respect. But there are other radical means of evading a wide territory of criticism of psychoanalysis – the hermeneutic and postmodern arguments about the nature of psychoanalysis, to which we will turn in Chapters 10 and 11.

Chapter 5

Reality and objectivity: concerning the 'psychoanalysis-as-science' debate

As Richard Rorty suggests, the question of whether psychoanalysis is a science, or not, is not so interesting. There is more passion than substance to it, more heat than light. The issue instead is to find out what kind of a subject psychoanalysis actually *is*.

When Freud modelled his work on scientific causality, he took with him his scientific baggage – not just causality, but generalisation and determinism as well. He believed he was following the correct principles of any science, 'the other view, which held that the psychical is unconscious in itself, enabled psychology to take its place as a natural science like any other' (Freud 1938b, p. 158).

However, that pre-supposed a general similarity between science and psychoanalysis, rather than argued for it. In other words, the experiential world of a patient composed of the meanings of his dreams and his symptoms, could be observed, and conceptualised, just as the medical components of his body, or the substance of any material thing. This overlooked the special characteristics of the experiential world. If we now bring back those special characteristics of personal experience, does that put us at the mercy of subjectivity and its supposed unreliable distortions?

The subject of psychoanalysis

Freud's intentions, to understand hysterical symptoms and dreams, were couched in the science of the time. Victorian science did not eschew finding evidence even for religion – such as life after death (Myers 1904). We are much more circumspect now. Science is believed to be a tool for investigating material reality only. The spirit world is by definition outside its area of efficacy; but does that area include a person's psychological experience? The barriers between the material world and the experiential world had not been erected so high in Freud's day, and for him there was simply no problem. However, not all disciplines conform to one method, design or logical model:

> psychoanalysts [must] stop asking (obsessive?) questions like 'Is psycho-analysis a science?' 'Was Freud a scientist or a littérateur?' 'Are psychoanalytic

claims objectively verifiable?'. . . . The founders of great and influential intellectual traditions quite often did not know quite what they were doing. The enduring impact of their work may have little to do with their original intentions.

(Rorty 2000, p. 822)

Whatever psychoanalysis is, we need to be clear about what natural science is, what sort of knowledge it is, and how it is established as knowledge.

Science now concerns exclusively a physical world contained within itself. Aristotle referred the origins of everything back to a 'final cause'; in effect, a divine purpose. Such a cause was purposeful, or 'teleological'. But the sense of purpose was eventually eradicated by the Enlightenment philosophers who proposed to go as far as they could to find ordinary material causes, called proximal, in contrast to the final cause. We know proximal causes as the laws of science, and in the modern era confidence grew that we can know the material world in a direct way not encumbered by non-material factors. One thing *in the material world* causes another thing *in the material world*. However, as many people now believe, in studying subjective experience we are dealing with a radically different 'substance' from the matter that natural science investigates. We study an immaterial substance, 'immaterial facts' as Caper (1988) dubbed them. Inner perceptions of our experiential world have no spatial extension we can measure, (though they do appear to follow a time dimension), and no measures of materiality – mass, density, acceleration, and such like. Instead, psychic phenomena have 'qualia', an example being 'redness', as opposed to the scientific characteristics of the measurable wavelength of light. Thus the psychoanalytic field of study diverges phenomenologically and ontologically from material science, and we should accept that psychoanalysis necessarily generates specific kinds of data which demand that psychoanalytic research develops uniquely in order to accommodate that kind of data.

The only measurable quantities we have are the numbers of experiences, but not their place, movement, intensity, and so on. Yet, by amassing numbers of instances, we preclude the uniquely personal *quality* of experience. As Wallerstein remarked:

> the data we deal with are not of the mechanisms of inanimate nature (the natural sciences) or of the operative mechanisms of the living world of flora and fauna where the phenomena of mind are not under study (the biological sciences), but are the quintessentially mental concerns of desire and will and intention in all their subjectivity and elusiveness.

(Wallerstein 2000, p. 29)

If psychoanalysis is to make generalisations it must avoid violating the individual subject.

The instrument for subjective observation

Psychoanalysts began to give up Freud's initial scientism during the 1950s. As countertransference has been increasingly used since then as a clinical tool, criticism of psychoanalysis as hopelessly subjective did not diminish. Despite the reasonable view that to observe a subjective field of study we need a subjective instrument of observation – that double embrace of subjectivity involved in using countertransference – the suspicion has doubled.

Whereas previously Freud (1916–17) had argued that interpretation must 'tally with' (p. 452) something in the patient, notions of countertransference today can lead to claims based rather simplistically on what *tallies for the analyst*. For instance, Paula Heimann stated anxiously, as early as 1960,

> I have had occasion to see that my paper [Heimann 1950] also caused some misunderstandings . . . [some analysts] referring to my paper for justification, uncritically, based their interpretation on their feelings. They said in reply to any query 'my countertransference', and seemed disinclined to check their interpretations against the actual data of the analytic situation.
>
> (Heimann 1960 [1989], p. 153)

Despite Heimann's alarm, the practice has continued. And indeed there is some justification for the practice, because if the analyst's intuition produces an idea that he finds himself pre-occupied with, that surely has *something* to do with the setting in which the intuition has come to him. And that setting is the one where analyst and analysand put their minds together. In other words what tallies for the psychoanalyst, must bear *some* relation to what tallies for the patient.

Psychoanalysis therefore contends with the twofold problems (and criticisms) ensuing from:

- the necessary subjectivity of the field of study; and
- the necessary subjectivity of the analyst's observations of the field of study.

Though this is accepted now by perhaps most analysts, the problem questions are:

- What precisely is the relation between what tallies for the patient and what tallies for the analyst?
- How could such a convergence be made to stand as data and evidence?

Heimann's suggestion, just quoted, is that the countertransference experience of the psychoanalyst needs to be checked against the actual data of the analytic session, and we will follow this up eventually (in Chapter 17) because any means of checking data is important in today's contests over what psychoanalytic data is (see Chapter 15).

In fact, scientific objectivity is also grounded in observations made by the same distorting human subjectivity, and debate in Western philosophy across two-and-a-half millennia has not come to a clear idea of how we know about the real, material world. On the whole, the assumption of most modern science is a so-called 'naïve realism'; that is to say, our senses perceive an exact replica of what is out there. It is also known as the correspondence theory of reality (and, somewhat derogatorily, as 'positivism'). It is the positive assertion that we can know what is out there; what we see corresponds to what there is. At the same time there is a strong tradition arguing that we 'see' more than the reality; we 'see' its significance. Also our sense organs have a limited 'coverage' of the available data – for instance, we cannot know magnetic fields in the way that birds use them for flying home; and the world perceived by a bat using its sonar system is pretty well unimaginable for us (Nagel 1974). All sorts of influences bear on and limit our certainty about the world we live in. However, human beings have improved on, and expanded, the biologically given senses, by inventing technological methods that convert hidden data from the real world to data we *can* sense. This has done a lot to support a realism that asserts we can know about our world as an exact and complete replica. Science offers a powerful confidence and conviction that the out-there reality can be discovered.

So, we need our subjective experiences in order to perceive our objective observations and to work with them, while our unique experiences ensure that we all vary what we see. It may be that this will be resolved by the creation of machinery that will itself generate knowledge without the dis-advantages of subjective experiencing. In that case, human beings are an expendable stage on the route to a benign, enquiring cyber-civilisation, which is not our own. Nevertheless, for human subjects experience is an ambig-uous ally in the creation of knowledge. Psychoanalysis is at the heart of that ambiguity, seeking to understand precisely those distortions without succumbing to their effects.

Objectivity and single cases

Pressures for managed care and an evidence-based practice which have leapt into the ascendant in general medicine, have swept through psychiatry too. The pressure is to gain objective evidence similar to that of material science. So, the standard method of achieving objectivity is to amass a large enough sample that will represent enough of a certain general category (or population) of people to warrant a claim that the sample results apply to the whole category. Typically the design is the iconic drug trial method based on randomly controlled comparative samples – the randomised control trial (RCT). The RCT requires two sample groups which match on all variables apart from one. Let us say that the differing variable is that in one sample all the individuals take 75mg of aspirin per day, and the individuals in the other sample do not (aspirin protects against suffering an embolism). Otherwise all individuals match in each sample – the same proportion of men to women, the same proportion of married people to unmarried ones, the same proportions in each age group, and so on and so forth. In that way it is possible to gauge the effect of aspirin on the single pathological variable of forming embolisms.

NICE (The National Institute of Clinical Excellence) was formed in 1999 as the tool for introducing evidence-based practice which has transformed the role of research in medicine and other clinical practices. From then on, professional practice has needed to be based on research evidence of that character. Almost without debate research became outcome research and was needed to legitimate forms of practice – and specifically to ensure the investment of government and other funders in those legitimated practices. The official approach produced a hierarchy of research methods. The various categories of evidence set out by NICE were:

Category I: Evidence from at least one properly randomised controlled trial.
Category II-1: Evidence from well-designed controlled trials without randomisation.
Category II-2: Evidence from well-designed cohort or case-control analytic studies, preferably from more than one centre or research group.
Category II-3: Evidence from multiple time series with or without intervention or dramatic results in uncontrolled experiments, such as the results of the introduction of penicillin treatment in the 1940s.
Category III: Opinions of respected authorities, based on clinical experience, descriptive studies and case reports, or reports of expert committees.
(Harris *et al.* 2001, p. 27)

Top of this hierarchy, and the 'gold standard' as it is called, is the RCT with the control being double-blind (blind because the patients do not know what drug/placebo they are being given; and double-blind because the treating doctor does not know either). What came bottom of the list was the single-case study, at least in its narrative (or process) form as is customary in psychoanalytic research. Though funding agencies may not make these exacting demands merely for the benefit of patients, their interests are best met by offering the most effective treatments. These demands are entirely reasonable, and good outcomes are the prime aim of effective treatment (see Richardson 2001; Leuzinger-Bohleber and Target 2002; McPherson *et al.* 2003; Mace *et al.* 2001).

Psychoanalysis has been caught up in this tide of opinion, but the RCT experimental design for evaluating outcome has proved difficult for psychoanalysis. Aggregated samples, control groups, and blind and double-blind trials are inherently incommensurate with the very personal and subjective quality of psychoanalysis. To look to descriptive case reports, and to single-case studies, is swimming against the tide (though an increasing body of such evidence is accumulating; see Shedler 2010).

In addition, good outcome has not always been the most appropriate means of advancing psychoanalytic knowledge. If we look at Freud's five major case histories, we find that Dora was a treatment failure, Little Hans was not a psychoanalysis (though he got better), Schreber was not analysed at all, the Ratman did improve and was a clinical success, and the Wolfman was never 'cured'. That is a score of 1 out of 5, a 20 per cent success rate; not a result to be very proud of. But of course Freud did not publish them for their treatment outcome, but for the advance in understanding they each produced.

Many people, however, have accepted the demands for outcome studies conforming, so far as possible, to the RCT standard. They believe the robustness of psychoanalysis will be shown by the outcomes of whole treatments, and many ingeniously designed (and necessarily expensive) projects have been conducted, or are in progress (Richardson *et al.* 2004; Roth and Fonagy 1996; Chiesa and Fonagy 2000; Chiesa *et al.* 2002; Bateman and Fonagy 2001; see also a recent compilation of American studies by Shedler 2010).

The evidence base

Scientific experiments, like psychoanalytic work, have to be carefully arranged so that the sequence of the experiment isolates a single cause–effect sequence. RCTs follow that model, starting with (a) the defined initial state; (b) an experimental action which is a cause; and (c) the effect on the initial state. The sequence, or process, demonstrates the existence of a cause–effect link. Taking a facile example of an experiment to test the theory that 'eggs are fragile', the essence of the experiment will be to place the egg on the laboratory bench and hit it with a hammer. The observable features are (a) the initial intact egg; (b) the hammer blow; and (c) the egg breaking (if it does). Parts (b) and (c) are called variables. The hammer blow is the independent variable, determined by the experimenter. The dependent variable follows on, linked to the independent variable, and showing the effect – the egg breaks, or it does not. For the experiment to be successful it is necessary to have only these two variables. If there is a third variable – say, the hammer is sometimes made of iron, and sometimes made of tissue paper – then the dependent variable, the breaking of the egg, will not necessarily happen with the hammer blow, only if the hammer is made of iron. Or a fourth variable might be the composition of the egg – a hen's egg, or alternatively a decorative egg made of marble polished into an egg-shape. This will add further complexities to the result. Ideally, a scientific experiment will have just one initial condition, and one independent variable (the strike by an iron hammer on a hen's egg), and the dependent variable (in this case two possibilities, the egg breaks or it does not).

When the numbers of variables increase the experiment rapidly becomes more complex. When the hammer might be made of two materials (iron or tissue paper) and the egg also (a hen's egg, or marble) then there are four different conditions. The dependent variable will sometimes be the broken egg, and sometimes not. A total then of eight possible cause–effect sequences. Not all will actually occur, but a pattern will of course become clear with enough eggs and enough runs of the experiment. If the dependent variable itself has more than two states – shall we say, (a) it breaks in a nasty mess on the laboratory bench; or (b) it breaks and a chick jumps out and runs away; or (c) it does not break – then more varieties arise to be correspondingly linked with the initial (independent) variables. Each of the four initial states could have three possible outcomes – 12 cause–effect links

The point is that sometimes science seeks to tackle very complicated systems with many more variables than this. This complexity of variables is so common in certain inexact sciences, notably medicine and psychology, that a whole branch of the mathematics of probabilities has developed to cope statistically. In medicine and psychology it is often the case that the variables are not only large in number but they are not all known. Numerous aspects of physiology may vary the uptake, and analgesic effect, of an aspirin. Physiology is not known in sufficient detail to identify all the possible variations in different people. With large samples, the expectation is that random variables will cancel each other out sufficiently to get some probable indication of the effects of a cause (the administration of a drug). The larger the sample, the more chance of cancelling out the extraneous variables. Large-scale sampling has become a standard method of assessing drug effectiveness, and comparing drugs.

Certain variables cause a variety of effects on drug effectiveness; these are the psychological factors. So RCTs are designed with multiple samples – some given the drug A, some given drug B, and some given an inactive placebo, and there are variants of this design, with combinations and variable doses, and so on; as well as cross-over trials in which sample groups change from drug A to drug B, or placebo. In addition, *blind* designs aim to eliminate psychological effects and focus on the physiological and pharmacological effects. However, blind designs (aimed at eliminating the psychology) appear to be at a disadvantage in investigating psychological methods for achieving psychological effects (Hinshelwood 2002).

Because many and complex variables demand more and larger samples for the necessary statistical methods, the accumulation of suitable psychoanalytic samples is unlikely. Blind experimental designs are also impossible; but despite all these difficulties at least some projects have been carried out, as mentioned above.

However, there is a further difficulty. Outcome of psycho-pharmacological medication and outcome of a psychoanalytic treatment are not the same thing. One prioritises symptom-change or at least relief, the second requires less tangible personality and relational changes. To reduce psychoanalysis to symptom change, or drug treatments (or other psychological treatments) to changes in unconscious aspects of personality and relationships, distorts each form of therapy. There is no true comparison.

In addition, a lot more research is needed than simply the effectiveness of a treatment. The complex nature of a psychoanalysis introduces new variables – notably, the theoretical views and the commitments of the conducting analyst. There is, as previously argued, a need to take account of some of these conceptual differences which intrude, probably with differential effects of one kind and another. Hence we need conceptual research. This corresponds in many ways to the initial R&D phase of drug development. Much work is needed to match chemical compounds to known physiological systems, for example, before the drug is trialled. Equally, the technology of psychoanalytic interpretation based on metapsychology has to be sufficiently understood before any really useful outcome of psychoanalytic treatment can take place.

Because of the limited knowledge of specific theoretical factors in the formulation of interpretations, comparisons across schools of treatment reveal only the grossest factors. This led to the influential results of Truax and Carkuff (1967) that therapeutic effects of many different kinds of therapy are nothing more than the effects of decent ordinary relations – empathy, non-possessive warmth and genuineness.

In general, the psychoanalytic use of the RCT-type research design has four main limitations:

1   *Like-with-like*: Psychoanalysis uniquely aims at changes in depth, at changes in object-relations, in unconscious phantasy, and this contrasts with the symptom change of most therapies; so hence there is not a possibility of comparing like with like – psychoanalysis with, say, CBT.
2   *Patient–therapist relationship*: The RCT was designed to exclude the influence of the medical bedside manner in order to isolate the effect of a drug on its own without psychological factors. However, in a relationship-based therapy like psychoanalysis, the very core is the analysis of the psychological relationship which is excluded by the RCT, and hence an RCT design works against itself with relationship therapies.
3   *Outcome studies*: Important though effectiveness in terms of eventual outcome is, such studies are unable to comment on the actual processes used in the practice of the therapy; and which bring about the outcome, and hence little can be said about outcomes if conceptual divergences and comparisons are ignored.
4   *Massification*: Though the amassing of psychoanalytic cases together is possible, it more or less requires that evidence has to be in the form of

non-clinical data that is collected separately from each subject. On the rare occasions where psychoanalytic case studies have been amassed – for instance, as in Wallerstein's (1986) 42 cases – the potential for generalisation has proved rather low. Even in psychoanalytic outcome studies the examination of those outcomes needs to be conducted on a single-case basis, with each case being considered for progress *in its own psychodynamic* terms if we are concerned with the specific dynamics of the inner world of each patient before and after treatment (see Chapter 2 on process research).

It is surely necessary to know the ideas, theories and practices of psychoanalysts by which the outcomes (whatever they are) will come about *before* outcome assessment is undertaken. So, psychoanalytic research must test the knowledge on which treatment is based, before any outcome research. We must rehabilitate conceptual psychoanalytic research, the old love of Freud and psychoanalysts (Dreher 2000; Haynal 1993; Freeman 1998).

The value of single-case studies will be considered in Chapter 14, where we will note the irony that, when we look beyond healthcare and drug trials, most research in the sciences does not use large samples. In fact, scientific experimental design frequently uses a single case, the experiment. And this is true occasionally of 'natural experiments' and fieldwork. As we will consider later, it only took *one* expedition by Christopher Columbus to ascertain that you do not necessarily fall over the edge of a flat Earth – with immense consequences for the history of civilisation. This design is potentially usable in psychoanalytic research, though there has not been a wide appreciation of this fact. Edelson is an exception; I have argued that the case study, now held in disrepute, is nevertheless necessary to test psychoanalytic hypotheses and, if properly formulated, can indeed test, not merely generate, hypotheses (Edelson 1986, p. 89). And earlier I reported a test study using material from a single case (Hinshelwood 2008).

Conditions for psychoanalytic knowledge

Despite Freud's insistent claim all through his life that psychoanalysis should join the natural sciences, there is good reason now to think that he was on the wrong track. Because of the problem of achieving a consensus between different groups of psychoanalysts adhering to different schools of thought, the question calls us to understand what conditions need to apply in order to claim a piece of psychoanalytic theory is knowledge, given the special characteristics of the field of study. As we have seen, consensus generation is hampered by several questions:

- Does the subjective nature of the data render it inadequate as data?
- What consensus-generating methods could we develop to test our knowledge?

• Does the need to take each case history on a single-case basis prevent the normal checks on subjectivity being applied?

We must take these three areas of concern into account in the logic of psychoanalytic research. Moreover, we have the more specific problem of what data we actually deal with and need. We will need to sort out carefully a rigorous method of observing and gaining appropriate data (see Chapter 15).

In conclusion, the unique set of problems facing psychoanalytic research suggests that the standard logical model in the natural sciences is not going to be relevant without modification. Our overall task will therefore be to see what modifications will be necessary to generate a logical model that *is* relevant to investigating subjective experience.

Chapter 6

What is knowledge?

In this chapter we will cover a few of the essential concepts necessary to grasp the main outline of knowledge-generation in general and how we need to conceive our psychoanalytic production of knowledge.

Justification

Plato required knowledge to be justified by some rational account, a reasoned argument. His actual claim (made here through the voice of Theaetetus) is:

> That is a distinction, Socrates, which I have heard made by some one else, but I had forgotten it. He said that true opinion, combined with reason, was knowledge, but that the opinion which had no reason was out of the sphere of knowledge; and that things of which there is no rational account are not knowable – such was the singular expression which he used – and that things which have a reason or explanation are knowable.
>
> (Plato, *Theaetetus*; trans. Jowett, p. 83)

Knowledge is belief (an opinion) plus something. Some 'thing' must distinguish belief from knowledge; in other words, he said: knowledge is justified true belief; or $K = B + J$.

J, justification, is the crucial term that makes a difference to B, producing K. Of course J may not give certainty, because new data, evidence, or theories may emerge which undermine the justification. The sun goes round the Earth is a view that received good justification empirically from ordinary observations of the sun. It lasted until accurate measurements of the planets could be made with a telescope, and the new evidence threw out the old theory and its justification, to be supplanted by Copernicus's heliocentric theory.

J is also problematic because there are various forms of justification, and therein lie the awkward questions. We can discern two main kinds of justification:

1   argument based on formal logic, like that of mathematics; and
2   empirical argument, that is to say, an opinion justified by observations (or 'facts').

The latter, empirical justification, turns to the real world and constitutes, broadly speaking, the field of science. Facts are gained from the experience of the real world – *Empeirikos* being the Greek word for experience.

Common sense would have it that we can simply check our opinions in the real world. Newton's law of gravity is simple enough to check with experience – just by dropping a stone. However, it is not so simple. Aristotle makes the subtle difference between fact and theory: 'knowledge of the fact differs from knowledge of the reason for the fact' (Aristotle, *Post and Prior Analytics*; trans. Ross, 1995). There are a number of problems with the common sense view.

Perception: We gain our experience from our basic sense perceptions, and they are not always reliable. People have different perceptions of the same thing – some people cannot distinguish red from green. 'No one now seriously believes that the mind is a clean slate upon which the senses inscribe their record of the world around us: that we take delivery of the evidence of the senses as we take delivery of the post' (Medawar 1982, p. 89). But more seriously there are many facts we need to know that are at the limit of, or beyond, the capacities of our perceptions. Then we make estimations which risk a point of view influencing what is perceived – for instance, the pitch of a car's horn is higher if it is coming towards you compared with one going away from you. It has proved possible to extend the capacities of our perceptual senses with technical inventions – like the telescope, microscope, night-sight binoculars, and so on, right down to the cloud-chamber to make visible the smallest particles of matter. On the whole, scientists are 'realists', which means that they think there is a good enough correspondence between the world and what we see to take a positive stance on there being a world out there, and that we can know what it is and how it behaves.

However, this is not uncontested. The problems with the observations made by the senses have led to doubt about the correspondence between what we see in our minds, and what actually exists out there in the world, or beyond. An element of influence *by our minds* can be incorporated in what we see. That influence on what there is, we call subjective. So, some philosophers are not so sure we can be as positive as realists want us to be. The ancient Greeks for instance argued that a very great deal of what we see is an interpretation. Red is not *in* nature – it is what we see. And we now know that what is out there is a 'wavelength of light', not the actual colour. The inferred qualities in nature, such as red, introduced by the interpretations by the mind, were called 'qualia'. It is difficult to know how far that interpretive activity means we live in a world of inferences. Kant for instance described certain interpretive schemes; in fact he thought that there were three basic categories introduced by the human mind when it interprets our perceptions. Those categories are 'time', 'space' and 'causality'. Our minds are *incapable* of eradicating those categories, and the question is whether the features of time, space and causality are indelible because they are out there in the world, or whether they are features of the mind which can *only* perceive things through the grid of those categories. This view that the mind sees things only in its own categories is known as an idealist view, and it contrasts with the realist one.

The idea that we cannot really trust our minds to be faithful in presenting to us a completely accurate picture is surely not a foreign idea for psycho-analysts, who work all the time with the distortions of transference. However, psychoanalysts do divide up. There are those more realist, who would claim that it *is* possible to get rid of distortions, so long as we conscientiously adopt Freud's role of the blank screen and the steely attitude of the surgeon. On the other hand, some psychoanalysts would say there is no unconflicted, undistorting functioning of the ego, and they hold a more idealist position. More recently, the latter view has moved to the fore with the investigation in great detail of the nature and effects of the countertransference and intersubjectivity.

Finally, a problem which will occupy us most in these Part II chapters is the way in which scientists use their facts. We will discuss the two alternatives, 'induction' and 'deduction'. They have considerable consequences in terms of what kind of confidence we put in our theories.

Inductive justifications

Induction is the mental process by which various observed instances can be seen to be related in a general way. By having some similar characteristic, those instances are then generalised. If the sun rises everyday, this has become a generally expected characteristic of the sun. If it has recurred every day so far, we can predict it will rise tomorrow. Induction is the emergence of a general rule, in this case about the behaviour of the sun, so that we can say that we 'know' it will rise tomorrow, and we can put our faith in the repetition every day of a sunrise and a sunset. Similarly, we can generalise that 'all swans are white', when we have only seen instances of white swans. If we see enough trees with green leaves, we can generalise that trees have green leaves. A generalisation is at a different level of knowledge from each individual experience of a tree having green leaves. Each instance of a tree might be called an observed occurrence, and a quantity of similar occurrences can be gathered together as a general discovery about the nature of some aspect of our world, which we can call knowledge. Further instances of the occurrence add to the confidence in the generalisation, or, we can say, *justify* it.

Generalisation based on multiple empirical facts from the senses is one form of giving an account, as Plato called it. Induction is not just a belief; it is more. If we say, 'angels have wings', we express a belief; but when we say trees have green leaves, the belief can be accounted for by recurring evidence from the senses – an empirical account. A belief in angel's wings cannot be accounted for by evidence of the senses. Induction on the basis of empirical evidence has a sort of concrete solidity which makes such beliefs into probable knowledge. In an inductive account of knowledge the justification, J, comes from empirical evidence from repeated instances.

Generalisation of this kind has been the stock-in-trade of scientific knowledge for many centuries. Linnaeus, for example, developed his hier-archical classification of a species, a genus, a family, and so on. Biology came of age as a modern science when Darwin took all the accumulated specimens from his voyage on the *Beagle* and generalised his theory of natural selection by the survival of the fittest. Darwin's classification of plants and animals in relation to the pressures of the ecological habitats in which they lived is a mass of data inductively generalised into theory. During the nineteenth century, science was largely the accumulation of facts about nature, the ordering of those facts, and insofar as it was possible, the development of general theories, or laws, based on the general occurrence of those facts.

Freud adopted induction in the creation of psychoanalysis, finding an accumulation of instances (such as the Oedipus complex), and generalising inductively from that to the theory that Oedipal fantasies are ubiquitous in the psychological development of all human beings.

Pattern recognition: Induction is akin to, or identical with, the intuitive and spontaneous function of pattern recognition, the quality of a gestalt that springs immediately to the mind apparently without effort, almost unbidden. It is a process in which a general form (visual, general, conceptual, etc.) is convincingly filled in from a sufficient selection of perceptual clues, giving the spontaneous experience of a closure to the pattern. Such an experience is not neutral. It is compelling, and people will spend hours doing jigsaw puzzles, for the satisfaction of completing a pattern. As the pattern is com-pleted and the gaps are closed a sense of significance or meaning is experienced. This satisfying sense of conviction occurs in the intuition of inductive generalisation.

However, the occurrence of a completed pattern is not necessarily evidence of actual regularities out there in the world. For instance the compelling meaningfulness of astrology demonstrates the unreliability of intuitions of this kind. The attribution of significance to the constellation of the stars, is an activity of the mind, and not of nature.

Verificationism: Any general rule predicts that further instances will conform to the rule. When repeat observations do conform to the theory, they verify it – another white swan confirms the generalisation that all swans are white. Continuing observations of the movement of the planets verify Copernicus's generalisation of the orbits of the planets. Each new psychoanalytic treatment which discovers a new instance of the Oedipus complex verifies the truth of the general theory.

Now, interestingly, verification may not always be exact. In the historical case of planetary orbits, it was found that some planetary measurements did not always fit Copernicus's generalisation. The heliocentric theory was not completely verified. A modified generalisation was then formulated by Kepler to take account of the anomalous instances – the orbits of planets are elliptical rather than circular. Such is the process of advance in science by induction and verification.

Enumerative induction: However, trying to check all instances is usually an impossibly large task. We are restricted to samples and have to make an assumption that a sample probably represents the whole class of all such instances. Errors of sampling can be reduced but they require increasingly complex sample selection, matched controls, and statistical handling. We have to accept probability rather than proof. Because induction concerns the problem of sampling, the nearest that we can come to a logic of induction is that of probabilistic statistics drawing on sample populations.

There is an important limitation to this form of inductive verification. As each confirming instance mounts up, the value of each instance, as a confirming verification, falls off. So after 1,000 observations of white swans, an additional sighting of a white swan will be a thousandth of the weight of the earliest sightings. It does of course verify the theory, but, as we approach the umpteenth million, that sighting is barely worth considering as empirical evidence any more.

Realism and verification: Those with a more realist point of view – minimising the distortions of the mind – tend to have more confidence in verification. This was the position of the logical positivists, a school of philosophy led by Moritz Schlicht that flourished in Vienna in the first half of the twentieth century. Their work elevated verification (Ayer 1936) to be the commanding principle of science, and knowledge-production in their project aimed at completely excluding metaphysics (i.e. eliminating Aristotle's 'final causes').

We can note here the emphasis placed on inductive knowledge generation by psychoanalysts. In many instances, new theories are advanced on the basis of a number of cases with a common characteristic.

Hume and problems with induction: There has been a long-standing concern about the confidence we can put in the process of induction. It is intuitive, and thus could allow a lot of subjective distortion. But that is not the only aspect of the problem. There is a concern that induction does not really stand up logically. Hume (1748) argued that to predict the future from past instances is not logical. If all instances of sighting swans in the past have shown them to be white, by induction we make the generalisation, 'All swans are white'. We predict that the next sighting will be a white one. However, Hume argued that this prediction is not the result of reason, and he could not see an argument which could establish this prediction with certainty – it is not possible to conclude with certainty, using this method, that black swans do not exist.

There are therefore several problems with induction as a valid form of knowledge-production:

- First, the observations may simply lead to incorrect generalisations, e.g. Copernicus's theory of circular planetary orbits.
- Second, the evidential weight of confirming instances progressively falls off, resulting in the decreasing weight of the evidence as the number of instances increases – this is the poverty of enumerative induction.
- Third, induction produces no logical certainty comparable to deduction.

However, the problems with induction do not necessarily invalidate theories built on such generalisations. More recent debate has engaged in defences of induction (Medawar 1969; Stove 1986; Williams 1947). Hanly (1992) makes a defence of inductivism as the basis for psychoanalytic knowledge, and the fact is that intuitive processes of generalisation (induction) do probably form the major part of theory building in all forms of science.

Prediction: Generalisations are in fact the articulation of predictions. When by the river we may well predict that the next swan we sight will be a white one. However, this is only one kind of prediction.

Another kind of prediction concerns causality. As we saw earlier, materialism is the view that events in the material world are caused by forces which are of that world. Causality is a general principle for making sense of process; one thing causes another. Thus when one thing happens we predict that its effect will follow on. Cause–effect links are the bedrock of science. They are also the Achilles heel of scientific theories, as we shall see (in the next chapter). But causality is problematic for psychoanalysis, too. Where do we place 'wishes', and 'intentions', the forces which psychoanalysis studies? We will eventually have to examine how (and if) causes and intentions fit together (Chapter 17). Whether cause–effect links can be a basis for theorisation in psychoanalysis has been extensively debated, and we will come back to that issue from a slightly different angle.

I have described how a rational account of knowledge can be based on induction. Though induction is important, especially in ordering and classifying observations, philosophers have gone in search of the kind of certainty that adheres to deductive logic. Because further instances of a generalisation may *not* always verify it, therefore a generalisation based on a restricted number of instances always risks the chance that one of the non-examined instances will be out of line with the rest, thus invalidating the generalisation – finding a black swan for instance (they do exist, apparently, in Australia). With only one instance, the inductive generalisation collapses completely – a powerful weight of evidence carried by a single case.

Deductive logic

Deduction is a different kettle of fish. It possesses a logical certainty. Aristotle is credited with the earliest form of deductive syllogism:

Major premise: All humans are mortal.
Minor premise: Socrates is a human.
Conclusion: Socrates is mortal.

There is an inherent conviction within the three steps of this argument. The conclusion follows with certainty from the truth of the two premises. This is formal logic, but it has been known for a long time that deduction can be useful in the experimental approach to science. In fact, Crombie (1953) showed that the distinction between induction and deduction was known to and described by Aristotle, and in the middle ages the twelfth-century monk, Robert Grosseteste used the distinction (though using the terms 'resolution' and 'composition') for formulating experimental approaches. In establishing the 'Oxford School', Grosseteste influenced no less a person than Roger Bacon (Hackett 1997).

Deduction is an a priori form of knowledge, in contrast to empirical observation, which forms the basis of induction. As a scientific tool, deduction formulates a scientific experiment like the logical syllogism of Aristotle. The scientific theory is the major premise, shall we say:

Major premise: Because a gravitational field bends rays of light, an eclipse will show this bending.
Minor premise: There was an observable eclipse in 1919 in India.
Conclusion: This eclipse will show light rays curving around the sun.

The conclusion predicted an actual state of affairs and therefore is amenable to empirical observation. Observations could then show if the conclusion is as predicted. If the conclusion is not predicted, then either one of the premises is wrong. In fact, a set of observations was made during the eclipse in 1919 by Arthur Eddington. His empirical measurements did show light being bent; so, the prediction was found and therefore the premises could be confirmed. The deductive process shows where and how to find empirical confirming instances. Take another classic experiment in physics, one done by Albert Michelson and Edward Morley. Here, the prediction was not found.

The ether theory stated that light travels through the ether, like waves across water, or sound in the air. So, a beam of light reflected back and forth in the direction of the flow of ether would take longer to return to its source than a beam reflected at right angles. This comparison can actually be measured by an apparatus known as an interferometer, invented for the experiment by Michelson and Morley in the 1880s. The delay in one of the beams will cause interference in the wave patterns when the two returning beams are superimposed. This can be set out in a form similar to a deductive syllogism:

> *Major premise*: The ether theory predicts that light will be reflected back quicker from a distant mirror at right angles to the motion of the Earth compared with light shone in the direction of the Earth's motion.
> *Minor premise*: There is an instrument, an interferometer, which can compare the speed of light reflected back from two directions.
> *Conclusion*: The speed light travels is the same in different directions.

The prediction that light travels at different speeds was not found – there was no difference in time of travel in the two directions. Unexpectedly, the prediction was not found, and so the ether theory was immediately dead (Michelson 1881; Michelson and Morley 1887). The deductive logic is lethal in its power to show a theory to be false. Such is the process of advance in science by deduction and falsification.

The divergence of induction from deductive logic has therefore been spotted for a long time, and the issues of induction, and verification and probability were revisited by the logical positivists in the early twentieth century. Reichenbach distinguished the 'procedure for finding' from 'the procedure for justifying'. This is the crucial area of uncertainty and confusion in psycho-analysis (see for instance Hanly 1992; Canestri 2003; or Ahumada 2006 who proposed varying arguments for defending psychoanalytic 'finding').

We therefore have two kinds of rational account that both give rise to the experience of something being true knowledge: either

1   an experience of empirical truth arises from the sense of a common characteristic and predictable repetition known as *induction*; or
2   in contrast, *deduction*, which is an a priori experience, is felt with a logical process worked from prior premises.

However, despite the logic being different in either case, the sense of conviction is common to both.

Nevertheless inductive and deductive processes of thought appear in practice to be both necessary; theory-building is an inductive process, and therefore provides the theories that need testing by a deductive process. *Both* induction and deduction are necessary in the production of knowledge. But we need to be clear that the evidential weight coming from the two processes is different.

Chapter 7

The scientific model of knowledge-production

Karl Popper, in 1930s Vienna, challenged the logical positivists' position on verificationism.[1] The English version of his book was published after the Second World War (Popper 1959). Popper exploited the asymmetry of certainty. The millionth sighting of a white swan carries little evidential weight compared with one sighting of a *black* swan, which falsifies the generalisation. Proving the validity of some inductive generalisation is uncertain; but proving it false can be definitive. The decisiveness of falsification led Popper to develop his *principle of falsification*. This led to the possibility of demarcating scientific knowledge from pseudoscientific theories. Genuinely scientific theories have a special property; *they can be shown to be false*. To be scientific, a theory must in principle be at risk of being falsified. Those theories which cannot be tested are not scientific (though they may be something else).

Non-scientific (or pseudo-scientific) theories do exist. They may be created by inductively recognising general patterns – like seeing the shapes of constellations in the sky. The 'truth' of the pattern of a constellation is *not* falsifiable, as it is not possible to devise a falsification of the theory that the constellation 'Orion' is truly the spirit of the hunter. It cannot be tested, and cannot therefore be falsified, so it is not a scientific theory. On the other hand, the circular orbits of planets could in principle be disproved, by further, more accurate, measurements – and they were (their orbits are ellipses). Popper wanted to make sure theories stand up when you try to disprove them. So, in Popper's terms, scientific theories are 'risky' – they must genuinely risk being false.

An important adjunct to the principle of falsification is the 'null hypothesis', a concept introduced by R.A. Fisher into evolutionary biology. Originally developed when statistically comparing a large sample with a control sample, the null hypothesis is that there is no difference between the samples, when one predicts that there is. The justification of a theory may not be easily decided definitively, but a hypothesis can be set up which is, as it were, the opposite of the research hypothesis, and that *can* be falsified definitively. So the falsification of the null hypothesis is said to be a more definitive support to the theory than a verifying confirmation.

Popper's principle of falsification became a watershed in the recent history of the development of science. Although Popper first published his theory before the Second World War, and in Vienna, it was really only after Freud's death that this notion of what science is began to be seriously debated, supplanting the older verificationism. To the consternation of psychoanalysts, one of the examples that Popper gave of a pseudo-science was psychoanalysis.

> I developed further my ideas about the demarcation between scientific theories (like Einstein's) and pseudoscientific theories (like Marx's, Freud's, and Adler's). It became clear to me that what made a theory, or a statement, scientific was its power to rule out, or exclude, the occurrences of some possible events – to prohibit, or forbid, the occurrence of these events. Thus *the more a theory forbids, the more it tells us.*
>
> (Popper 1976, p. 41)

In fact, he was also in difficulties over the Darwinian theory of evolution by natural selection, though eventually decided it could pass muster as a science. He was not so generous to psychoanalysis.

In line with the new scepticism, Sydney Hook organised a large symposium in New York, in March 1958, on psychoanalysis and scientific method, gathering a prestigious group of psychoanalysts, philosophers and social scientists to discuss the psychoanalytic method (the proceedings were published in the same fateful year as the English edition of Popper's book, 1959). Hook challenged psychoanalysts with his thought experiment: 'what kind of evidence were they [psychoanalysts] prepared to accept which would lead them to declare in any specific case that a child did not have an Oedipus complex?' (Hook 1959, p. 214). This points to a fundamental principle: it is necessary that the research procedure includes the possibility of a negative result. If the only outcome of the research is to confirm what you already expect, then you have in effect done nothing. The *possibility* must exist of finding evidence that your hunch (believed knowledge) is wrong. In the same symposium, Ernest Nagel (1959) gave a keynote address, similarly criticising the apparent vagueness of psychoanalytic ideas which made them difficult or impossible to verify. Heinz Hartmann (1959), in the other keynote paper, languidly gave a satisfied account of psychoanalytic ideas which amply confirmed Nagel's concern that they remained essentially unreliably verifiable.

Hook's question is a crucial one: is it possible *in principle* to find evidence that a theory is wrong (or at least not generally the case)? The emphasis is on the negative, the disconfirming instance.

The logical model of science

This logical model promoted by Popper starts with a theory, not with data. He was not interested in the generation of theories, which being inductive lack the rigour of a logical scientific method. Science, therefore, is putting theories to the test. If we make a generalisation based on experience that, for instance, 'eggs are fragile', then an experiment can be devised: put an egg on the laboratory bench and hit it with a hammer. If it breaks, the theory has been tested and survived (though the egg doesn't). This entails a logical structure, based on deduction. The theory will allow us to deduce a general *prediction* – 'an egg will smash when hit with a hammer'. That prediction can then be confirmed with an experiment: 'If I hit an egg with a hammer, will it smash?' The prediction is tested – the egg either smashes or it does not. The model has a number of steps, and resembles the syllogism used in the last chapter:

- a hypothesis
- a deduced prediction and
- a decisive set of data.

The third of these steps, collecting the decisive data, is to set up the experiment that will generate this precise data for the purpose of testing the prediction (the second step).

Having it both ways: Central to Popper's assigning psychoanalysis to the category of pseudoscience is the common accusation that psychoanalysts have it both ways. Freud knew this supposed criticism:

> in giving interpretations to a patient we treat him upon the famous principle of 'Heads I win, tails you lose'. That is to say, if the patient agrees with us, then the interpretation is right; but if he contradicts us, that is only a sign of his resistance, which again shews that we are right. In this way we are always in the right against the poor helpless wretch whom we are analysing, no matter how he may respond to what we put forward. Now, since it is in fact true that a 'No' from one of our patients is not as a rule enough to make us abandon an interpretation as incorrect, a revelation such as this of the nature of our technique has been most welcome to the opponents of analysis.
>
> (Freud 1938c, p. 257)

If psychoanalytic interpretations are always correct, they cannot be adequately tested. In Hook's terms, there has to be some conception, however imaginary, of what someone without an Oedipus complex would look like. This is the epistemological challenge for psychoanalysts.

Consequences for psychoanalysis: This 'hypothetico-deductive' paradigm has given 'science' a different logical structure from the scientific thinking that Freud knew. In fact, he specifically described induction:

> The true beginning of scientific activity consists rather in describing phenomena and then in proceeding to group, classify and correlate them. Even at the stage of description it is not possible to avoid applying certain

abstract ideas to the material in hand, ideas derived from somewhere or other but certainly not from the new observations alone. Such ideas – which will later become the basic concepts of the science – are still more indispensable as the material is further worked over.

(Freud 1915, p. 117)

Freud could not be giving a better description of the *inductive* method of generating theories. Psychoanalysis tends still to rely on the inductive accumulation of supporting data. For our purposes, we might regard psycho-analytic clinical research as having two stages; *both* (a) accumulating facts to generalise a theory – induction, and (b) testing those theories. Until we can do both (not just create theoretical novelties), Freud's 'science' has been left behind by the rest of science. That means we need a logical model for *testing* psychoanalytic theories – not just generating new ones.

The interesting question is not whether psychoanalysis is a science, but whether deductive testing of psychoanalytic theories is possible. In other words, can psychoanalytic research proceed in a way similar to, or by analogy with, the procedures of natural science? Can deductive processes of falsifica-tion be developed in the investigation of the immaterial world of subjective experience? The answer I will give is that it can. We *can* develop a parallel logic which compares with the rigour of present-day scientific investigation.

Are psychoanalytic theories falsifiable?

In the last 50 years, the hypothetico-deductive model of science has made demands on scientists to present their research in a specific way. However they came to their conclusions, scientists now need to be able to formulate their thinking in this logically deductive way. The development of this logical model of science, implies psychoanalysis should follow suit with a comparable model for psychoanalysis, however psychoanalysts come to their conclusions.

There are various ways of responding to Popper's ruling, but there are two epistemological strategies. One is to challenge Popper on the status of psychoanalysis, and argue that it is falsifiable, and therefore real science; and the other strategy is a more global challenge to Popper's view of what science is, like that of Kuhn. Kuhn's tendency to simply say, based on a sort of social psychology argument, that science is what scientists do, has seemed to be a God-sent justification for doing what psychoanalysts do. However, one philosopher–psychoanalyst has cautioned, 'it is misleading for psycho-analysts to rely upon the anti-objectivist thesis of Kuhn as though it were uncontroversial in philosophy' (Hanly 1983, p. 395).

Grunbaum's repudiation of Popper: Adolph Grunbaum (1984, 1993) criticised Popper on the first grounds. He argued that Popper held completely the wrong idea of psychoanalysis. Freud did in fact lay himself open to the risk that his theories were wrong, and constantly discarded inadequate ones. Grunbaum claimed Freud's theories could be tested and falsified; and so they are 'risky' in Popper's sense. Grunbaum argued that predictions can be made, just as in natural science, and established this with Freud's statement that: 'After all, his [the patient's] conflicts will only be successfully solved and his resistances overcome if the anticipatory ideas he is given tally with what is real in him' (Freud 1916–17, p. 452).

Grunbaum calls this the 'tally' principle – tallying is the *necessary condition* for a patient to recover. Only psychoanalysis can produce the correct insight into the patient's unconscious that will effect a cure. After interpretation, the patient may get better, but without interpretation he cannot. This 'necessary condition thesis' (NCT) is a falsifiable claim. Like the black swan example, it would take only one case in which a patient gets better without psycho-analytic interpretations to falsify Freud's claim for psychoanalysis. So, risking being falsified, psychoanalytic theory is scientific. Therefore, Freud *was* doing science.

As is well known, having rescued Freud from Popper by showing that Freudian theory is 'risky' in the sense that it can be properly falsified, Grunbaum then claimed Freud's theories did end up falsified! This is Grunbaum's second claim. Only one case is needed to falsify Freud's risky claim that neurotic patients *only* get better with interpretation, and Grunbaum showed from Freud's own work that patients sometimes do get better by spontaneous remission or by suggestion! The necessary condition is not necessary.

Many psychoanalysts reject Grunbaum's second claim, using two main arguments:

1   The quoting of Freud is highly selective when we know his writings were often polemical and political as well as scientific. Grunbaum is right that Freud does in his earlier writings emphasise psychoanalysis as inherently very different from suggestion, involving insight without suggestion. Freud's claim in 1917 was in response as much to the claims of dissenters such as Jung and Adler as well as the French suggestive therapies, as it was a scientific claim. So there is here a small sleight of hand on Grunbaum's part. Later, however, Freud relaxed his distinction between psychoanalysis and suggestion after about 1920. Hence Grunbaum's reliance on later writings to falsify early theories is inconsistent. Grunbaum mistook the stress Freud placed on the distinction between psychoanalysis and the effects of suggestion, and overlooked Freud's political intentions as if they were just scientific ones. This does not mean that Grunbaum is not right to subject Freud's early claim to rigorous philosophical enquiry, but to do so in ignorance of the specific progress of psychoanalysis, and Freud's well-known propensity to modifying his ideas, weakens Grunbaum's argument.

2   Grunbaum's use of Freud's process evidence – if you make a correct interpretation, the symptom abates – as a genuine cause–effect process is a little dubitable. Freud's early work had a very short timescale – typically

Anna O was hypnotised, and the effect was a modification of the symptoms immediately when she came out of the hypnotic state – but this is very anachronistic and impractical in the later Freud when treatment began to take a number of years with innumerable interpretations. And symptom-change is even more impractical today when much more subtle, internal and unconscious changes would be taken as the confirming effect of an interpretation. So Grunbaum used the complexity of the later technique as if it were no different from the simple short-term causation of the earliest technique.

Now to another challenge to Popper.

Thomas Kuhn

Popper's work on the nature of science in general has been debated and challenged (Kuhn 1962; Lakatos 1976; Feyerabend 1975; see also Fuller, 2003). Kuhn (1962) argued that Popper's falsification principle was in error *in general*. In practice, Kuhn argued, scientists do not follow the ideal model laid out by Popper, in two respects:

- Instead of discarding falsified theories, scientists tend to modify them, a manoeuvre Popper condemned as a 'conventionalist strategem' (Popper 1963, p. 48). It may include redefining the class – for example, the class of swans will only include white ones. Scientists are conservative; they stick to their theories as long as possible (of course, psychoanalysts are not so conservative, and embrace new theories in an almost promiscuous way – but unfortunately not always on the basis of old ones being adequately falsified).
- In any case, a theory cannot be discarded until there is an adequate alternative. Scientists need to go on explaining things even if imperfectly. For instance, the wave theory of light is known to be inadequate, as light also behaves as if it were a stream of particles; and indeed the particle theory is inadequate as well. To this day no adequate theory has replaced these imperfect and falsified ones. Falsification does not lead to discarding a theory as Popper required.

Kuhn described a very different pattern to the progress of science. In practice, new theories are adopted under quite different conditions from those Popper claimed. Kuhn's more historical observations led him to two conditions for the emergence of a new theory:

1   when the unexplained anomalies a theory fails to explain build up to a serious level; and

2   when a theory capable of explaining the anomalies, or some of them, makes its appearance.

Kuhn addresses what he claims actually happens, rather than an ideal model. He took account of the phase of research that comes after discoveries – that is *dissemination* to other scientists who form a consensus in accepting the theory. Its continuing acceptance means it is a paradigm, before it, too, gets displaced eventually when there are too many anomalies it cannot explain and another theory can. This strategic argument was adopted by the psychoanalyst Marshall Edelson (1983). Edelson argued that research in psychoanalysis only discards a theory if there is an adequate alternative. Truly, one cannot continue to practice therapeutic psychoanalysis if the theories one uses have been discarded by research and no alternative is yet forthcoming. One uses the best there is, however imperfect.

Kuhn might subscribe to the view expressed by various people that 'Philosophy of science is about as useful to scientists as ornithology is to birds.' Nevertheless, if science is not actually done according to the precise logic, that logic is still necessary. We need the hypothetico-deductive model for formulating the results of experiments, and to defend the body of knowledge. New knowledge needs to be argued for using that logical form, even if that may not be how it was originally gained.

Conclusions

The idea that a paradigm theory is a consensus captures the allegiance of an established group of people who research and practice in the field is important. Various methods, some mentioned in Chapter 4, operate explicitly or implicitly to create this consensus in any field of knowledge including the psychoanalytic. Development of course involves debate, dispute, and contention, as well as the important process of consensus generation. Given the particularly fissile history of psychoanalysis, we require reliable methods for achieving this consensus. In other words, we need such a logical model as science has, even though the psychoanalytic logical model may not conform to the scientific one, and in my view it has to diverge very significantly, due to the subjective field of study.

This chapter has given some idea of the ingredients of the models of knowledge which are current. We will now go on to explore how these can be applied to psychoanalytic knowledge, and with what sort of research design.

Chapter 8

Single-case studies: their validity

As mentioned earlier, NICE put the narrative reports of single-case studies bottom of its list, as the least valid form of evidence. Research designs using large samples of subjects were developed in experimental psychology as a means of controlling numbers of variables. A plethora of variables makes psychology more like fieldwork than experimental science. However, in the history of psychoanalysis, case studies have provided the staple data. Psychoanalytic knowledge production originated in the detailed analysis of single cases, including the very first, Anna O. That makes psychoanalytic research suspect in its context of medical and psychological research. However, single-case studies do not carry such low status in the physical sciences; quite the reverse. The strategy of experimental science is to design experiments that can be specific in a single instance, like dipping a litmus paper in a solution to determine if it is acid or alkali. Natural science aims at specifying all the conditions that will isolate (a) the independent variable, such as wielding the hammer, and (b) the dependent one, the fate of the egg which hangs on the effect of the hammer. Thus, natural science developed a method not followed by academic psychology or medicine. Given that sciences differ in their methods, psychoanalysis may be free to differ too.

A mediaeval single case

Long ago, in the Middle Ages, there was a hypothesis that the Earth ended just beyond the horizon and if you went further you will fall off. In fact, it only needed one expedition to go beyond the horizon, and return, for the theory to collapse. Columbus decided that he would make the journey, and find whether he would fall off the Earth's rim, or find new territories for the king of Spain. This might have seemed a reckless venture, and indeed the hard-headed merchants of Genoa had refused to support him. So Columbus had to go to the king of Spain for his research funds. We know the result. It was a decisive one: the Earth is round. The point is that it needed only *one* expedition. It did not need a whole sample of expeditions of numerous Columbuses to set sail.

It doesn't really matter if this was intended from the outset as an experiment, or whether it was some adventurer seeking to make his fortune. My claim is this is a good example of a decisive single-case study, so decisive in fact that it radically changed the course of European and world history to the present day. Implicitly the experiment followed the line of argument on the asymmetry of truth; the confidence in the theory was tested, and tested by a single instance.

This experiment was successful because only one variable was involved. It could decide whether the Earth is either a flat disc or a round globe. This is a binary question. The single variable is the crucial step in this research design, because it produces a binary question, and one answer only can destroy a generalisation.

Generalisation and binary questions

The Columbus example is rather unusual since there is only one Earth to investigate. In this case, the whole of the class of 'earths' is merely one, and a 'sample' must simply be one case. The usual situation is that the sample is only a proportion of a much larger class of instances. Generalisation is therefore to make the assumption that what is true of the instances in the sample is true of the total number of instances in the whole class. So all the swans that have been found have been white leads to the generalisation that this bird is always a white one. This is why there is a risk that a counter-example, a black swan, will exist among the whole class, but has not been a part of the sample. This is the risk with sampling, but it also gives the possibility of certainty through definitive falsification when a counter-example is found.

Freud's great generalisation was the Oedipus complex as a central feature of all human personalities. One counter-example would demolish the theory, as Jung and Adler threatened. His response was to write his phylogenetic phantasy, *Totem and Taboo* (1913), arguing, with Frazer's (1890) *Golden Bough* as support, that Oedipal issues stamped their mark on society throughout history and pre-history. In reaching into non-psychoanalytic territory, to fend off his dissidents, he in fact brought down more criticism from the anthropological world. Bronislav Malinovski, Elliott Smith, W.H.R. Rivers and others actually went out to visit the tribes who told the myths that Frazer had used, and found family constellations so different that it was difficult to see how an Oedipal configuration could arise.

However, because the stakes were high, and generalisations vulnerable, it was necessary to assert the psychoanalytic discovery, and Ernest Jones (1925) wrote a detailed and well-informed rebuttal of the anthropological criticisms, using the unfortunate psychoanalytic tactic of arguing that if the facts do not fit then it is because of resistance from the tribal unconscious. It was hardly a debate-winning argument and the discussion between the two disciplines has continued to the present (e.g. Johnson and Price-Williams 1996).

The point is that generalisations are risky, and this can be exploited with a binary question. Any instance of the general class can be asked if it supports the generalisation. If so it is added to the accumulating enumerative induction, or if a counter-example, then it makes the general theory untenable.

However it is a matter of experience that a generalisation which is flawed may still be useful, and cannot be simply regarded as false. Thus a more or less generally true theory may still have some value. This has been the position in medicine and psychology. Most people with a *Staphylococcus* infection will get better with penicillin – except people allergic to penicillin, or if the organism is a resistant strain. That still means penicillin is useful – based on the experience of people infected in general.

Exceptions are perhaps even more wanton in psychology, where individual variation is both more pronounced and also less understood in terms of the variables that would allow for prediction of exceptions. And this may be the case with psychoanalytic theories. However, a psychoanalytic treatment is not like a course of penicillin. It is not a probability exercise, it is about finding all the hidden variables, different but discoverable in each individual case. This makes the probabilities involved in a generally true theory irrelevant.

Psychoanalytic single cases

Like Columbus's adventure, psychoanalysts do not set out to design experiments as such. However, you can't conduct a psychoanalysis without finding it is a research investigation of what we know, and what we don't yet know. Freud's inseparable bond between therapeutic work and knowledge-production means that psychoanalytic cases are natural experiments. As Ernest Jones rather defensively claimed, 'Most criticisms of single-case research apply to the uncontrolled, informal case study, and it is important to distinguish between these and the more formal and systematic study of the individual case' (Jones 1993, p. 100). In fact the condition is to follow a precise design with a carefully developed question which keeps the variables to a minimum, preferably two – the independent and dependent variables. And this condition the psychoanalytic setting is eminently suited to meeting.

A case that disconfirmed theory: Freud's (1905) case of Dora may be formulated as a test of a science-like hypothesis. On the strength of his theory of dreams (1900) Freud believed that their interpretation was the basis of a psycho-analysis. He constructed the theory, utterly reasonable at the time, that since the dream represents the repressed in disguised form, then the interpretation of the dream brings those repressed contents of the mind back into consciousness. Freud proceeded on this basis with Dora's two key dreams. However, the benefits of insight gained in this way were not confirmed. Dora dramatically disconfirmed the theory, by leaving the treatment with some disaffection. Had Freud formulated this as an experiment in a formal way he might have:

- formulated a binary question: if the dream elements are interpreted are the symptoms relieved?
- made a prediction – that the interpretation would relieve the repression; and
- observed, as a result, that the symptoms modify (or not).

The result in the case in question was that such interpretation did not modify the symptoms; and this falsified the generalisation based on his theory of repression. One case was necessary to achieve a falsification, and Freud appreciated this decisive result. His theory did not hold, and he spent some years before publishing, not just the case history, but the modification of theory required – the notion of negative transference. Thus it is quite possible to reformulate case histories, even from the early history of psychoanalysis. Modern experimental design employing the principle of falsification and a single case is quite adequate in many instances for describing the progress of psychoanalytic knowledge.

The 'placebo' design

The Dora case conforms to the pattern of the Columbus case. An independent variable is applied (an interpretation), and the dependent variable has two forms (arising from a binary question). However, an alternative design is common in the psychological and medical arena. This is the withholding of the independent variable. A successful outcome after *no* treatment is an equally crucial single case. This is also achievable in psychoanalysis.

The necessary condition thesis: When Grunbaum (1984) postulated the necessary condition thesis (NCT) he rescued psychoanalysis from Popper (see Chapter 7). The thesis is that *only* a psychoanalytic interpretation will cure a neurosis. However, he continued his argument by examining how the NCT can be put to experimental risk – as Popper demanded. A cured case of neurosis can be examined to see whether the cure involved psychoanalytic interpretation, or not. This is comparable to the design that compares a drug to a placebo. If the necessary condition is the interpretation (the independent variable), we have a binary question: did a specific improved case result from an interpretation? This question has two possible answers: either (a) the symptoms disappeared after interpretation or (b) they disappeared without interpretation. The question decides categorically and convincingly between two clear-cut answers. It takes only one case demonstrating the latter, improvement without interpretation (in effect, a placebo), to conclude with certainty that the NCT is false – interpretation is *not* necessary.

Conclusion

Thus, psychoanalysis *can* test its theories, given an appropriate research design; either applying the independent variable with a negative result (the Dora case), or not applying the independent variable with a positive result (Grunbaum's NCT test). The experiment has a litmus-like effect. Only one case is decisive. The 'experiment' is not designed as such, as the Grunbaum example explicitly shows. In both cases, however, the material is comparable to fieldwork in social science, or more to the point, like Eddington's observation of a naturally occurring eclipse. A psychoanalytic generalisation (like one in physics) is vulnerable to a single case that does not conform, provided the research question is posed as a binary question. The conditions for a single-case research design *can* be met by psychoanalytic clinical work.

Chapter 9

Freud's claims

Psychoanalytic ideas are not easily accepted, and so we can ask, what valid methods are there for making our claims? What in practice should convince us? As Freud confided, 'There is too much that is new and unbelievable, and too little strict proof' (Freud to Fleiss, 14 December 1899; Masson 1984).

In this chapter, I will look briefly at some of Freud's methods of convincing his public, since they are surprisingly varied and represent existing methods of dissemination and consensus-generation.

Freud was familiar with, and was reconciled to, the uphill task of persuading others to take psychoanalysis seriously. As a scientist early in his career, he believed psychoanalysis to be scientific knowledge, and science provides an effective discourse for convincing colleagues in the medical and psychological professions. However, Freud also knew psychoanalysis was akin to the humanities, and regarded psychoanalysis as potentially bringing them a scientific rigour. Interestingly, around the same time, there were high-status attempts to use the scientific method to evidence religious beliefs, and the survival of human beings after death (Myers 1904). This research was conducted by the well-endowed Society for Psychical Research (Oppenheim 1985), of which Freud was a corresponding member. The use of the scientific method to establish the validity of knowledge outside the material world was a movement in full swing when Freud was developing psychoanalysis. Thus in the climate of the time, science was expected to colonise those disciplines – sociology, the humanities and religion – with its characteristic rigour and use of evidence.

However, Freud did not restrict himself to a scientific method of discourse. He explored and exploited a range of methods. He had reason for moving beyond the narrow scientific method of disseminating knowledge, prompted by the stubbornly dismissive medical reaction. Hence, he endeavoured to draw into his circle people from any walk of life, and he was ready to speak to them in whatever way they could listen.

However, psychoanalysis is *about* that very object – the human mind – *to* which Freud was disseminating his new ideas. Psychoanalysis being the most personal of 'sciences', everyone has their own authoritative views about their mind and that of others. Because people make their own observations, theirs are as valid as anyone else's. Moreover, curiously, while science is an Enlightenment project rooted in human reason, psychoanalysis takes seriously that most subversive of human attributes: our passions. So, all human beings practice their own 'folk psychology' with each other all the time, and then they employ *all* their faculties in assessing psychoanalysis, and not just those restricted ones permitted by Enlightenment reasoning. Hence Freud was probably right that one has to appeal to all sides of human beings when trying to inform them of themselves, and to convince their minds of his discoveries about their minds.

I distinguish Freud's four main methods as:

1   The scientific, exemplified by Anna O in *Studies in Hysteria* (Breuer and Freud 1895) and based on the cause–effect link in which clinical outcome stemmed directly from medical intervention.
2   The free association method, evolved later, in his own self-analysis, exemplified by the Irma Dream (chapter 2 in *The Interpretation of Dreams*; Freud 1900), and based on an inductive argument quite different from scientific causality.
3   Genetic continuity, exemplified by the Wolfman (Freud 1918), which is a quasi-historical method, seeking a hidden thematic continuity between the infantile Wolfman and Freud's adult patient.
4   A more literary/dramatic mode, as used in *The Psychopathology of Everyday Life* (Freud 1901) and *The Introductory Lectures* (Freud 1916–17), which attempts an evocation of experience in the reader's own reflective understanding of human beings.

These comprise four *kinds* of arguments.

Scientific causality

Anna O: Freud's early training as a medical scientist carried through into his study of human beings. At the end of the nineteenth century the dominant psychology was associationist; that is to say, the human mind is conceived as the association of perceptions, memories, thoughts, and so on, with each other. The discovery of the reflex arc in the nervous system enhanced the notion of the mind as contents associated together, and therefore the mind like the brain was the outcome of similar processes of connection. So it was anticipated that when the mind goes wrong the linking associations go wrong. Complexes of mental contents could come apart – i.e. dissociate – and reform in arbitrary ways, which may feel compelling to the patient but are nonsensical.

Breuer and Freud were fascinated that in the case of Anna O, emotional stress provoked disruption in the normal associative processes, and quite unpredictable and inappropriate links were made between perceptions and behaviour. Via such paths, Breuer and Freud thought Anna's traumatic stress could become a direct causal determinant of hysterical symptoms. Breuer called the state of mind which was conducive to these random associations, the *conscience secondale*, and he found he could access it by hypnosis. Then, like an ordinary medical scientist he *caused* a therapeutic effect by interrupting the abnormal associative links by bringing them back into the normal state of consciousness. The nature of the condition is a causal one – trauma causes symptoms. Freud could claim to his audience the scientific causality of hysteria.

The dream of Irma's injection

Later, Freud adapted Breuer's therapeutic method, and dropped hypnosis. But he retained the notion of association – and dissociation. He experimented with an associative method using his own dreams. Francis Galton in England and Wilhelm Wundt in Germany had already conducted experiments with psychological associations. And Carl Jung with Franz Riklin in Switzerland was using associative tests to access the dissociation believed to be at the root of severe psychosis. We can follow Freud's thinking very clearly in 'Analysis of a sample dream' (Freud 1900: ch. 2). In this process Freud moved towards a conception of association that differs from Breuer's. It is an association of themes – those *similar* themes that crop up within different elements of the dream. Naturally he regarded this as the ordinary, non-pathological, form of association. However, he still saw it as occurring in a 'second' conscious-ness – or as he called it by then the Unconscious, kept distinct from consciousness by the activity of a 'censor'.

There is a continuity with the associationist theories of the Anna O case, but causality has been dropped. Freud was not appealing as a scientist. He was not presenting a deterministic causal link, but instead a more subtle *thematic* link. Of course it is true that by then he was operating with a different model of the mind – one in which the *conscience secondale* was no longer pathological, but a 'normal' Unconscious possessed by everyone. The method by which he tried to grab the attention of the reader is to show a common theme represented in disparate forms in the dream associations. He asked us to look at this thematic pattern and not at a time-dependent causal sequence. He understood that the human mind is highly influenced by seeing patterns – the common theme, gestalt (as named by Wundt). There is no causality to be interrupted by therapeutic intervention – and indeed how could a dream be 'cured' in the way Anna O's symptoms were? Underlying the dream are themes leading to the discovery of a trauma (or at least a serious discomfort). And this contrasts with the scientific work with Breuer, in which knowledge of the trauma could lead to the discovery of causal links. Freud thus added to his armoury a second method of gaining attention for his new ideas – a thematic affinity.

Reconstruction in the Wolfman case

Freud's write-up of the Wolfman case (Freud 1918; analysis conducted in 1913–14) has endured as a paradigm of the therapeutic method in psycho-analysis. In this he established the principle of genetic continuity as a pillar of clinical psychoanalysis. The plausible appeal is that early experiences structure adult psychodynamics. For a long time Freud had claimed a continuity from early stages of development to the later emergence of symptoms and character problems, using his principle of fixation points. He had checked the validity of this extrapolation back, with the Little Hans case (Freud 1909a), by showing that the early genital stage postulated in adult treatments actually did occur in a four-year-old boy. But the Wolfman, by presenting a dream from his fourth year which was analysed when an adult, showed how the dynamics of the childhood dream emerging in the adult analysis must have been operative at the time of the dream in childhood, and continuing into adult life. The Wolfman, arriving in Freud's practice at a time when the crises with Jung and Adler were at their height, offered a special opportunity to weld in place the theory of infantile sexuality and its enduring effects, in answer to the dissident voices. The case is itself both a major exemplar of the use of genetic continuity, and a major justification of the principle.

Interestingly it bears traces of both the two previous claims – the causal aetiology of hysteria, and the thematic affinity in the dream elements. Like Anna O, there is an associative link between a trauma as a cause and its later effects in adulthood. The trauma of the primary scene at the age of 18 months led, via the dream at four years, to neurotic symptoms more than 20 years later. The timescale is enormously extended compared with the causal links of Anna O's case, so the demonstration of the Wolfman case does not turn on the interruption of this causal link, as did Anna O's treatment. Instead, the link is presented in another way. Our conviction is requested on the basis that the later dynamics (the passive identification, etc.) matches the dynamics as discovered in the analysis of the earlier dream from childhood – this is a thematic similarity and compares to the affinity of themes in a dream. The case therefore turns on the similarity of themes in past and in the present, which can then be construed as a cause, from the theme in the past to the theme in the present. Freud appeals therefore to an intuition that early experience is linked with later ones, and represents a causal link *as well as* a thematic affinity. The plausibility of this long-standing link did convince colleagues so effectively that the reconstruction of early psychodynamics has been a central feature of classical psychoanalytic treatments ever since.

Literary evocation and everyday experience

Appealing to the reader's own intuitive response to create a sense of plaus-ibility was one of Freud's great gifts which, as argued above, may be entirely appropriate when dealing with the discoveries about the human capacity to intuit a psychological life in other humans. Freud's literary gift enabled him to exploit this form of argument in certain of his works, notably his *Psychopathology of Everyday Life* (Freud 1901) and his *Introductory Lectures* (Freud 1916–17), the latter being delivered to a live audience. The method is remote from science. It is an attempt to convince through evoking in the audience a dramatic sense of plausible 'stories', and their explanation. Freud relied on his audience being, in fact, human beings who could identify themselves with the players, or identify the players with those they already knew. Because people have the capacity for self-reflection, they can place themselves within the experience of the figures in the stories. He appealed not just to reason and evidence, but to an evoked response just like a novelist or dramatist does.

I have discerned four main methods by which Freud described his discoveries with varying success to different audiences. Other people studying this may discern other methods Freud used. Nevertheless, his methods do vary – from the neutral principle of causality, to a principle of thematic meaningfulness on different timescales, to plausible self-reflection. As Freud clearly demonstrated, though hardly acknowledged, if this is a science it is a science with one foot in meanings, intentions and values. It also demonstrates an understanding that conviction may be aroused in various ways, and we will look in the next chapter at the power of conviction of meaningfulness and narrative.

Chapter 10

What about hermeneutics?

A number of psychoanalysts have pulled the rug from under the criticism that psychoanalysis is not a science, by agreeing that it is not – that it is something quite different.

The hermeneuticist conception of psychoanalysis is to a large extent a radical attempt to invalidate methodological criticisms made against psychoanalysis. Instead of trying to answer charges about the unverifiability of psychoanalytic propositions one by one, they want to discard them as irrelevant (Strenger 1991, p. 40).

The alternative 'something else' that psychoanalysis might be, has two forms

1   psychoanalysis is a *hermeneutic* discipline engaged with meanings rather than causes; and
2   psychoanalysis is a *post-modern* approach to a co-constructed event that arises intersubjectively between analyst and analysand. The very possibility of objective knowledge and truth is then called into question, completely ruling our naïve realism.

In this chapter we will consider the first of these, the tempting movement known as the hermeneutic turn (Spence 1993) the post-modern approach Chapter 11 will consider.

Thematic affinities

Freud's fundamental investigation of dreams – their meaning and interpretation – has led some philosophers and psychoanalysts to approach psychoanalysis as an investigation of just that – meanings *rather than* causes; 'The methodological goals of the interpretive sciences are radically different from those of the natural sciences' (Steele 1979, p. 391). Starting with the meaning of dreams, turning to the age-old narrative of Oedipus, and recently concentrating on the immediate dramas of transference and transference-countertransference enactments, psychoanalysis has always been a narrative discipline tracking down meanings – as well as a contrasting 'physics' of psychic energy. The seduction of Dora, the Wolfman's trauma arising from the primal scene of parental intercourse, to the contemporary emphasis on enactments between the two analytic partners, focuses us on the subjective narratives of inner reality: 'I want to argue that narrative appeal and narrative persuasion lie deep in all of us' (Spence 1983, p. 458).

This focus on meaningful narrative rather than causes had not been Freud's original intention; but he may have misunderstood what he was doing, a 'scientistic self-misunderstanding' as Jurgen Habermas called it (Habermas 1968, p. 246). That is to say, Freud misunderstood his own work, believing it to be about scientific causality when it is actually very different.

In Freud's move, between 1895 and 1900, from analysing the causal structure of hysteria to interpreting the meaning of dreams, he made a number of changes. Explicitly, he substituted the free association method for the hypnotic cathartic one. Moreover, in dream analysis, there is no instrumentality – the dream link (its wishful meaning) is not tested by revealing it, the dream does not 'disappear' as Anna O's causal hysterical symptoms did, by consciously recognising the cause (see Chapter 9). Though Freud did think he was looking for a cause–effect link – the painful wish causing the dream – it is not what he found. He found a similarity, themes recurring in a number of the chains of associations to the dream elements. Thus the link was a similarity of theme (and of its affective quality). In the theory of dreams, the meaningful theme supplants causality. If the nature of the link (thematic not causal) is so different, then it might require a different form of study, and the hermeneutic approach is waiting to supply that alternative.

Therefore, the hermeneuticists say that psychoanalysts *should* regard their work as the study of meanings and meaningfulness, rather than causal determination. Grunbaum, however, scathingly mocked the motivation for this view:

> This stratagem has likewise had much appeal to a good many analysts. For, faced with the bleak import of sceptical indictments of their legacy, they are intent on salvaging it in some form. Hence, some of them will be understandably receptive to a rationale that promises them absolution from their failure to validate the cardinal hypotheses of their clinical theory . . . Be of stout heart, they are told, and take the radical *hermeneutic* turn. Freud, they learn, brought the incubus of validation on himself by his scientistic pretensions. Abjure this program of causal explanation, the more drastic hermeneuticians beckon them, and you will no longer be saddled with the harassing demand to justify Freud's causal hypotheses.
>
> (Grunbaum 1984, p. 57)

Despite the ridicule, it could still be possible, in principle, that Freud *was* wrong in his view of psychoanalysis as a science. Both philosophers (Habermas 1968; Ricoeur 1970) and psychoanalysts (George Klein 1973; Schafer 1976;

Spence 1983; Brook 1995) have argued that psychoanalysis is a hermeneutic discipline. Instead of causality, we must seek the meaningful significance in the patterns of personal history and narrative. The rationale for a psychoanalytic treatment is then to help the patient create a more coherent meaningful narrative of their lives. The aim of knowledge-generation is converted to meaning-generation, with the guiding principle of intelligibility – not prediction. Rules of interpretation of a text do not exist in the way that rules of experimentation exist for testing the validity of a scientific theory; so that individualistic meanings support the uniqueness of persons, but defy general application.

Hermeneutic philosophy and the hermeneutic psychoanalysts

The philosophers

Hermeneutic philosophy was developed in the twentieth century, particularly by Gadamer (1975), who, following Heidegger, investigated the nature of understanding. He rejected the narrowness of science, and its increasingly severe demarcation of scientific truth from human understanding in general. In contrast to the absolutist objectivity of science, truth for Gadamer comes from a consensus within an interpretive community. He explored the historicity and cultural relativity of the way a community understands its world.

Paul Ricoeur (1970) argued that psychoanalytic material, notably dream content, is articulated in language; rather like the social relativity of Gadamer's emphasis on community. Similarly, Ricoeur recognised the fact that psychoanalytic material is not objective as is that of physics. Psychoanalysis is an immaterial, semantic field of observation, without the physicality of natural science. Psychoanalysis is concerned with meanings embedded in symbolic utterances, meanings may even be *hidden* there. So, the occurrences in a semantic field – expressions in words – are driven by reasons, intentions, and meanings. The driving force is the pain of a meaning – in the Irma dream it was Freud's fear of being an incompetent doctor. The pain that activated the dream elements, is a hermeneutic form of description, different from a description of libidinal energy cathecting a memory image – Freud would have said they are the same kind of description.

Undoubtedly, psychoanalysis is an interpretive activity; so it is not a big step to claim that intelligibility of meaning is test enough. A psychoanalytic treatment is concerned with the agency of the person to make meanings and generate experiences and intentions. Habermas (1968) pursued this agentic aspect. He described psychoanalysis as an emancipatory practice, and thus as an extension of liberatory politics. He started with Freud's earliest work, showing that the unconscious contents of the mind are causal factors that have determinant effects on conscious thought and behaviour. Psychoanalysis, he argued, is a means by which the conscious individual may free him/herself from those unconscious determinants. Consequently, the critical contribution of psychoanalysis to understanding human beings is not the causality embedded in the metapsychology, but the clinical theory which releases the agency of the person *from* unconscious causality. He therefore developed a very sophisticated proposition in which the social determinism for capitalist and consumerist economics can be dissolved through the agency of the subject in exploring and understanding the distortions in his dialogue with 'others' from a different class. Through the dialogue between analysand and analyst (like dialogue between any two people) the hidden and underlying determinants – both social and psychological – are challenged and therefore open for conscious thought. Such a conscious activity then emancipates them both socio-politically and psychologically. Psychoanalysis could therefore entertain the hope that in its dialogical functioning, it promotes the political project of social tolerance, and exposes false consciousness (Lukacs [1923] 1974).

Thus, a central focus of these writers has been the contrast between determinism and free will. This in turn transforms into other polarities – subjective experience versus physical evidence, and reasons versus causes (Hopkins 1982); the latter opposition was debated by philosophers as far back as Toulmin in 1948 (see also Eagle 1980).

The psychoanalysts

While Ricoeur and Habermas addressed philosophical questions, some psychoanalysts have focused on the treatment method itself (initially, George Klein 1973, and Gill 1979). Metapsychology was important to Freud as it created a body of abstract theory comparable to the advanced natural sciences. Metapsychology elaborated psychic determinism and founded psychoanalysis on the principle of causality and the psychic economy of the libido. However, what drove Freud was not what drove his patients. His patients were struggling persons looking for solutions and resolutions to their conflicts. They were not interested in abstractions about their psychic energy. The body of theory, especially that called 'drive theory' within ego-psychology in the American tradition of the 1940s to 1980s, radically contrasts with the clinical encounter theorised in terms of the transference, countertransference and the therapeutic alliance. That contrast has been of focal significance for the hermeneuticist psychoanalysts.

George Klein distinguished two separate psychoanalytic activities: 'Explanation in terms of process versus explanation in terms of motivation' (Klein 1969–70, p. 520). The first explanation, he said, was connected with the theoretical principles of metapsychology and consisted of the operation of mechanisms operated by drives, while the second was what he called a 'clinical theory' addressing the suffering patients' struggles. In opposing metapsychology to 'clinical theory' he wrote:

We need an entirely different theory of sexual development to replace the libido drive concept. Let me add that I believe the clinical theory of psychosexuality does offer the basis for such a revision, but it is the clinical theory sans the drive metapsychology. It still occasions some surprise to say that Freud's conception of psychosexual development – the clinical theory – is not synonymous with, and even does not require, the libido drive concept.

(Klein 1969–70, pp. 519–20)

George Klein was arguing for the separation of clinical theory, concerned with the person, from metapsychology, concerned with generalised notions of mechanisms and forces.

However the methodological problem hermeneutic psychoanalysis addresses is that 'One glaring difficulty with the conception of a systematic motivational explanation is that the problem of criteria for evaluating such an explanation is not dealt with' (Eagle 1980, p. 336). With the hermeneutic approach such general criteria of evaluation are not necessary if the aim is to make sense to the patient. It is the meaningfulness of the new narrative for the patient that is the criterion.

The rejection of generalisation expresses the hermeneutic turn towards the individual person with meaningful intentions. Related to this was the development that Schafer made, to develop a 'new language for psychoanalysis'.

[Freud] relied on a mixture of two languages, one suitable for natural science propositions and the other for the utterly unsystematic discourse of everyday life. But Freud had no warrant to expect either the language of the laboratory or the home to be suitable for expressing his data, He seems never to have realised that the discipline he was creating would have to have a language peculiarly its own before it could attain systematic dignity and elegance.

(Schafer 1976, p. 123)

The role of Schafer's new language is 'to identify a network of intelligible actions where none was thought to exist' (Schafer 1976, p. 127). In this sense, the person is an agent of whatever happens in his internal world, whether he accepts that or not, even if he claims a passive subjection. This attempt to gain intelligibility through posing the person as agent, was elaborated into a psychoanalytic system of narration, 'I designate as narration whatever qualifies as a telling or as the presenting of a version of action' (Schafer 1992, p. xiv). In this sense a psychoanalysis is the construing of a life as a sequence of intelligible actions, and hence the narration of a personal biography which is coherent in terms of the meaningfulness of the events, and of the sequence of them, or incoherent for those mentally troubled.

The analysts who have most prominently thought this through are those working in relation to (and perhaps in reaction to) the ego-psychology tradition where drive theory pushed psychoanalysis into its most scientistic and deterministic forms. Hence these writers are mostly American, whereas British and European psychoanalysts of the last 50 years have tended towards an emphasis on object-relations, rather than drives, with therefore a less mechanistic, and more humanistic style. And those British authors attempting to rewrite drive theory, such as the Sandlers (e.g. Sandler and Sandler 1994) and Target and Fonagy (1996), have gone less far than the radical inter-subjectivism of some American writers (e.g. Renik 1998b; Ogden 1992); and that is probably because the British version did not need to go so far.

The main points of the hermeneutic debate

In summary, the scientific view rests on the realist assumption that there is something in the patient to be discovered; while the hermeneutic view rests on the assumption that a joint agreement on meaning constitutes a relative truth for both partners. We have covered a number of points in support of this approach, which I will summarise before addressing the problems:

- Gadamer postulated that there is a world of human knowledge that is not empirical in the scientific sense, but attracts a sense of conviction because it has social 'meaning', not because it is logically supported by induction or deduction.
- The pattern, meaning, significance, or narrative must be intelligible and coherent; internally and externally.
- Ricoeur developed this by giving a special importance to language as the vehicle of meaning. Since psychoanalysis is the talking cure and is about the nature of human experiencing, then psychoanalysis is a privileged case for this new 'philosophical hermeneutics'.
- Habermas, however, took this in a different direction, and was interested in hidden meanings and false consciousness, for which he turned to psychoanalysis for inspiration and liberation.
- George Klein followed this trend by giving psychoanalysis a new direction, separating the complex metapsychology from clinical theory; the first being theory-building (perhaps for its own sake), and the second being theory in action, necessary for understanding the treatment process and the experiences of that process.
- Schafer pursued the notion of psychoanalysis as focused on action, intention and responsibility. Patients need to own their part in the creation of their biographical narrative. Psychoanalytic language has the form of intended action in the world, and he moved away from elaborate theoretical structures to establish that psychoanalysis elaborates wishes, meanings, and the biographical narrative.

Problems

These steps in developing a hermeneutic philosophy of psychoanalysis have taken a different direction from those of the scientific approach to psycho-analysis. It has, however, met with difficulties and criticisms of its own.

Relativism: The problem of a permissive view of truth and the means to achieve it, is that we can slip into a simplistic relativism, in which meaning for the sake of it is sufficient. Gadamer's 'intentional community' implies a relativism which scientific experimentation avoids. The scientific demands for validity and reliability no longer apply to meaning generation. Without that rigour we could be compelled to enter an 'anything goes' territory. And indeed psychoanalysis exemplifies that, being pushed apparently helplessly towards such a Tower of Babel.

Meaning systems: It is probably true that meaning is more or less an exclusive property of the human mind. However, it does not follow that human beings live only in a world of meanings. On the contrary, people are active beings who use their physicality as well as their mentality (not least their bodily sexuality, as Freud tirelessly stressed for the benefit of his dissidents). And the physical world demands at least some respect so that meanings can fail to provide direction in the real world.

Emancipation: Habermas's argument has been criticised (notably by Grunbaum 1984) for the rather easy equation of causal determinism with the unconscious, and agency with the consciousness. It is not likely to be the case that conscious effort in the course of psychoanalytic treatment unlinks the determining causes from the symptoms, the traumas from their effects. Instead of working by abolishing the trauma–symptom link, Grunbaum argued, a psychoanalysis abolishes the cause (the unconscious trauma) and therefore the effect disappears in the absence of its cause. Causality itself is not abolished, only certain instances of causes.

Reasons versus causes: The sharp and defining difference between meaningful reasons and mechanical causes has been disputed. For instance, Davidson (1963) argued that the brain is a physiological mechanism organised on cause and effect principles, and yet operates with perceived reasons based on meaningful experiences. The evident correlation of mind with brain implies the impossibility of dividing reasons from causes. In quite general terms this may be the case, but his detailed correlation of causes with agency remains impractically abstract.

The paradoxical conclusion

Inevitably, as with much theorising, psychoanalyst's differences become oppositions. In this case, the opposition of causes versus meanings. If we unpack the set of views that comprise the hermeneutic turn, we have to acknowledge that there is a hidden belief that hermeneuticists rely on. This is a belief that adopting a new meaning changes the patient. In this case, it is a change in the patient who comes to live his life with a new narrative, more coherent and more healthy. Thus an interpretation conceived by a hermeneuticist psychoanalyst is believed to *make a difference* – that is, to have an effect on the subject (as Renik 1998b conceded). This implicit theory approximates to the causality of science. Can the hermeneuticist really eliminate causal thinking, when it comes to the actual practice of psychoanalysis? As a result, the structure of hermeneuticist thinking is much the same as that of the scientist – both include an intention to have an effect.

At the same time, an account of a psychoanalytic treatment from a scientific point of view, describes a series of occurrences which proceed from the interpretation to its effects, and this in itself is a narrative, a set of intelligible occurrences arranged in a coherent sequence, and with intention. The process of scientific enquiry is a narration!

The paradox exists; the hermeneutic approach aims to *effect* some result, and scientific causality is an intelligible *narrative*. This should lead us to suspect that we are not dealing with such a radical opposition as claimed by the hermeneuticists. The hermeneutic and scientific approaches are not two separate, distinct and alternative explanatory domains. There is a perceptible interpenetration between them, which could lead to a more synthetic view. We may instead be dealing with something like the contrast between a vertical perspective and a horizontal perspective on the same identical domain. I will come back later to this resolution of the apparent opposition in Chapter 20. We will find that, in fact, both scientific knowledge and meaningfulness need to be engaged together to fully understand the nature of psychoanalytic knowledge. And how else could it be?

Chapter 11

Is there a post-modern approach?

Central to the hermeneutic development is the post-modern premise that truth is socially generated: 'Science in origin and essence is the mechanic's mode of enquiry' (Home 1966, p. 45). The notion of truth in a subjective science is inevitably contentious (see Hanly 1983, 1999). Questioning the very existence of reality and objectivity has relevance for psychoanalysis. Interestingly, it leads to the view that psychoanalytic truth is the joint property of two (or more) subjectivities, not a view of the relationship with truth. Turning epistemology on its head also turns aspects of psychoanalysis on its head. However, the really important aspect of this approach is that it acknowledges that the field of study is a subjective – and an intersubjective – one, and *not* one of the physical material world (see Hinshelwood 2012, for variants of the notion of intersubjectivity in psychoanalysis). It turns away radically from the scientific past of Freud and seeks to undo the excessive scientism of drive theory and ego-psychology. As such it is a post-modern version of hermeneutics. Whereas the hermeneuticists acknowledged that the interpretation of meaning was individually and culturally specific, the intersubjectivists take the micro-culture of the analytic pair as central, so that the therapeutic micro-culture constitutes all of what psychoanalysis is.

I will touch on this unconcluded current debate by looking at the exchange between Owen Renik and Marcia Cavell (Renik 1998a, 1999; Cavell 1998a, 1999).

Renik's postulate

Renik takes as problematic a current contradiction:

> on one hand, tolerance for and interest in the intensely personal nature of an analyst's participation in clinical work has gained an increasing place in our thinking about psychoanalytic process and technique; but on the other hand, the theory we retain still conceptualizes the patient's psyche as a specimen to be held apart for examination in a field as free as possible from contamination by elements of the analyst's personal psychology.
>
> (Renik 1993, p. 555)

The elimination of the analyst's personal psychology, and an unremitting focus on the patient's perspective, has, over the decades, proved impossible. So a more subtle approach towards countertransference has gained a hold. Discovery is not a process of finding clues and evidence for some objectively existing entity, Renik argued;

> there are those of us who see an analyst's subjectivity as irreducible, and conclude that an analyst can only present his or her own reality (including, of course, the analyst's subjective perceptions of the patient's reality) to the patient for the patient's consideration.
>
> (Renik 1997, p. 281)

The nub of the problem is that by excluding subjective distortions we risk excluding subjectivity which is the whole field of study. In line with a post-modern view, the psychoanalyst's view is merely a subjective one, like that of anyone else, including the patient. The old notion of 'contamination' by the psychoanalyst's subjectivity is rather underplayed because psychoanalytic work, like any discourse, becomes the mutual construction arising simply from two different points of view:

> When two individuals with roughly similar neurophysiological equipment view the same thing or event and each sees it differently, it is not necessarily true that one is incompetent or even wrong; rather, it may be that they each observe with a different theory.
>
> (Goldberg 1976, p. 67)

If the partners are tracking down some *thing*, it is elusive because every momentary attempt to entrap it changes it. It is a moving target, a mouse running under the carpet in unpredictable directions. As Susan Isaacs remarked apropos of the field of study:

> our material changes from moment to moment. Our patient's thoughts and feelings and intentions do not stay still while we examine and compare them. The changes occurring are themselves part of our evidence. They not only bring us new data, but are themselves data by which we gain understanding of the patient's history and present life.
>
> (Isaacs 1939, p. 156)

But Renik's psychoanalytic version of this post-modern, co-constructionist view threatens to throw out objectivity altogether, on the grounds that if the psychoanalyst is irreducibly subjective then objectivity cannot exist. However, Renik denies this and instead discusses an interesting angle on the relative subjective positions. He turned to pragmatism; the best view of something is the one that meets the objectives. The importance of a theory is its practicality, not its objective truth. Each party is subjective simply because each one has his own *objectives*, the wish to achieve something effectively. Thus their views are moulded by their wishes, desires, and so on. Any 'interpretation' is little more than a suggestion from the analyst's subjective point of view, refracted through the field of study, based on his own motivations/objectives. Objectivity is replaced by the meeting of two sets of objectives. As Renik claims, 'In other words, objectivity is a pragmatic concept: it refers to objectives as well as to objects' (Renik 1998b, p. 491). He moves our view from a supposed entity out there seen in a misty, wobbly representation, to a view of the inner realities of both the psychoanalyst and his patient. However, a problem here is to establish the nature of the objectives, as Renik is conceiving them. It appears he has in mind some objective view of the motivations, conscious and unconscious; but who is there left to make such an assessment of each?

Cavell's criticism

Renik's view was critiqued by Marcia Cavell (Cavell 1998a, 1999). First she credited pragmatism, which

> did philosophy a good turn in reminding us that the concept of truth is tied to human interests and does not somehow descend on us from above. Pragmatism also freed us from the Cartesian idea of truth as correspondence to a reality with which we can never immediately be in touch. As I have written elsewhere, this Cartesian idea is endemic in psychoanalytic theory. But pragmatism does not show us how to dispense with the idea of objectivity.
>
> (Cavell 1998b, p. 1200–1)

She argued that what is objectively 'true' is *always* seen from a perspective. A truth is never the whole truth. Two people observing from different perspectives see things differently, but they see the same objective thing (see Cavell 1998a; also Sayer 2000, on a transcendental realism). Two points of view on an occurrence do not cancel out the possibility of an objectivity. Some entity out there can still be said to exist, and can be the object of study. The intent can remain to find the truth about the entity, rather than *just* about the observers holding their perspective-dependent views.

Cavell's solution

Taking Renik's example of a hiker finding his direction from the sun rotating around the sky, and the NASA scientist calculating the Earth's position as the Earth rotates round the sun, Cavell agreed they view differently which object is rotating – the sun or the Earth; and they do so because of the purposes they intend. However, she makes the point that the hiker would not stick to his point come what may – he will, if shown the NASA calculations, probably agree that the truth is that the Earth rotates around the sun. Thus it is possible to recognise a gap between what is true and what works. And the pragmatic view of what works, does not cancel a view of what is true – or what works from another point of view. In creating that gap, objective truth has some place in which to survive. To give up resignedly on objectivity could be making the 'best' the enemy of the good. We, and our patients, must as always make do with 'good enough'.

Cavell is really pointing to a perspectivism, not exactly subjectivity. It is like the half-a-dozen blind men trying to find out what an elephant is; they can each feel a part, a tusk, a trunk, a leg, a tail . . . each one discovers a part of the whole, and that whole still remains actually existing despite the fragmenting perspectives of separate blind observers. As Cavell conveys, the distortions of a limited perspective of the hiker/scientist kind is different from the inner distortion due to the subjective factors we are interested in – the psychoanalyst's anxious defensiveness, or his many other pre-occupations.

This limitation on the possibility of knowing objective truths does not have to lead to pessimism; as Jonathan Lear remarked about Plato's phantasy of men in a cave trying to make sense of their shadows on the wall, they do in fact manage to make some sense of them. It is not all failure, 'The cave is often taken to offer but a bleak prospect for human life, but I think it is the most optimistic metaphor in Western Philosophy' (Lear 1993, p. 741). In other words, *something* of the 'out there' is still knowable despite both the defensiveness and the limited perspective of the observer.

Bell's critiques

As a footnote to Cavell, there is Bell's (2009) hard-hitting rejection of post-modern psychoanalysis. Bell argued that Renik's pragmatism is over-wrought, throwing the baby out with the bathwater; indeed he claims it is un-psychoanalytic. If psychoanalysis is based on a deep understanding of the distinction between appearance (e.g. symptoms) and the real determinants (unconscious conflicts), then post-modernism's emphasis on the surface equality of all points of view rules out the psychoanalytic project of exploring beneath these surfaces – even though it can reward us with 'a great democracy of truth' (Bell 2009, p. 333). However, Bell's critique goes further, and in a psychoanalytically sophisticated way understands post-modernism as having a deep structure itself. By allowing all appearances to have equal status, none can be wrong, and everyone can claim an equal virtue in their own point of view. In short, no-one need relinquish a narcissistic omniscience – an authority deeply dyed in solipsism. This appears to be a counter-accusation against the post-modernist view that 'modernists', those who claim a real truth to be discovered, are asserting a hegemonic authority and privileged ownership of the truth (see also Goldberg 2001). Exchanging accusations of over-claimed authority, or omnipotence, is helpful for neither side. A more nuanced view of the 'truth'-value of a point of view, a perspective, needs attention.

The perspective on perspectives

A perspectivist position was also argued by Gabbard, on the grounds that, 'Even though the analyst cannot transcend the intersubjectivity of the analytic couple, part of that intersubjectivity involves a perspective outside that of the patient' (Gabbard 1997, p. 15). However, Cavell made a second main point; two perspectives on some entity make a triangle, a state of affairs she calls a triangulation, somewhat similar to the use of the term later in the next chapter (and Chapter 17). Cavell's significant point is that there needs to be an awareness of the point of view actually being just that, a point of view. It has a location. There has to be a perspective on the perspective. Because there is never a 'view from nowhere', the importance of triangulation to Cavell is that it must presuppose the capacity to take a point of view while knowing it is just a point of view. As she wrote about subjectivity:

> This means, as Wittgenstein and others have argued, that [a subjective being] is able to make attributions of mental states to others (see Strawson 1963 and Evans 1982); it understands that the mental states of others are available to him in a way they are not to one's self, as one's own thoughts are accessible to one's self in a way they are not to others.
>
> (Cavell 1998b, p. 460)

This is the familiar notion of mentalisation, knowing another has a mind, a capacity that autistic individuals are so bereft of (Mitrani 1992), and maybe even borderline personalties (Fonagy 1989). But the capacity to know there is 'knowing' going on, depends on the capacity to represent, in words but also in pre-verbal forms of representation, called phantasy and unconscious phantasy. Thus, just as the triangulation of a surveyor is his comparison of two perspectives *on* a feature of the landscape, a psychoanalytic triangulation must include an awareness *of* the two perspectives.

The concretistic approach

This distinction between the personal psychology of the psychoanalyst, and his perspective as an analyst, is important. Unfortunately, Cavell's responses to Renik were mostly referring to an entity conceivable in an 'out there' fashion which has a material presence, like the sun in the hiker/scientist illustration. However, at one point Cavell (1998b) did say about her own distortion in one of her cases that it was provoked by her own experience of her mother at the time. Renik is right to maintain that as psychoanalysts we are not dealing with subjective distortions of, or perspectives on, an entity out there; we are dealing with an entity which is itself formed of our subjectivities. But on the other hand, it is not sufficient to collapse the problem into the view that everything perceived is only one solipsistic perspective among many equal others.

The 'entity'

If we follow Cavell that there is some enduring objective entity about which we seek the truth, and we also accept that it has radically different properties from entities in the material physical world, then the question is what is that subjectively formed and studied entity? Freud thought that the entity was the patient's view, his transference. As quoted earlier, Freud regarded an interpretation as an observation by the psychoanalyst on something in the patient which the interpretation *tallied* with (p. 65).

However today, psychoanalytic discovery is no longer a process of finding clues and evidence for some *objectively existing entity*, the transference. That emphasis has been superseded by the addition of the countertransference as an observable and informing phenomenon in the setting, leading to current interest in the transference-countertransference enactments – 'discovered' by various analysts, including both contemporary Kleinians (Joseph 1989; Hargreaves and Varchevker 2004), as well as relational and intersubjectivist analysts deriving from Sullivan (including Renik 1998b and Ogden 1992 – see Hinshelwood 2012).

The change of level from an objective truth about the patient to a subjectively nuanced appreciation of the intrapsychic/interpersonal level involves acquiring a new meta-perspective – taking a perspective on the perspectives. This is the psychoanalytic attitude, and moreover one which we expect our patients to identify with. It is the observing ego, and this may be the central problem to be recognised in certain cases. As Steiner put it, 'I want to make a distinction between *understanding* and *being understood*, and point out that the patient who is not interested in acquiring understanding – that is, understanding about himself – may yet have a pressing need to be understood by the analyst' (Steiner 1993, p. 132).

The acquisition of that reflective meta-perspective – to understand oneself as well as to be understood – is a gauge of the psychoanalytic work. Rather than leaving the understanding to the psychoanalyst, the patient goes away from the psychoanalysis with a newly acquired or enhanced capacity of his own for understanding himself. For instance, 'The observing and criticizing ego [achieves an] objectivation . . . This is necessarily followed by a changed attitude of the conscious ego towards its behaviour which it has up till now wrongly ordered and understood' (Bibring 1937, p. 180).

A progressive objectification results in 'this enlarged state of consciousness' (Bibring 1937, p. 182). The terminology contrasts with that of Steiner, but the nature of the processes each is describing corresponds surprisingly well (Zetzel 1956).

The patient takes away a new perspective on his/her perspectives, and thus leaves the session (or leaves treatment) with an immaterial entity. We will return to the nature of the subjective entity that stands in for the data of objective physical science in the next chapter. The post-modern celebration of relativism, perspectives, subjectivity and the great democracy of truth lays the ground for the psychoanalytic entity that stands in for data.

Chapter 12

Inference and occurrences

Psychoanalytic observations are increasingly viewed with some suspicion, and this comes from various disadvantages, which we have discussed. But it may also be as Tuckett chided: 'I assert that by and large our standards of observation, of clarifying the distinction between observation and conceptualisation, and our standards of discussing and debating our observations are extraordinarily low' (Tuckett 1994a, p. 865). This is a correctable problem, though not without overcoming some difficulties.

One of the difficulties is that our data is refracted through a special instrument we use for making observations: 'Every science is based on observations and experiences arrived at through the medium of our psychical apparatus. But since our science has as its subject that apparatus itself, the analogy ends here. We make our observations through the medium of the same perceptual apparatus' (Freud 1938b, p. 159).

Freud did at times bravely acknowledge this discrepant course for psychoanalytic research. The analogy with the research data of science only extends so far. The data from the psychoanalytic process is a subjective matter, not physical matter. Our observational data, made on our patients, is much the same as our observations of ourselves. We will begin to address this reflexive problem in determining the clinical material to be used as data for research.

Inference

Much anguish is caused by the fact that we cannot 'see' our psychoanalytic phenomena, the Oedipus complex, or a projection. This is felt to create unacceptable uncertainty.

In the course of our analytic work we intervene on the basis of what we infer, and it is the outcome of our interventions which is the test for us of how good our model of the patient is. But neither the analyst nor the patient ever actually knows what goes on beneath the surface material brought by the patient. It can be conceived of, but not perceived (Sandler and Sandler 1987, p. 332).

However, it is one of the most pernicious problems, and it has to be solved in research of all kinds and not mere research data in psychoanalysis. Inference is the stuff of science.

In natural science, the field of observation yields data which is selected for its relevance to the research question. Darwin's research question was: what are the causes of the variation between species? While investigating the Galápagos finches – as well as many other biological organisms on his voyage around the world on board *HMS Beagle* (between 1831–6) – he formulated a hypothesis that the form of a species was an adaptation to the ecological niche in which they survived. The beaks of the various species of finch were ideally selected to form a set of data with which to test his hunch. Hence, a selection takes place influenced by a theory to be established or to be tested:

facts → inference in relation to a theory → meaningful data

Meaning comes from the application of theories to an array of facts. The data can be used then (a) to summate, which increases the weight of inductive support for the hypothesis (enumerative induction), or (b) to test logically an already formulated theory from which a prediction has been deductively made, and which will indicate particular results to be expected. In science, the term 'data' is often used both for what is produced by observation of the field of study, and what is selected from those observations as meaningful and significant for research.

It is different in psychoanalysis. What is observed is itself already meaningful. A segment of the material composed of free associations, dreams, and so on is composed of meanings and narratives. Such a segment of meaning acquires further meaning, or a sort of meta-meaning through the application of psychoanalytic theories (a metapyschology as Freud called it). The generalities of psychoanalytic discoveries, such as the Unconscious, or the Oedipus complex, exist as super-ordinate (or meta-level) organisers of the individual world of meanings in which each individual idiosyncratically lives.

Meaning as substance: Thus, the place of meaning in the two types of investigative disciplines, science and psychoanalysis, is quite different. The very substance of the psychoanalytic field of observation is meaning itself and meaningfulness:

segments of meaning → inference in relation to a theory → psychoanalytic occurrences

The outcome of the same process in psychoanalysis is the production of psychoanalytically meaningful meanings, which I would prefer to call 'occurrences' in the flow of material.

While it is possible to treat the patient's utterances as an objective set of data, and various designs for 'process research' do just that (see Chapter 2), in practice the clinical status of the patient's material is not objective. The patient's associations are his/her expression of personal experience, and he infers meanings from *his* field of observation, and then he communicates these as the segments of the clinical material. The psychoanalyst is alert to that experiencing through his own subjective intuition and empathy.

Dimensions of meaning: Psychoanalytic data occurs apparently in one dimension only, unlike the data of science in the four dimensions of time and space. Subjective experience is located only in time. However, there is a kind of spatial dimension that exists for psychoanalytic data, since subjectivity comes to an end at the boundary of the person, and clinical material expresses that boundary by being the communication of experience and meaning between one subject and another, an 'interpersonal' dimension in actual space. In fact, psychoanalytic meanings also exist in the dimensions of a *semantic* space, not shared with animals even. To a major degree these non-physical, semantic dimensions are idiosyncratic for each person (Wisdom 1943; Nagel 1974). Such data therefore is estranged from the scientific kind. Their characteristic is *being from a* perspective. Really it is a combination of observations from two perspectives, or triangulation.

Perspectives and meta-perspective

The same kind of occurrence may be inferred very differently by differing psychoanalytic theories which isolate a segment of material for their own reasons. Take for instance the following two sets of inferences.

1   Anna Freud wrote of certain moments of hesitation in the flow of free associations, and she conceptualised it thus:

> the ego bestirs itself again, repudiates the attitude of passive tolerance which it has been compelled to assume, and by means of one or other of its customary defence mechanisms intervenes in the flow of associations. The patient transgresses the fundamental rule of analysis, or as we say, he puts up 'resistances' . . . The analyst has an opportunity of witnessing, then and there, the putting into operation by the [ego] of one of those defensive measures against the id . . . and it now behoves him to make it the object of his investigation.
>
> (Anna Freud 1936, p. 14)

She selected the segment – the hesitation – and inferred its theoretical meaning. The meaning of the hesitation she inferred as the manifestation of a defence that had come into play at that very moment. The 'occurrence' of resistance comes from the ego deploying a defence against a derivative of an instinctual impulse.

2   But that hesitation could be given an alternative meaning, according to a different framework of theory. From early on Klein observed a similar phenomenon in the play of children; she called it an inhibition of play:

> in far the greater number of these inhibitions whether they were recognisable as such or not, the work of reversing the mechanism was accomplished by way of anxiety . . . only when this anxiety was resolved was it possible to make any progress in resolving the inhibition . . . the completeness of our success in removing inhibitions is in direct proportion to the clearness with which the anxiety manifests itself as such and can be resolved.
>
> (Melanie Klein 1923, p. 78)

Here, inhibition is linked with anxiety overwhelming the ego; theoretically (in this alternative view) the cause of inhibition is anxiety, and resolving the anxiety relieves the inhibition.

While the clinical occurrence is remarkably similar – the interruption of a free flow either of associations, or play – there is a sharp difference in what is inferred. While similar segments are identified, different theories gave significantly different meaning. On one hand, an ego bringing effective defences into play, and on the other hand, an ego so overwhelmed by anxiety its symbolising functions become ineffective.

Clearly the occurrences are different: (1) the ego starting to function defensively, or (2) the ego paralysed by anxiety. Thus a very similar segment can be used to generate two significant occurrences that are different, and as a result each supports a very different theory. We will end up then with occurrences used by different schools of psychoanalysis, which are not strictly comparable; 'a ten-minute silence in the middle of the hour is not a psychoanalytic fact, but merely a matter of record' (Spence 1994, p. 916). We are not truly comparing like with like. And there is no immediate means of deciding between them. In such a vacuum of indecisiveness it is not surprising that authoritative opinion can step in as a substitute for evidence.

Selection and inference

Not only are similar segments of material the subject of different inferences, for theoretical reasons, but different segments are selected according to the theoretical preferences of the clinician. For instance, to take a published example; for many years the *British Journal of Psychotherapy* published regular 'Clinical Commentaries'. Two or three people comment on a session; the following fragment of one set of commentaries illustrates how selecting segments varies for purposes of making inferences. A man in his late twenties had failed to develop a life independently from his elderly parents, and came for therapy because he both craved for and feared a sexual relationship. The female therapist reporting the session said:

> [he] arrived two minutes late for a session at a changed day and time. As usual he took an extra cushion for himself before settling on to the couch.
>   [Patient says] Well (Laughs) continuing Monday's session – it was a good one for me, very positive. (Stops) You're looking very smart tonight. (Pause) (I thank him).
>
> (Clinical Commentary 1987)

Two of the three commentators (both psychoanalytic psychotherapists) picked up on that opening sequence. One commentator wrote of this event:

> The session begins flirtatiously . . . [the patient] offers a flattering pleasantry about the previous session, and says, 'you're looking very smart tonight'. He has come along to be cosy and in no way is his entrance that of someone arriving for serious work.

This commentary selected the rather off-hand manner, and the distinctly flattering comments. This inferred the patient anticipated the therapist as a 'woman who allows him sexual rope but who requires nothing in the way of serious masculinity from him'. Such a reading of the material, immediately, implies the enactment of a mildly sexual encounter which defensively avoids serious contact. One can see that the commentator is operating with a theory of a defensive pulling away from sexual encounters that must be felt as dangerous in some way.

In contrast, the other commentator pointed to something else – the change of the day and time: 'I would probably have related his compliment to the change of the session, a change to a day and time (tonight) when he no longer experiences her as a therapist but as an exciting and castrating "very smart" woman to be tamed by flattery.'

This take on the material has some similarities to the first commentator, but with a crucial difference. In this case the commentator inferred a much more engaged situation in which the therapist is the seducer and the patient is to tame her.

We can see first of all that different parts of the material were selected – the off-hand manner and flirtation, or alternatively the changed time. The different selections come from different theoretical pre-conceptions. The route to the different conclusions was determined by the selection of the material allowing inferences to be made according to different theories. Of course it is unfair to make too much of the variance in the selection of significant material, since neither commentator was in the actual transference–countertransference situation of the therapist. However, different theoretical slants put weight on different segments of material with the creation of different evidential occurrences. One can presume without much difficulty what the theoretical biases operating in each commentator were, which led them to different inferences and selections. The first one is working with the notion of the struggle between passive and active identity, crucially posed in the sexual situation, while the other appears to depend on regression to phantasies of phallic conquest.

Circular argument: Although in both cases the occurrences drawn from the field of observation are already theory-rich, the problem is multiplied when such occurrences are used as instances to justify the very theory that was used to infer them. What is claimed as evidence has, in truth, been selected using the very theory it is then used to support. We would seem to have a self-fulfilling circular argument – the theory used to select the occurrence is the same theory that is under test by the selected occurrences.

The laws of 'psycho-optics': The problem does not arise from the fact that data comes from a personal (therefore subjective) awareness. Even scientific data does that. The problem is that the observer is in essence just like the subject observed. That is to say, meaning is the 'substance' of the occurrence for both patient and analyst.

Taking science as an analogy, a field of observation is studied by means of an instrument, the microscope shall we say, which leads to generalisations, theories and laws about, perhaps, the life and reproduction of a certain bacterium. Therefore, the theories under study are not those theories used in constructing and operating the microscope. There are two separate sets of theories; those governing a microscope are the laws of optics, and they are quite distinct from the kinds of laws investigated *through* the microscope in the life of a bacterium. Thus there is a separation of the laws governing observation and the laws discovered and tested *by* the observations.

The psychoanalytic instrument of observation, the analyst's mind, is, like the microscope, also designed to make visible what is not normally seen – in this case, objects of the unconscious mind. However, the instrument of observation (the psychoanalyst's mind) operates with the same laws as those governing the operation of the mind under observation (the patient's). There is no comparable separation in psychoanalysis of the laws of observation from the laws of metapsychology. We need to understand how the theories of observation in psychoanalysis (comparable with the laws of optics of the microscope) separate from the metapsychology theories under study (comparable with the laws of bacterial life). We will effect this separation in Part III (Chapter 16).

Chapter 13

So far . . . concluding Part II

Freud used his authority to adjudicate which theories were psychoanalytic and which were not. One effect was to suppress a lot of otherwise necessary debate with his dissenters. Part II has tried to distinguish those aspects of conviction which arise from personal causes such as allegiances, and those which might transcend individuals by having an independent logical weight. That weight does not always carry through into the wider acknowledgement of well-judged theory. For instance, it is particularly difficult even today for a psychoanalyst to disentangle him/herself from theories given Freud's signature. Doing science is different, as Freud himself said:

> Science, in her perpetual incompleteness and insufficiency, is driven to hope for her salvation in new discoveries and new ways of regarding things. She does well, in order not to be deceived, to arm herself with scepticism and to accept nothing new unless it has withstood the strictest examination.
>
> (Freud 1925, p. 213)

It is as well to have pre-armed ourselves with what natural science is, and how psychoanalysis needs to differ.

So, Part II has dealt with a number of epistemological questions about justifying knowledge in general, and about convincing others, which have been addressed since ancient times, and psychoanalytic versions of those questions and issues have hopefully been clarified. I shall summarise these issues that crop up when establishing psychoanalysis as a particular form of knowledge.

Epistemological issues

Objectivity and subjectivity

The instrument for making observations of the human mind is another human mind. Personal experience can only be observed by another mind capable of registering personal experience, so nothing can know a mind except it is itself a mind. This is an axiom of psychoanalysis – and perhaps of everyday experience. However, this inevitably gives rise to grave suspicions that reliable data cannot be collected in a field so flooded with personal subjective forces. It is true that intense subjective needs and emotions may come to the fore, and this leads to an enquiry into whether the emotional and cognitive problems of subjectivity are of such a degree that they rule out our observing instrument for research use.

Causality and narrative

A strong argument has often been made that psychoanalysis is about meaningful narratives, exemplified in Freud's *Interpretation of Dreams*, and is not about causal processes, so that psychoanalysis is distinguished absolutely from natural science. I have suggested an argument (to be developed later) that the distinction between meanings and causes is not oppositional, and does not demand a choice between one or the other.

External and inner facts

Natural science is objective and based on facts solidly based in the four-dimensional space–time of the physical world. In contrast, psychoanalysis uses facts about the inner world, with a very different kind of dimensionality. Natural science aims to find data that can be given meaning through generalisation, whereas psychoanalysis investigates meaning as the very data it works with. However, those distinctions will be shown not to rule out finding 'inner', immaterial facts usable in a 'science-like' way – not science, but maybe a para-science. However, the selection of 'facts' will demand certain conditions, to be examined in Part III.

Deduction and induction

The problems of psychoanalytic research derive in part from the reliance on induction, central to science in Freud's day. Psychoanalysis may need to catch up with more recent trends which exploit the hypothetico-deductive model of testing, or some analogous version adapted to the unavoidable subjectivity of our field of observation.

Meanings and causes

Because I shall argue that being concerned with meanings does not mean there cannot also be causes, I shall have to deal with the nature of the interaction between meanings and causes (in Chapters 16 and 20). If a particular pattern of interaction between meanings and causes dissolves the opposition between science and hermeneutics, we could have answers to a raft of questions asked of psychoanalysis.

Can we justify our knowledge?

It is often concluded that psychoanalysis is naturalistic observation, like social science, anthropological fieldwork, or the medical clinic. As a result, the rigour of scientific results is believed to be out of reach, and like social science in general there can only be inductively generated theories not amenable to strict testing. In consequence there is a temptation to turn to other sciences, to use the 'softer' research methods of social science, or to turn in a completely different direction – to philosophical hermeneutics. However such 'choices' may be an illusion since the harsh interface between objectivity and subjectivity can, as we shall see, be unexpectedly eroded.

Interestingly, the rigour of the psychoanalytic setting approaches that of the laboratory experiment, and therefore in principle it could be seen as an 'inner' laboratory, the interpretive laboratory. Because of the highly controlled parameters of the psychoanalytic session, appropriate research designs could exploit the rigour of the setting to isolate variables as effectively as in the physical sciences. Grunbaum argued that psychoanalytic research could conform to a hypothetico-deductive method as prescribed by Popper. Psychoanalytic theories can be 'risky' and therefore tested scientifically. This implies that we attend to the way research questions are asked, and how the research design answers them.

Part III will have to take account of all these issues. The strategy will include a specific research design based on binary, either-or, questions, and the scrupulous use of precise predictions that can distinguish between confirming and falsifying occurrences in the analytic setting. Most crucially, we will have to tackle the difficult problem of psychoanalytic data so different from that of natural science, being both (a) immaterial and (b) meaningful, narrative experience.

Part III

Justifying psychoanalytic knowledge

Part III will set out the ingredients of a logical model for testing theories about subjective experiencing, and achieve Wisdom's goal: 'it will be seen that there is such a thing as the clinical testing of clinical hypotheses, but that it is vastly different from the testing for home-truths that goes on in day-to-day life' (Wisdom 1967, p. 47).

The generation and survival of knowledge depends on a cycle of two phases; first the intuitive generalisation of a theory based on the accumulation of clinical occurrences, and second the testing of theory through a model research design using a precise protocol for generating occurrences (data) that can falsify the theory. As Edelson tells us, 'It is a common mistake to suppose that because psychoanalysis is concerned with meanings or purposes it is not concerned with causal explanation' (Edelson 1986: 102), and research designs involving *both* causes and meanings are quite possible.

The research design entails a binary question formulated to be answered with a single case. One of the serious impediments to this kind of design is to establish clinical occurrences that will do the job in a way that can be generally accepted. Chapters 15–17 therefore concern the establishing of 'facts' that can be robust. Because of the circular argument used in finding occurrences to test theories, the method has to keep metapsychological theories, including those we seek to test, out of the process for selecting occurrences. Instead, the selection of occurrences needs to be done using theories that are more generally accepted by competing schools of psychoanalysts – those will be the theories that Wallerstein defined as the common ground of clinical theory. But first, we will turn to research designs using single cases.

This part develops the logical model offered as a parallel to the scientific model. We will aim at the laudable goal of the editors of the *International Journal of Psychoanalysis*, who 'hope to build bridges between different psychoanalytic schools and begin to topple the tower of Babel that has created barriers between colleagues around the world' (Gabbard and Williams 2002, p. 2).

In fact the aim is not merely to build bridges, but to build them in a specific way, by comparing separate concepts and their proprietorial schools of thought with the purpose of beginning a more rigorous evaluation than is current today. We proceed on the basis that, 'if analysts are given a common vocabulary and a relatively theory-free set of descriptors they can agree on what constitutes an ideal psychoanalytic process, at least at the level of a single session' (Ablon and Jones 2005, p. 563).

Perhaps psychoanalysts do not always keep faith with the hope, and they hide behind a diverse vocabulary. Nevertheless, that should not prevent an attempt at a common language and logic with which agreement can be sought.

In Part IV, this model will be exemplified, with a number of case records subjected to the required rigours in order to illustrate its use.

Chapter 14

Certainty and single cases: research designs for psychoanalysis

In response to the Schreber case Freud postulated that latent homosexuality underlies schizophrenia. He made this a general assertion. Later, he reported a further case that appeared to run counter to that theory (Freud 1915). The generalisation is therefore a risky hypothesis in the scientific sense, and will fail if a case is found that does not show this dynamic. In fact, Klein and Horwitz (1949) found some *80 per cent of cases* falsify the theory! Despite this more or less annihilating finding, psychoanalysts seem little deterred from Freud's theory – see Lingiardi and Capozzi's (2004) recent review, which fails to mention (or reference) the Klein and Horwitz account at all. Empirical results have had little influence on accepted psychoanalytic theory. However, it is essential we respect and debate such. In this chapter, I shall begin to discuss how such debate might develop – first with a focus on research designs suited to single cases.

To start this we will take a natural science hypothetico-deductive model off the shelf, as it were, and modify it for psychoanalytic research while retaining the same rigour of investigation as the natural science model. The design consists of the setting, the logic (and research question), and the data.

- *The setting*: The psychoanalytic setting is highly controlled, and the technique precise if the rules of free association and abstinence are applied, if certain operational rules of prediction supplement clinical interpretation, and if the purchase on countertransference subjectivity is adequately managed. Although some writers in this area consider psychoanalytic observation to be akin to social science and anthropology, in fact the clinical setting is not naturalistic observation. The case study is observation under laboratory conditions.
- *The logic*: Using the operational rules for interpretation as described in Chapter 18, it is possible to make predictions as effectively as in natural science. The logic of the experiment in science is to provide a definitive answer to the research question arising from the prediction (see Chapter 7).

- *The data*: Empirical data needed to provide the 'litmus paper' test of the
  logical prediction is the biggest stumbling block in psychoanalytic
  research, and requires the most careful adaptation of the research model,
  as well as the careful observation of the clinical occurrences that form the
  data. We observe a clinical 'process', that is to say a flow of associations
  which exist within the medium of the ever-changing occurrences in the
  relationship between psychoanalyst and analysand. So, careful attention
  needs to be paid to how specific occurrences are selected and their
  meanings inferred. This will be addressed in Chapters 15–17, using the
  distinction between clinical theory and metapsychology. Their recombina-
  tion into the final model will be considered in Chapter 20.

In this chapter, I shall begin by looking at the single-case study, which is
supposed to make psychoanalysis so unreliable compared with other
psychologies and therapies. I shall argue that the single-case study brings
psychoanalysis closer to natural science experiment than to psychological
or medical research.

The case as experimental setting

Earlier (Chapter 8), I suggested that the expedition of Christopher Columbus
could be seen as a research design involving a single critical case. One
occurrence decided the truth (or falsity) of the flat Earth theory. The fact that
Columbus returned from his voyage is decisive evidence that he did not fall
off the Earth when he sailed beyond the horizon.

So, the hypothesis – that the Earth is a flat disc – led to a prediction: if
the Earth is flat, a mariner will fall off its edge at some point at, or beyond,
the horizon. This prediction is posed in the form of an either/or question, and
we need the appropriate empirical data to answer the question. The result,
in the form of an answer to the question, will confirm or disconfirm the
prediction.

In 1492, Columbus sailed over the horizon. In 30 days, he came back and
confirmed there was land beyond. The horizon was not a precipitous edge.
The prediction was therefore *not* confirmed. So, his test yielded a negative
result (although positive for Columbus, you could say). In this research design,
the theory was a 'risky' one (in Popper's terms). One single critical case was
definitive. Like a litmus paper, indicating either red for acid or blue for alkali,
this simple research design works because a logic ensues from the way the
research question is set up. Two, and only two, quite distinct results could
occur: either he came back or he did not. So, we can endorse the view, 'The
case study does not necessarily imply deviation from the canons of scientific
method and reasoning. It should not be relegated to the context of discovery.
The case study can be an argument about the relation between hypothesis
and evidence' (Edelson 1985, p. 611).

However, we must follow through this irony that the single case is definitive in ordinary science, by examining its possibility for psychoanalytic research.

The alternative hypothesis research design: A variant of this 'falsification design' is the 'alternative hypothesis design', which in fact is more common. We can illustrate it by the same historical example. There is an alternative to 'the Earth is flat'. That is: 'the Earth is round', a hypothesis which lies, as it were, in waiting if the first, 'flat Earth' theory, falters.

In fact, Columbus did not sail completely round the globe. However, another expedition, led by Magellan from Seville, did make a further test in 1519. Magellan's expedition sailed around the tip of South America and eventually found its way back from the east. The second research design amenable to being decided by a single-case study decides between the two alternative theories. In this case the two theories are:

- the Earth is a flat disc; or
- the Earth is a round globe.

If one theory is proved false, then the other will survive as the more likely one.

One piece of test data – returning to the starting point while travelling only westwards – can decide between the two theories. This 'alternative hypotheses research design' tends to be closer to how science (and psychoanalytic research) is *actually* done.

Modifying theories: Columbus falsified the flat Earth theory. One option is to rescue falsified theories. A modified theory for instance could be – the earth is not flat, but a curved disc, so that it stretches beyond the horizon, so you don't fall off till a good deal further on; and Columbus never reached that point. Thus you can go beyond the horizon even if you cannot see beyond. In fact, commonly, a theory is patched up in this way. As we saw, Kuhn described how scientists hang on to theories as long as they can. In effect Magellan's expedition was the definitive case study that disposes of the hypothesis of the earth as a disc, in both its original and modified forms, flat or curved.

Research designs for psychoanalysis

These single-case designs work in geographical exploration. The question is whether such designs are appropriate for psychoanalytic research. The answer is 'yes', since many questions debated in psychoanalytic publications could in fact be formulated in terms of one or other of these designs. Mostly they are not so presented, but they could be, were there a tradition to think of psychoanalytic research as requiring this logical design. In the rest of this chapter, I shall give some examples that could have been formulated in terms of one or other of these designs. The question of adequacy of test data (the clinical occurrences) is a serious difficulty that will no doubt be noted, but we will address that problem in Chapters 15–17. The aim here is to show what clinical research might look like if it is reported in a manner that replicates the rigour of natural science. The formal presentation includes (a) the hypothesis; (b) the prediction arising; which leads to (c) a specific research question; so then (d) the data, like a litmus test, can decide whether the prediction is true or false. I shall give two examples from the psychoanalytic literature that exemplify the falsification research design, followed by one that exemplifies the alternative hypothesis design.

Falsification of a single hypothesis

The first example is Grunbaum's test case, the necessary condition thesis (NCT) that we have already considered. In fact his logic was explicit. The second is a hypothesis claimed by classical psychoanalysis concerning the experiential world of endopsychic perception.

The necessary condition thesis: Following Popper, Grunbaum (1984) sought to test whether psychoanalysis could be scientific (see Chapter 7), which serves as a good example of the falsification research design. Grunbaum extracted from Freud's writing a necessary condition – the condition for the cure of a neurosis is a psychoanalytic interpretation. As we saw, he derived this from Freud's *Introductory Lectures* (Grunbaum 1984: 140). Grunbaum then claimed that this psychoanalytic theory, the necessary condition thesis (NCT) is risky (as required by Popper). It is capable of falsification; in fact, only one case that gets better *without* psychoanalytic interpretation proves the thesis false. Grunbaum believed he had rescued Freud from Popper's criticism by showing that this psychoanalytic theory (the NCT) is falsifiable (Popper's criterion for science).

Then he tested the hypothesis, the NCT, by referring to experimental studies, suggestive therapies, spontaneous remission, and to Freud's later writing, to show that psychoanalysis is not the *only* cure of neurosis. For our purposes, this is 'doing science', indicating the existence of a case study that definitively found the theory false. The risky theory predicted that a case cannot be found to remit without psychoanalytic interpretation. When data, a case that got better without interpretation, was reported, the theory would be falsified. This result has a logical certainty, based on its premises. Ironically, the assertion by Popper that psychoanalytic theories cannot be falsified, is itself a risky theory. It requires only one example to falsify it. Grunbaum's risky NCT falsified Popper's view of psychoanalysis!

Grunbaum's conclusions showed that a core psychoanalytic theory, though scientific, was false. Naturally a blizzard of refutations erupted from many analysts far and wide, although Grunbaum, addressing every point in his second volume (Grunbaum 1993), never conceded anything.

Experience of psychic structure: The second example comes from a more clinical debate that could have been formulated to conform to the falsification research design. Joe Sandler committed himself to a view on the unconscious phantasy of psychic structure and function: 'structural organisation [of the mind]. . . lies outside the realm of conscious and unconscious experience' (Sandler 1990, p. 869).

This is a helpful formulation because it is clear and categorical enough to allow dispute. It is entirely at risk from finding evidence of cases in which patients do show an experience of psychic structure. It is therefore satisfactorily scientific, 'risky' by Popper's criteria and refutable by a single case. In fact only one case would falsify Sandler's theory as stated. Is there such a case? In fact, Freud reported one – the Ratman:

> [In obsessional neurosis] repression is effected not by means of amnesia but by a severance of causal connections brought about by a withdrawal of affect. These repressed connections appear to persist in some kind of shadowy form (which I have elsewhere compared to an endopsychic perception), and they are thus transferred, by a process of projection, into the external world, where they bear witness to what has been effaced from consciousness.
>
> (Freud 1909b, pp. 230–31)

Freud clearly described some sort of awareness in obsessional neurosis of psychic connections that had been effaced, displaced and unconscious. They indicate there is an experience of an aspect of the mind's structure and its distortion (the severed connections). The Ratman is certainly only one case, but it is all that is needed. (To my knowledge, Sandler never dealt with this counter-example).

Alternative hypotheses

The alternative hypotheses design selects between two theories that cover the same facts. Edelson (1985) argued for this design as appropriate for psychoanalytic clinical research. Justification is based on judgements whether

> The test hypothesis has the power to explain the kind of observations made and reported in the case study, and some rival hypothesis has not. The observations are predictable or expectable if the test hypothesis is true, but are not predictable or expectable if the rival hypothesis is true instead.
>
> (Edelson 1985, p. 598)

In this design the alternatives are not for or against a theory, but for one theory or for an alternative theory. However, like the previous research design, the condition is to pose the question clearly and the data needed will then be equally clear. The following example from the literature was indeed cast in the logic of the alternative hypotheses research design.

Joseph Weiss and paradoxical relief: In Chapter 2, we saw how Weiss contrasted his new 'higher mental functioning' hypothesis with the classical 'automatic functioning' hypothesis. Miss P, reported in Weiss and Sampson (1986, pp. 23–6), decided to finish treatment. Weiss's argument is that this is explicable in different ways by the two theories: (a) the classical, automatic functioning theory predicts more repression, while (b) the higher mental functioning theory predicts a test-plan which, if successful, will lead to relief and the lifting of repression. The crucial research question boiled down to two clear-cut alternatives; whether there is more repression or less.

When the psychoanalyst refused to accept her decision, Miss P did paradoxically experience a relief. Moreover, a little later, she recovered a long-repressed memory indicating the lifting of repression rather than triggering a stronger repression. The new theory of sophisticated mental functioning at an unconscious level was supported.

This table presents the logical argument in a formal way with two mutually exclusive alternatives. The research data, a recovered memory, decided decisively against the old 'automatic functioning' theory. It is no longer possible to hold the simple generalisation that unpleasure always promotes a stronger repression.

Table 14.1 Weiss's Miss P

	Automatic functioning theory	*Higher mental functioning theory*
Hypothesis	The unconscious copes with pleasure and unpleasure without the use of higher functioning, secondary process	Higher functioning (secondary process) occurs unconsciously as well as primary process
Prediction	Miss P's wish to terminate comes from an automatic trigger that strengthens her repression by avoiding any more psychoanalytic insights	Miss P's wish to terminate arises from a sophisticated plan to test the analyst's willingness to reject her
Research question	Did Miss P increase her repression, or follow a sophisticated test-plan?	
Research data	Miss P's recovered memory	
Data analysis	The recovered memory is indicative of less repression rather than triggering more	
Result	The automatic functioning theory precluding secondary process was not confirmed	The higher mental functioning theory prediction was confirmed

Comparative research: The alternative hypothesis research design may be particularly applicable for comparing different schools. It is in the nature of the different schools to use different theories and a direct comparison of two theories is possible using the alternative hypothesis design.

The fate of tested theories

Testing theories in this way strongly indicates which theories should be eliminated. If questions are posed in this binary, either/or, form they can be definitive. However, Kuhn pointed out that not all theories falsified are necessarily discarded. This is one of the problems with the stress placed on 'evidence-based practice' which claims that theories without the necessary evidence should be excluded from practice. In fact, that is not a scientific approach. There are other strategies that can be employed before discarding a falsified theory.

Modifying the theory

The theory may be modified, and Freud gave a lot of space to modifying theories in the light of evidence that disconfirmed his previous theory; for instance, describing a case of paranoia which ran counter to the established theory. Also, Dora confounded Freud's expectations and left treatment precipitously, so he modified his theory of transference to include a negative version.

Fit for purpose

Theories may continue to be used in practice if they are sufficient for the purpose. Taking an example from physics, Newton's theories are still not discarded, even after an alternative (the theory of relativity) has been postulated and tested to show it explained more of the evidence. In most areas of application (apart from the subatomic field and the hugely astronomical), Newtonian physics is preferable because it is good enough, and simpler to use in practice. This often makes the Newtonian theory the one most fit for the purpose, though not the most 'true'. Something comparable might be said in psychoanalysis about the theory of the death instinct. Many analysts would say that although it is now known that the theory of the libido is not enough and that Freud postulated the death instinct (Freud 1920), in the practice of analysing neurotic people who are not too disturbed, the classical theory of libido may be good enough. In some circumstances, even if the chosen hypothesis explains the facts better than an alternative hypothesis, it still may not be abandoned if the alternative hypothesis is so unlikely that it is believed it could never apply. For example, during the Controversial Discussions (King and Steiner 1991), one of the arguments against the Kleinian theory of unconscious phantasy was that although the theory could be consistent with certain facts about pre-genital phenomena (the oral Oedipus complex, for instance), the chances of infants having the capacity for such sophisticated phantasies was so remotely unlikely that the theory of unconscious phantasy was discarded by classical Freudians, despite it apparently explaining more of the facts.

Absence of alternatives

A theory may go on being used even though it fails to explain certain anomalous phenomena. In natural science, Newtonian physics went on being used, despite anomalies it could not explain. Anomalies were tolerated because, until 1906, there was no alternative. Only later, Einstein's theory of relativity explained the constancy of the speed of light, and the effects of gravitational field on electromagnetic ones. Similarly with the field of psychoanalysis, Freud continued to use his theory of neurosis as repression of conflict to explain psychosis (e.g. the Schreber case; Freud 1911) because there was no alternative until he postulated that there were early anxiety-situations and correspondingly more violent mechanisms of defence (Freud 1926).

Conclusions

In this chapter, I have set out the logical structure of two different research designs – the falsification design, and the alternative hypothesis design. Many psychoanalytic conclusions from clinical work could be re-arranged according to a form of logic that renders them 'risky'. And indeed many responses to papers are in the form of counter-examples which could be formulated as falsifying evidence if presented in the appropriate way. However, at present, papers do not usually spell out the explicit structure of the logic, and the force of the vignette from a single case is lost.

The important condition in these research designs is that there is a set of two alternatives – either confirm or falsify – in the falsification design; or, theory A or theory B in the alternative hypothesis design. These either/or choices are *binary*, and that binary form is the *sine qua non* for the effectiveness of clinical material from a single case.

Of course the fact that theories are not necessarily discarded when falsified does not mean (as Kuhnians have tended to argue) that the falsification criterion is not useful, nor that it is not an excellent form of thinking for developing rigour. It is indeed both, but it just means that the demands of practice may require a rigour that is different from that required for reporting new knowledge.

The upshot of this chapter is that single-case studies have a wide potential scope as research. The two designs are more in line with the natural science experiment and less aligned with the more standard large sample methods common to research in psychology and medicine. Levels of certainty are higher with single-case research designs, and therefore, surprisingly, we could expect psychoanalytic research to produce more certain results than much psychological or medical research.

The weak point of these designs is that the results can be contested on the basis that clinical material is unreliable as data, and can be subject to alternative inferences according to the rival theories that need support. Thus, the selection of data from the clinical process is problematic, and this is where a logical model for psychoanalytic work must begin to deviate from that of natural science, and it is the issue we will go on to address in detail in the next chapters.

Chapter 15

Selecting facts: circular arguments

This chapter is about facts; they are the actual occurrences in our clinical work, and we need them for research purposes. Psychoanalysts lack a consensus about how we connect theories to facts. Partisan special pleading often substitutes for research. As we have seen, allegiance to theory can determine the selection of, and inferences from, the significant segments of clinical material (for example, in Chapter 12, the alternative theoretical positions of resistance/inhibition). Simply *because* a theory can explain something in the flow of clinical material does not mean either (a) that it is the best theory to explain that occurrence or (b) that the occurrence is the significant thing, methodologically speaking, that needs explaining at that moment.

Take a debate from surprisingly early on, but still unconcluded, which is admirably cast in the form we discussed in the last chapter. The 'results' depend wholly on one crucial case in which the data is *highly* determined by a prior theoretical position.

A nervous tic

In 1921 Ferenczi published a paper, 'Psychoanalytical observations on the tic'. The classical theory of libidinal development at the time, Freud's *Three Essays on Sexuality* (Freud 1905), held that prior to object-love there was self-love, and the first form was auto-erotic, distinguished from narcissism, the second form of self-love. Auto-erotism is characterised by being object-less. Ferenczi argued that a tic exemplified just such an objectless discharge of impulses. A tic is therefore a possible example of auto-erotism, to support Freud's postulation of an auto-erotic phase, and to give it empirical substance. Ferenczi concluded by claiming – 'In Tic . . . it would seem that no relation to the object is hidden behind the symptom' (Ferenczi 1921, p. 13).

Abraham commented on Ferenczi's conclusions briefly in the same year (1921) to the Berlin Psychoanalytic Society. He took the opposite position and did not agree that a tic is a primary object-less phenomenon, and declared, 'In my analyses, however, I have found a double relation to the object, namely, a sadistic and an anal one' (Abraham 1921, p. 324). So, there *is* a hidden object-relation behind the tic. However, Abraham gave no clinical material. His comment was entirely opinion. He appealed to his own authority and not to evidence.

In terms of the two positions, this is an exemplary debate. Two theories exist:

1   that the tic is an objectless auto-erotic discharge (Ferenczi); or
2   that object relations underlie the tic (Abraham).

In principle, one single clinical case in which an object relation is demonstrated, is enough to decide against Ferenczi's generalisation and therefore to allow the alternative theory instead. Can we find a case?

Well, a case was soon reported in which the tic was associated with an object relation. In 1925 Melanie Klein wrote a paper which drew on clinical material to demonstrate an object-relationship, *in phantasy*, in a child with a tic. The phantasy was of a sadistic intercourse between the parents in which the patient participated. The 13-year old Felix was analysed over three-and-a-quarter years.

> The tic comprised three phases . . . At the beginning Felix had a feeling as though the depression in his neck, under the back of his head, was being torn. In consequence of this feeling he felt constrained first to throw his head back and then to rotate it from left to right. The second movement was accompanied by a feeling that something was cracking loudly. The concluding phase consisted of a third movement in which the chin was pressed as deeply as possible downwards.

In order to bring the tic within the scope of the analysis, it was necessary to obtain the patient's free associations to the sensations associated with the tic and to the circumstances which gave rise to the tic (Klein 1925, p. 109). Very detailed associations were brought, which showed that

> Felix played three roles: the passive role of his mother, the passive role of his own ego, and the active role of his father . . . With this boy the phantasy of taking the mother's place in relation to his father, that is the passive homosexual attitude, was concealed by the active homosexual phantasy of taking the place of his father with a boy.
>
> (Klein 1925, pp. 109–10)

Felix was therefore, in his own mind, in relation to his two parents in the moments when he performed the three tic movements. The tic represented his complex relationships with his two parents at an age when both the Oedipus complex and its inverse were intertwined.

Table 15.1 Nervous tic and the alternative theories research design

	Auto-erotic (Ferenczi)	Object-related (Abraham)
Theories	Tic represents an objectless auto-erotic discharge of libido	Object-relations underlie nervous tic
Prediction	No object relation will be found	An object relation will be found to underlie the tic
Research question	Is there an object relation?	
Test data	Klein's case showing underlying object relations	
Result	The case made this theory false and it should give way to the alternative	The case was compatible with Abraham's alternative theory

At face value, this single-case study would demolish Ferenczi's general-isation that there are no object-relations underlying the tic. It would be decisive, like a 'litmus-paper' test, judging between the two theories. Ferenczi's hypothesis must be given up in favour of Abraham's.

The debate has a logical structure that would be called research in any other discipline. However, I have referred to this set of contributions (Ferenczi, Abraham and Klein) to demonstrate problems of evidencing in psychoanalysis.

Consequences of the debate

This debate demonstrates serious problems. One concerns problems of allegiance, and another concerns the ensuing problems of data collection and use.

Problems of allegiance: Mahler (1949) revisited the tic debate, bringing it up to date; and subsequently Cohen (1991) reviewed it, too. Both Mahler and Cohen examined Abraham and Ferenczi's papers, but ignored the apparently clinching paper of Melanie Klein – perhaps not so clinching. It is tempting to consider that a selective reading resulted from allegiances to anti-Kleinian points of view (Mahler to ego-psychology, Cohen with a neurobiological interest). It is not that the paper of Klein's was considered and rejected for specific reasons, it was simply ignored.

Of course, it may be that I am equally partisan (i.e. *towards* Klein's work), and I have to acknowledge that setting aside my own allegiances is easier said than done, even in a passage about setting aside allegiances. The degree to which allegiances can trump logical content cannot be overemphasised. That does not mean I, or anyone else, should give up on debate based on good clinical work presented with logical force. In fact, the reverse, the future of psychoanalysis will depend on how we do manage issues like this. One resource for dealing with such personal factors is to have at hand an effective logical model.

Problems of data collection: Leaving aside the intense personal aspects, Klein's argument falls down in a very familiar manner. The clinical data used to settle the object-relatedness of tic, was selected on the basis of an object-relations approach. The data selection by a psychoanalyst who was assuredly primed to find object-relations, duly found object-relations. Such circularity cripples the data, and nullifies the results. What kind of psychoanalytic 'facts' would avoid that pitfall?

The 1994 symposium on facts

In 1994, David Tuckett, then editor of the *International Journal of Psycho-analysis*, had a similar question. He published 31 papers from a wide selection of people across all the continents where psychoanalysis is practised. They were written in answer to his question: What is a psychoanalytic fact? These papers are thoughtful and intelligent, and they express a great deal of reflection and contemplation, while varying enormously in what the authors think are 'facts'. It is worrying that a lack of consensus emerged so strikingly. It appeared that if you ask the question of a number of analysts, you would get as many answers as analysts. The wide disparity must hamper or seriously obstruct discussions so that research evidence is very frequently disputed, or equally frequently just ignored.

Disputed facts: We saw, in Chapter 12, an example where hesitation in the flow of associations can be given different significance according to two different theories; either an ego bringing rigid defences into play, or an ego overwhelmed by anxiety. These two kinds of occurrences start as similar clinical events – interruptions in the train of associations. Two theories lead us in two different inferential directions. Once these divergent meanings of the occurrences are established in the minds of different analysts, the formulations of interpretations must diverge as well.

Given the different inferred meanings, and contrasting interpretations, psychoanalysts will look for different types of response to their interpretations (see the opening to Chapter 2). In the Freud/Klein example (Chapter 12), the expected response will be that the troublesome drive derivative will emerge more explicitly into consciousness; in the second, managing the anxiety will release the play from inhibition. At times, the expected responses may look rather similar, so that a similar response gives justification to either theory, with added confusion and ambiguity in debate.

Selection and inference

A further example, also in Chapter 12, was the divergence in parallel commentaries on a session with a male patient experiencing being seduced by his female therapist. Different segments of the flow of clinical material were identified by different commentators and thus selected for different theoretical reasons.

The inferring of a psychoanalytically meaningful occurrence from a segment of the associations, is complex and unreliable. We may 'see' the Oedipus complex, primary narcissism, projective identification, and so on and so forth in the clinical process. Then we select those occurrences on the basis that the Oedipal theory (shall we say, or primary narcissism, projective identification, etc.) explains it, while ignoring other occurrences. Then a theory has no trouble in making sense of the occurrences which have already been selected on the basis that the theory makes sense of it.

When an electron microscope produces spots on a photographic plate (or on an electronic screen), the blip is already selected for the observer as a discrete perceptual datum on the basis of the algorithms of the electronic programme which displays the blip. Similarly the laws of optics, via the telescope, reveal the sequence of positions of a planet in the sky. The observer then infers mitochondria from the blips, on the basis of molecular biology; and Brahe used mathematical theories to make sense (the heliocentric theory) of his tables of observations and measurements of the positions of the planets. On the whole it is assumed that psychoanalytic inference works the same way. But there is a difference as we argued in Chapter 12. In psychoanalysis there is no equivalent of the electron microscope. The observer is the instrument that selects the data to make sense of, and is then the observer who makes sense of the data. In natural science, selection of a datum *because* it can be explained by a theory, is sufficient *so long as* the theory used in observation is *distinct from* the theory that is being tested.

The selection of occurrences, and their use, are different processes separated by the use of different theories. But psychoanalysis transgresses this rule, and we risk a circular argument. This circularity is not easily spotted by the casual reader, or indeed the psychoanalytic reader who, typically, reads for clinical purposes according to the biases of their own theoretical group.

To put it another way, the instrument of observation of a subjective field of study, is the mind of the analyst. But a significant part of the subjectivity of that mind is the stock of theories to which he/she has a special allegiance. The circularity which results risks seriously distorting any results. We have to consider if that distortion is eradicable. Although in the present state of affairs, it remains strongly present, I will argue that it is potentially possible to eradicate it, but that will require making a distinction within psychoanalytic theory. We need to pay close attention to the theories we use to select the occurrences; they should be different theories from those the research aims to test. In effect, we will distinguish 'clinical theory' for selecting occurrences from metapsychological theory which we aim to test.

Chapter 16

Causal theories and hermeneutic theories

Because in psychoanalytic research the observing instrument is the psycho-analyst's mind working in just the same way as the patient's mind that is being 'observed', the inferential process in *selecting* the research occurrences and the *use* of those occurrences are usually related in a circular manner which largely invalidates the research. The potential confusion demands that we be much more alive than the natural scientist to the theories that underlie the selection of observations. Generating occurrences and using them must be two different forms of inference, requiring different kinds of theory for making the inferences. We will consider how to define a bounded set of psychoanalytic theories to use in observing and selecting clinical occurrences. If that were to be successful then we would have a workable parallel to the laws of optics governing investigations with the microscope.

'Clinical theories'

On what grounds does the psychoanalytic instrument, the psychoanalyst's experiencing mind, make his observations? It is a very immediate, momentary activity. We may not need all of our elaborate metapsychological ideas and theories. For instance the theory that there is a continuity between an early trauma and the configuration of the transference is not usable as part of the task of clinical observation. The early trauma theory is used *after* we have made the observations on the transference, and to give psychoanalytic meaning to that relationship. It is the theory of transference we need for observing the occurrence.

Interestingly, we saw in Chapter 10 that George Klein (1973) explored the notion of 'clinical theory' as distinct from the theories of motivation (roughly 'metapsychology'). 'Clinical theory' was a term also adopted by Wallerstein (2000), in his discussion of a common ground that unites psycho-analysts. His claim was

> that our overall and overarching general theoretical diversity and pluralism can be fully consonant with the shared clinical theory, basic clinical

method, and common observational data that I trust I can demonstrate to be our psychoanalytic common ground, that unites all the diversity represented in this hall today.

(Wallerstein 1990, p. 12)

He particularly identified the theories of resistance, defence against anxiety, conflict, object-relations, and transference/countertransference (Wallerstein 2005). Gabbard took up this drive for common ground among psychoanalysts:

the subject of countertransference has been emerging as a common ground for groups as diverse as the modern Kleinians, the American ego-psychologists, the relational theorists, the 'middle groupers' of the British School, and the constructivists. This consensual view involves an awareness that countertransference is generally a joint creation involving contributions from both patient and analyst. The exact form of the countertransference is inextricably linked to a 'fit' between what the patient is attributing to the analyst and the internal self and object representations within the analyst that may or may not provide a 'hook' for what the patient is projecting.

(Gabbard 1996, p. 260)

We might therefore look to the observing instrument to operate with such clinical conceptions when selecting research-usable occurrences (see also Kernberg 1993; White 2001).

Currently, research practice is so often the search for clinical patterns of occurrence that confirm metapsychological theories – a strategy of support by induction. However, supposing we use only a restricted set of theories, 'clinical theories', to select occurrences? The advantage is that, following Wallerstein, clinical theories are what *unite* psychoanalysts; while the metapsychological theories are what divide us. Then a research model could develop on the basis of observational theory that is properly distinct from (metapsychological) theories to be tested; clinical theory distinct from metapsychology.

Hence if we really wanted to make comparisons of our *diverse* theories we could have some common ground from which to do the job. If clinical theories are (more) generally accepted and can deliver us occurrences for testing *disputed* theories, then we have struck lucky. However, what exactly is it that we need to observe? And are the concepts of clinical theory good for the job?

Observing effects

When we intervene in a session, we expect it to have some effect, and we want to select occurrences from which we can *infer that effect*. We noted in Chapter 2 the analyst's interest in the response to an interpretation, that is, whether there is a confirming effect. We are considering the very short-term effects, the results of a particular interpretation; and not outcome studies on a long timescale, assessing the overall benefit of a psychoanalytic treatment or later. The response to interpretation is the occurrence which can say something about the actual interpretation, and the metapsychological theories used to formulate it. The interpretation has an immediate effect (or not) depending on its correctness, and that correctness can be assessed by the immediate response.

We are looking at a sequence that resembles what happens in a laboratory setting. The experiment would be the interpretation, and the results would be its effect. So, we are looking for occurrences with an inferred meaning (giving rise to a metapsychology-rich interpretation), and how the associations subsequent to the interpretation reveal an occurrence demonstrating the interpretation's effect. Since we identify the post-interpretive occurrence as the effect of an interpretation, we are seeing the interpretation as a cause; it causes an effect. Thus we are conceptualising the relations between the two occurrences as a cause–effect link just like the scientist who Freud thought we needed to emulate.

Meanings

Metapsychological theories – the ones that Wallerstein says divide us, and we seek to test – provide the framework for *formulating* interpretations, and they comprise the 'cause'. Metapsychology is the meaning element at the primary process, or the dream, level of the unconscious, and our interventions – interpretations – are concerned with this surging ocean of meanings. But having identified such a meaning occurrence and formulated an interpretation, we expect an effect. But 'having an effect' is a different kind of occurrence. We are distinguishing two kinds of occurrence: (a) the meaning occurrence prior to interpretation (say, castration anxiety), and (b) the causal occurrence, some sequence in which a change occurs from before to after the interpretation. So a meaning occurrence and a causal sequence are both involved in clinical material. They are intertwined in the same events. The causal occurrence, or sequence, is in fact a change of the initial meaning occurrence caused by interpretation.

Sub-sets of theories

In both clinical practice *and* research we therefore attend to two dimensions. On one hand we are interested in formulating interpretations, and, on the other, we are interested in the effects of those formulations. We seek out meanings, *and* we observe the way those found meanings change the patient's meanings. We gauge the effect of an interpretation, by the changes in transference, the transference-countertransference relationship, resistance (and inhibition) or its reduction; this is the realm of causal experiment. When we are grasping, formulating, interpreting meanings we are in the realm of hermeneutics.

Table 16.1 Two classes of theory

Type 1 theories (causal theories)	Type 2 theories (hermeneutic theories)
Process	Content
Changes/effects	Meanings/narratives
For testing	For interpreting

The claim is that psychoanalytic theories form two sub-sets – Type 1 and Type 2 – and are adapted to separate functions.

Type 1 theories

These are used to select cause–effect links (sequences) from the clinical flow – we can list resistance, defence against anxiety, conflict, object-relations, and transference/countertransference), those theories which are experience-near (as Wallerstein called them) in the psychoanalytic session,. They are specifically the resources to understand the effect of interpretation, and are the ones likely to be generally accepted by psychoanalysts.

Type 2 theories

These are the narrative or discursive theories of metapsychology with which we understand the way the patient constructs and manages his meanings, and his experiences.

Conclusions

Psychoanalysts have always been interested in the effects of their interpretations, and that means a sequence from before to after interpretation. To avoid circularity we need Type 1 theories to infer effects, whereas the occurrences that contribute to the interpretations whose effects are to be gauged must be inferred by Type 2 theories. Without that respect for the distinctness of the inferred causality and the interpreted meanings, no clinical material can settle an inter-group dispute.

We now need to check the actual kinds of clinical occurrences that are commonly used by the clinician and assess them for use as research data. At this stage, it is worth warning against a self-defeating perfectionism. Arguments will easily spring up on the basis that different groups have different views of transference, of resistance, and so on. This is true and clinical theory is not completely purified of metapsychology, so some variance exists. However, the point is that there is an important issue of degree – there is going to be much more agreement over, say, the concept of transference as compared with the metapsychology of narcissism, of the death instinct, of guilt, and so on.

In addition, complaints will be made about focusing simply on interpretation. There are many other forms of interventions that psychoanalysts use, but this is not the place to debate which count as psychoanalysis and which not, though much debate has taken place. The intention is simply to use standard interpretation of the unconscious as the specific intervention of use in conceptual research. Such interventions embody more clearly than others, the concept used in making meaning of an occurrence. Therefore such interventions are the most suitable for testing those concepts.

Chapter 17

Theories and meaning occurrences

As described in the last chapter, theories are of two kinds: theories of causal effects (Type 1), and theories of meanings (Type 2). Inferences from these theories constitute data for use as evidence in research. One problem was identified a long time ago: 'we have no exactly formulated view of the concept of "interpretation" itself, no precise knowledge of what "interpretation" is and what effect it has upon our patients' (Strachey 1934, p. 127). Here we need to recognise more precisely what an interpretation is. I shall move away from any notion that it is a simple and intuitive idea of the analyst. Though that may well be what happens in practice, we need to formulate it precisely for the rigour of a logical model. In this case, I will take the interpretation to stretch backwards towards the material which provoked it, and to stretch forward to the further associations that are provoked by the interpretation. This is a sequence in time within the session. There is a complexity arising from the kinds of evidence involved in spotting this sort of sequence.

Because the theories are of two kinds, consequently, evidence is of two corresponding kinds in our research. Clinical theory illuminates *sequences* around the interpretations. And meanings from metapsychology identify segments of free associations, which I shall call '*occurrences*'. For purposes of keeping the discussion clear I shall use 'sequence' for the changes after an interpretation compared with before, and 'occurrence' for a segment of the associations chosen for its meaning.

So, there are two jobs to do, each informed by a different type of theory. The division is important in order to avoid circularity, and makes a significant formal difference from natural science, where only one general category of datum exists. Psychoanalysis needs both causal sequences and hermeneutic, meaning occurrences. These separate types of evidence are not independent of each other. Both are needed to observe the effect of interpretation.

Observations inferred from Type 1 theory demonstrate the interpretive process. The actual interpretation is based on the meanings that are inferred in the material on the basis of Type 2 (metapsychology) theories. Such meaning occurrences need to be found at two points in the process: before and after the interpretation. It is clearer if we discuss these meaning occurrences first, arising from Type 2 theory, in this chapter; causal sequences (Type 1) will be considered in the next chapter.

There are several kinds of meaning occurrence commonly used by practising clinicians (perhaps readers may contribute more):

1   contiguity: two associations in close proximity in the material;
2   thematic affinity: two associations linked by a common theme;
3   genetic continuity: a symptom linked to a prior trauma, over a long time-scale
4   triangulation: a piece of material linked by a common narrative to the psychoanalyst's countertransference.

I will describe each systematically with an example.

Clinical occurrence 1: Contiguity

Contiguity is a standard method for listening to free associations. Associations that are adjacent in time in the session are deemed to have an unconscious link between them. Such an associative link implies a psychoanalytic significance to be inferred. This linking together of what is put together emerged for Freud with the elements of a dream (Freud 1900). Two elements in a dream compose the meaning of the dream. Meaning is inferred from their juxtaposition, or contiguity. Condensation and displacement exemplify the characteristic linking in the unconscious, primary process. They are hidden connections that point back to an implicit theme/meaning that is unacceptable, or traumatic. Symptoms are mental contents linked together (a compromise formation), and derived from the associationist psychology prevalent during Freud's early career during the nineteenth century. Freud later formalised this as the free association method for working with the fully conscious patient. Two adjacent associations in an analytic session point to hidden links between them.

A simple clinical example is the following from my own practice: a patient described a tiring journey he had made in his car over the weekend (this was a Monday session). I knew he often talked of a quite severe depression in terms of tiredness and endlessness. He continued with the thought that he had endured the journey because of the beauty of the landscape which helped him to feel alive and contributed to an inner feeling of resourcefulness. After a short pause, as if going on to the next item on his agenda he had come with, he talked of the previous session (on Friday) when he said I had made a difficult interpretation which he felt he had not understood sufficiently.

Though these associations – the tiring journey and the difficult interpretation – appeared separate items, they were adjacent and so suggested a significant link. The long tiring journey, and the struggle with the interpretation, could be the same story, which I understood to be about keeping something alive inside him during the weekend.

The two elements were contiguous. Their close position together is not serendipity; it is unconsciously meaningful. This is not a claim that the interpretation is necessarily correct, only that this is one kind of occurrence that is believed to be evidence of the unconscious. The link between (a) the patient's long tiring journey, and (b) his difficulty with my interpretation, is a segment of the associations, and is worth testing. The link is selected by the analyst who inferred a meaningful story about keeping an internal object alive, inferred meaning from the theories of the depressive position and internal objects (Type 2, hermeneutic, theory).

Clinical occurrence 2: Thematic affinity

Thematic affinity is also a link between two associations, but it differs from contiguity. The associations are recognised by a common theme; instead of their closeness in time (as with contiguity), they have a common content/narrative.

Take for instance a case of Freud's that concerns the traumatic theme of impotence on the wedding night of a woman patient:

> Over a period of time she used to repeat an especially noticeable and senseless obsessive action. She would run out of her room into another room in the middle of which there was a table. She would straighten the table-cloth on it in a particular manner and ring for the housemaid. The latter had to come up to the table, and the patient would then dismiss her on some indifferent errand. In the attempts to explain this compulsion, it occurred to her that at one place on the table-cloth there was a stain, and that she always arranged the cloth in such a way that the housemaid was bound to see the stain. The whole scene proved to be a reproduction of an experience in her married life which had later on given her thoughts a problem to solve. On the wedding-night her husband had met with a not unusual mishap. He found himself impotent, and many times in the course of the night he came hurrying from his room into hers to try once more whether he could succeed. In the morning he said he would feel ashamed in front of the hotel housemaid who made the beds, and he took a bottle of red ink and poured its contents over the sheet; but he did it so clumsily that the red stain came in a place that was very unsuitable for his purpose. With her obsessive action, therefore, she was representing the wedding-night.
>
> (Freud 1907, p. 121)

The table-cloth ruffled up to display a stain has an affinity with the bedclothes similarly ruffled and stained. There is a common visual theme, and a narrative affinity.

The stained table-cloth represents a meaning displaced from the bedclothes with their traumatic association to her husband's impotence. The meaning of the occurrence is inferred from Type 2 theories of sexuality, impotence and castration, and is a segment of material selected on the basis of an inference using a Type 2 theory.

A problem of thematic affinity was pointed out by Grunbaum (1984). If complex chains of associations go on long enough without limit to proximity in time, more or less any theme could eventually be echoed in the material. The risk is that the inferred meaning will arise from the theoretical ingenuity of the observer, rather than necessarily from a repressed meaning in the patient.

A footnote to this occurrence is an approach based on probabilities. The likelihood of a specific link of this kind could be computed on the basis of the number of all possible links, their distance apart in the flow of associations, and their individual rarity. In fact, Freud endorsed this computational method (in a footnote in 1924) citing an argument by Bleuler:

> This short analysis [of the 'aliquis' parapraxis] has received much attention in the literature of the subject and has provoked lively discussion. Basing himself directly on it, Bleuler (1919) has attempted to determine mathematically the credibility of psycho-analytic interpretations, and has come to the conclusion that it has a higher probability value than thousands of medical 'truths' which have gone unchallenged.
>
> (Freud 1901, p. 12n)

However, it implies that this kind of occurrence needs mathematical and extra-clinical support to be usable for research, a conclusion which Freud would probably have resisted.

Clinical occurrence 3: Genetic continuity

The principle of genetic continuity relies on the plausible assumption that all symptoms and their underlying dynamics have a direct continuity with preceding dynamics at an earlier period in the person's history (the term 'genetic' means generated in the past, and not the action of the genes). The occurrence is selected on the basis that a common dynamic can be extracted from both a developmental period and the current symptom.

A vivid example of reaching into a pre-verbal stage from a later period was given by Susan Isaacs:

> a little girl of one year and eight months, with poor speech development, saw a shoe of her mother's from which the sole had come loose and was flapping about. The child was horrified, and screamed with terror. For about a week she would shrink away and scream if she saw her mother

wearing any shoes at all, and for some time could only tolerate her mother's wearing a pair of brightly coloured house shoes. The particular offending pair was not worn for several months. The child gradually forgot about the terror, and let her mother wear any sort of shoes. At two years and eleven months, however (fifteen months later), she suddenly said to her mother in a frightened voice, 'Where are Mummy's broken shoes?' Her mother hastily said, fearing another screaming attack, that she had sent them away, and the child then commented: 'They might have eaten me right up.'

(Isaacs 1948, p. 85)

The flapping shoe was thus seen by the child as a threatening mouth, and responded to as such, at one year and eight months, even though the phantasy could not be put into words. This example illustrates in a simple way how an understanding at nearly three years can throw light on a dynamic situation at half the age.

However, typically, genetic continuity is an affinity over a longer timescale than this. Freud's use of genetic continuity in the Wolfman case was great. Anxiety states starting before the age of four, when the Wolfman had the famous dream of stationary wolves sitting on a walnut tree, could be understood in terms of symptoms as an adult in his twenties. The idea derives directly from Breuer's tracing of symptoms to a prior trauma. Hence, there are causal implications, which makes genetic continuity *more than* a thematic affinity.

The common dynamic in the Wolfman case was inferred from the theory of castration anxiety, linking the Wolfman's fear of the wolves in the child dream to the primal scene experience, and the infant's identification with either parent, active or passive. Genetic continuity is good at generating narratives on the basis of early core phantasies which are repeated in later development, personal relations, and symptoms. Such narrativity on a long timescale, has remained universally important for clinical interpretation. But explanatory value makes such occurrences useful *only* for accumulating more instances for enumerative induction, The timescale makes it quite impractical for hypothetico-deductive testing.

Clinical evidence 4: Triangulation in the setting

Originally a concept in social science (and taken by social scientists from surveying), 'triangulation' referred to the simultaneous examination of two perspectives. This allowed two kinds of data, quantitative and qualitative, from the same sample to be combined; the qualitative gave *meaning* to the raw quantitative facts. Triangulation is now a broader strategy. Campbell (1956) used a questionnaire and also direct observation to measure a single construct – leadership effectiveness – and he is attributed with the first use of the term 'triangulation'. Denzin (1978) described various kinds of triangulation including: different methods of data collection on the same sample (methodological triangulation), or the same methods on different samples (data triangulation); using more than one investigator (investigator triangulation), or using more than one theory for data analysis; and combinations of these (multiple triangulation). In many of these variants both perspectives are qualitative data. Franke (2006) – from whom the general background for understanding triangulation has been taken – used a method of psychodynamic observation in different settings, with an analysis of their commonalities.

Psychoanalysis is particularly suited to this kind of occurrence as it always involves a dual perspective. A piece of material can be looked at from two points of view *in the session*:

- the *content* of the immediate free associative material; and
- the transference interaction (or *enactment*) of the moment.

The best clinical work analysts do nowadays looks from these two different directions, and offers a potential for an intrinsic triangulation in the clinical session. As Bion remarked, 'Evidence for interpretations has to be found in the countertransference and in the actions and free associations of the patients' (Bion 1954, p. 113).

So, in an ongoing therapeutic process a psychoanalyst has a dual perspective. That the transference–countertransference enactment can replay the content of the associations in a dramatic form in the session is a recent realisation. In the following example, my summary of an extract from a conference presentation, the content in the form of a dream displays something that occurs in the act of presenting the dream:

> A colleague presented at a conference a dream from the middle of an analysis, most of which is not relevant here. The dream was: *A caravanserai in the middle of a desert*. The psychoanalyst found herself full of interesting ideas, but a bit perplexed because the patient had no associations or any affective response to the dream even when asked. There was therefore an interactive process here between the two states of mind (analyst and analysand), both exaggerated in the telling of the dream – the analyst's intra-psychic state became more lively, and the analysand's less lively. The point is that the dream represented visually a 'desert' as well as the 'oasis', the caravanserai. But that division – desert/oasis – was also represented in the psychic enactment (the two minds, one more lively and the other less lively). Thus the content of the dream and the enactment between the psychoanalytic partners converged. Importantly, the *content* of the dream is a commentary, as it were, on the process of presenting the dream.

There is a similar inference arising from both content and countertransference that correspond with each other. The selection is on the basis of those theoretical inferences – not spelled out – but apparently a theory of mutual projection. The convergence seems to give a confidence in interpreting that narrative.

This dual perspective is quintessentially a psychoanalytic occurrence. It requires listening not just to the verbal content, but also 'with the third ear' as we say, to pick up the intuited, 'felt' nuances of the presentation. 'We analyse,' as Segal said, 'the dreamer not the dream' (quoted in Quinidoz 2009, p. 94). And analysing the dreamer entails both the content of the dream and the process of presentation which enacts the transference-countertransference.

So, this occurrence is selected by finding a common inferred meaning in two modes – in the content of the association, and in the unconscious enactment of the transference–countertransference. Just the content, or just the transference process, could each seem convincing. But the convergence from the two very different unconscious communications impresses. First, the patient conveys something through the manifest dream and, second, s/he is also successfully conveying something through setting up an interaction with some activated part of the analyst's unconscious. When these perspectives are not checked against each other in this triangulating way, they are unreliable. Heimann (1950), who encouraged the use in clinical work of the counter-transference, eventually became anxious about an unbalanced reliance on it, and we have already noted what she said:

> I may mention that I have had occasion to see that my [earlier] paper also caused some misunderstanding in that some candidates, who referring to my paper for justification, uncritically, based their interpretations on their feelings. They said in reply to any query 'my countertransference', and seemed disinclined to check their interpretations against the actual data in the analytic situation.
>
> (Heimann 1960, p. 153)

There is here an appeal to use the countertransference together with the analytic data (the free associations) as checks upon each other. More recently, Busch stated a similar position, 'I worked with the transference throughout this material, and used my countertransference reactions as a backdrop to my interpretations' (Busch and Schmidt-Hellerau 2004, p. 702). Whether the associations check the countertransference, or the countertransference checks the content of associations, the occurrence is selected when the two perspectives converge on one inferred meaning.

In the first three occurrences described in the chapter, the meaning of two associations coincide, but in a triangulation two quite different modalities are brought together. The pattern in the patient's unconscious, and then in the analyst's experience, is an improbable chance happening, and it gives a special charge of conviction.

Gabbard (1996, pp. 262–3) reported a session with an unmarried woman who was alternately desiring of him and angry with him. The analyst had a strong reaction to her, but needed the evidence of the material (her dreams and phantasies) as well, to understand his reaction, and what they were enacting between them. After one occasion when she saw the previous patient – a woman – leaving, she accused the psychoanalyst of deliberately causing her jealousy. Gabbard wrote:

> As I sat in session after session with her, engaging in my own process of reverie and self inquiry, I had a persistent feeling that she was dangerous, that she somehow wished to destroy me, and that I had to be on my guard with her.
>
> A dream she brought into the analysis just before a one-week absence of mine shed further light on what was transpiring between us. In the dream, Ms D was standing in a shower washing male genitals that were unattached to a body. In her associations to the dream, Ms D commented that she had read in the New York Times that they were arresting prostitutes in Manhattan and then printing the names of the men who visited them. She then told me, 'I have a fantasy of taking you to the cleaners.' She went on to say, 'It must be related to literally castrating you. I can see you standing around missing your vital parts. But I don't want to leave here feeling I damaged you. I want to make sure everything's in its place. I don't want to be castrating toward you. I'm terribly afraid I'll damage you and lose you.'

We can see here a correspondence between the analyst's countertransference, his sense of danger, and the patient's own fear of being damaging; an explicit dream about castrating a man. A little later she was crying,

> My father always said no man would put up with me. What I fear is that you'll see that behind my wish to seduce you and to become your lover is a desire to bring you down. I derive such a sense of power over men when I have sex with them. I feel like I literally bring them to their knees. I reduce them to my level.

There is a correspondence between

- the *content*, the dream of being castrating; and
- the *countertransference* danger.

Thus there is a correspondence between two perspectives, and the two views can be sensibly combined – 'The patient's dream and her associations had made it clearer to me why I felt a sense of danger and needed to be on my guard with her' (Gabbard 1996, p. 263). The content and countertransference held a common inferred meaning based on a Type 2 (metapsychological) theory – castration and penis envy.

As in the previous categories of occurrences described in this chapter, triangulation represents the overlap of meaning derived from a Type 2, metapsychology theory. Such triangulations comprise the same meaning/narrative twice over. However, triangulation differs from other meaning occurrences because the two things linked together are *not* both the content of associations; only one is. The other element comes from the *psychoanalyst's* experience. They are two different perspectives, consisting of both the experience of the patient (conscious and unconscious) and the interacting experience of the psychoanalyst (conscious and unconscious). So, triangulation is significantly different from the three occurrences given above. Naturally errors will occur, but the meaning occurrence formed in this way is measured against itself by two interacting systems, rather than one observed by another (the patient observed by the analyst). Whereas any of these four kinds of occurrences described in this chapter are suitable for generating meaningful interpretations, perhaps the double perspective of triangulation does make it more reliable. A triangulation expresses a convergence of *both* minds, drawing very different kinds of contributions from each.

Conclusions

In this chapter, we have considered four kinds of evidence psychoanalysts habitually use for formulating their interpretations. Interpretations require meaning occurrences, and are derived from Type 2, hermeneutic theories, from metapsychology. They are important clinically for the work they do in generating interpretations and, as we shall see, they are important too in understanding the response to interpretations.

When it comes to research, the theories by which meanings are inferred are inevitably tested in the analytic process. They cannot therefore form the whole of the theoretical background to the testing process. We need now to consider, in the next chapter, the process to which we apply the Type 1, causal theories. That process is the sequence of change that occurs in the meaning occurrence, under the impact of the interpretation (i.e. by comparing the meaning before and after the interpretation). A change in a 'meaning occurrence' *is* the change sequence.

Chapter 18

Change sequence as evidence

The discrepancy between the pre- and post-interpretive occurrences has been regarded as a significant piece of micro-process ever since Breuer's Anna O (Chapter 2). Though Freud expanded this causal relationship between trauma and symptom into the elongated timescale of the Wolfman case, we can see that the micro-process has potential for testing the theory on which the interpretation was made. With hindsight these two models of causality (the Wolfman timescale and the micro-process within the session) have become opposite ends of the spectrum of psychoanalytic causality.

The research sequence, or causal process (Type 1, clinical theories)

Clinical psychoanalysis is the fluctuating process of associations. However, included in that flow, there is an intentional process as well – to effect a change. Analysts make a number of other interventions, but a systematic interpretation intended to give insight into the unconscious is the key activity in a psychoanalysis – and to no other therapy. So, the response to interpretation has always been a prominent means of assessing the validity of the work. There have been various attempts to systematise that process, as Wisdom (1967, p. 46) said: 'an interpretation embodying a clinical hypothesis is corroborated if the response to it can be interpreted by means of the same clinical hypothesis . . . [N]otable discussions have been given by Freud (1938c), Isaacs (1939), Kubie (1952), Brenner (1955), Ezriel (1956) and Paul (1963).'

Subsequent contributors are numerous. Chapter 2 reviewed developed projects attempting to get an objective leverage on that process.

Inferences before and after: If an interpretation tallies with something in the patient, an observable change can be expected (the rules for predicting the change will be considered later). The causal process (or change sequence) is different from the meaning occurrences in the last chapter. The latter depended on the comparison of *two* meaning occurrences (before and after interpretation). As Money-Kyrle commented, 'we distrust an interpretation if the inference from the response does not support the inference on which the interpretation was originally made' (Money-Kyrle 1958, p. 343).

Each of the two meaning occurrences must be inferred according to *the same* Type 2 theories. For instance in Gabbard's example of the woman wishing to castrate him out of penis envy, we will expect, after interpretation, to find a response from which meanings are still inferred according to precisely the same theories – castration anxiety and penis envy – though the representation of those meanings will have changed in some way (provided that the meaning was correct).

So, for research purposes, as the interpretation drops into the flow of the clinical process, we observe the effect on the flow of associations. That particular segment of the temporal flow I am calling a 'change sequence'.

Contiguity, thematic affinity, genetic continuity and triangulation give material which constitutes meaning occurrences, for formulating interpretations. To put it simply, the research process is not inferred from meanings, but from a change of meaning.

Dynamic and historical causation

Of course meanings have a root in the individual person's past, but the therapeutic effect is worked out in the present, 'only such forces as exist at a certain time can have effects at that time' (Ezriel 1956, p. 35). Ezriel called it the dynamic here-and-now, ahistorical process; and distinguished it from the alternative long-term process, the historical genetic process, that which Freud most exhaustively and fruitfully described in the Wolfman. The here-and-now process has here-and-now causes; and Ezriel pointed out the likeness between that process in a psychoanalytic session, and the experiments of natural science (see Chapter 6). Ezriel claimed, 'The customary method of investigation in the natural sciences is to observe events in the "here and now", i.e. while they are taking place in front of the observer, either spontaneously or under experimental conditions set up by him' (Ezriel 1956, p. 30).

And he refers to the experimental conditions set up by the psychoanalyst making interpretations. Observation can be made on the ensuing events, just like a scientific experiment.

The research process, as just discussed, is the immediate here-and-now change that takes place in the transference. It is independent of what the transference is exactly at any particular moment, in any particular case. The data here is the *change*, not the content. We require the interpretation do more than fit the facts, it must change them.

An example of the combination of the dynamic (process) and the historical (content) was a particularly submissive patient, mentioned by Ezriel (1956). 'The patient's father had died when the patient was in a rebellious phase in childhood leaving him with an uncomfortable sense of responsibility arising from his rebelliousness and the coincident death.' A dynamic process occurred in childhood:

rebelliousness → death of father → reactive submissiveness

Turning to the present, it can be predicted that this same dynamic process *also* determines his adult submissiveness such as that with his analyst – rebelling against the analyst will result in the analyst's death, so therefore the patient submits. This is transference as a 'new edition' of a past relationship. At both points in time, the same dynamic results in the submissive outcome; but the historical sequence from the earlier point in childhood to the later one in the analysis is *not* the experimental dimension. The transference is *both* a historical relic *and also* a currently lived dynamic event. So, history is important, and the current lived relationship is not in opposition to the historical approach. They run together because of the common narrative. But they are conceptually different – the genetic link *with* the past is a different concept from the dynamic link *in* the past. What links the past with the present is the unconscious dynamic; that dynamic force of the idea is, in this case, that submissiveness is the outcome of a fatal rebelliousness. At both points in the patient's life there is the same *dynamic* compulsion. The past is a dynamic past, but the present is similarly a dynamic present. Even child analysis is predicated on the need to rework now, the experiences earlier in infancy.

The interpretation (the personal narrative meaning) is the change agent, but it changes the present dynamic interplay of rebellion and submission, however much it *uses the historical narratives*. The change process is quite different from the historical link. Interestingly, Freud mixed up these two levels in his metapsychology, no doubt because the theory of psychoanalytic change was relatively undeveloped at the time he was working.

Psychoanalytic work and experimental results

The psychoanalytic work done to effect a change, as in a scientific experiment, goes on in the process in the present. This might remind us of Strachey's (1934) ideas on the mutative interpretation. By interpreting to the patient, the analyst enables the patient to reality-test his/her transference perceptions of the analyst now. The analyst in reality does not bear the unduly exaggerated characteristics of transference. He/she is not an angel, nor a demon. So, Strachey understood a psychoanalysis as a here-and-now working through to test reality; no longer teasing out pathological connections with the past. Strachey's paper may have been ahead of its time and was rarely mentioned before 1950 (on PEPWeb, there are only 24 hits in the 15 years up to 1968, prior to republication of the paper, and 336 hits in the 42 years since). This emphasis on the fact of therapeutic change being focused necessarily in the immediate here-and-now has later been argued by Gill (1979) and by Stone (1981). See also Gill (1982), Gill and Hoffman (1982) and Wallerstein (1984).

The change agent, the interpretation, is a construction of the history, but the change process is something personal between two people now. Ezriel, again,

The analyst deals with material which is unconsciously selected for him by the subject of his investigation, the patient, as dynamically significant and belonging together . . . While patient and analyst had ostensibly started their work like two friendly archaeologists trying to dig up the patient's past, they were in fact two human beings interacting with one another.

(Ezriel 1956, pp. 31–2)

Ezriel was indicating that the modern understanding of the dynamic inter-action of transference and countertransference was left out by concentrating on the psychic archaeology. Only around 1950 did the process of two human beings 'interacting with one another' come more into focus (i.e. the process itself gradually became the content for analysis). The rules of countertrans-ference have greatly assisted the task of separating the subjectivity of the observational instrument from the subjectivity of the observed field, as discussed in Chapter 16.

However, there remain problems. Many intruding personal factors can disrupt the smooth understanding of the dynamic and historical dimensions of psychoanalytic research. So, psychoanalysts and their critics alike remain wary of claims based on clinical observation. Wallerstein (1964) discussed this extensively and, though it was some time ago, his points are not outdated. Schafer puts this well, too:

We have enriched our attitude toward the patient's response to inter-pretation so that its evidential value has been enhanced well beyond what Freud chose to emphasize concerning the ambiguity of the patient's acceptance or rejection of an interpretation. Particularly important now is the patient's subjective experience of being at the receiving end of a particular interpretation or of any interpretation at all. And we do not limit subjective experiences only to what is conscious or immediate; what is unconscious or delayed is crucial but may not be decidable until long afterward. Be all that as it may, an interpretation may be experienced as a blow, a moral judgment, a reassurance, a seductive move, a rape, an insult, and so on. Thus, what is registered or heard may not correspond to the conventional sense of the analyst's action or his or her words. Moreover, there may be a countertransferential gap between what the analyst consciously intended and what the analyst conveyed, as, for instance, when an interpretation of an implied hostile feeling in the trans-ference is conveyed with so much tentativeness or anxiety that it may well be warranted to say that the analyst is conveying fear of the patient's aggression or fragility and in either case sending a message different from that consciously intended.

(Schafer 1999, pp. 505–6)

Deviation from the interpretive sequence could therefore lead to many things that are difficult to decipher in terms of the psychoanalytic process – we might call them para-psychoanalytic. To refine the logical model, we need a means to protect those changes that are genuinely due to the impact of the interpretation (showing it is correct) from other changes which are, in effect, false positives, or disconfirmations of the interpretation. Change must be in terms of the actual interpretation that was given. Any other change, resulting from factors such as many in Schafer's quotation, would in effect be *false positives*. Is such a weeding out process possible? The answer is, yes it is; but we need one more ingredient in the model.

Turning to the scientific model for further inspiration, the key element we need is the capacity to make predictions of exact changes we expect of an interpretation, to be clearly distinguished from any old change that simply says an interpretation has been experienced as 'something', as Schafer pessimistically said.

In the next chapter, I want to examine the way in which psychoanalytic research can generate predictions which will distinguish between true and false positives.

Chapter 19

Prediction: results and false positives

As indicated previously, psychoanalysts are alert to the fact that 'it is the patient's specific response to interpretation that will be decisive' (Horowitz 1987, p. 190). Since interpretations are expected to result in changes, it is, in principle, possible to make predictions about what change a given interpretation is expected to make. If this is precise enough, then it should exclude all other changes an interpretation is *not* expected to make. But what sort of prediction would do this?

An interpretation that makes a difference should affect the dynamics between unconscious and conscious meanings. Hence a prediction will need to specify an exact change in what is unconscious and what is conscious. The dynamics of the transference and countertransference are expressions of these relations between conscious and unconscious that are directly observable, now. So, in effect, that means a change in the transference-countertransference relationship. The following continues to depend on Ezriel (1956).

The structure of psychoanalytic prediction

The structure of the transference relationship has three levels:

1   There is the overt transference relationship as we normally consider it, which according to Ezriel is that which the patient requires to exist between him and the analyst – the *required relationship*; and, in the example of Ezriel's patient mentioned in the last chapter, it was the patient's required submission to the analyst.
2   The patient requires himself to be submissive in order to *avoid* another kind of relationship – which would create a great deal of anxiety in the patient – this is an *avoided relationship*; in the illustrative case, it was the patient's rebelliousness.
3   If the avoided relationship became manifest it would threaten a *catastrophe*, the death of the father/analyst.

Ezriel recommended that this tripartite structure of the transference should be the structure of the interpretation, to include the required relationship, the avoided relationship, and the catastrophe (sometimes called the 'because clause'). He called these the 'operational rules' of psychoanalytic interpretation. The predicted change after the interpretation is a *specific* one – a movement in the here-and-now transference from the required relationship towards the avoided one, *and towards no other*. Ezriel's example is:

> If the analyst then gives a here-and-now interpretation – that is points out the hidden dynamics of the patient-analyst relationship in terms of these three object-relationships . . . the subsequent material produced by the patient will contain the avoided object relationship in a clearer, i.e. less repressed, form.
>
> (Ezriel 1956, p. 13)

He gave a brief example of this clearer expression of the repressed, as follows:

> one of my patients started a session by unconsciously giving vent to hostile feelings towards me in the form of an attack upon the Government. After my interpretation he criticised the Clinic. The object of his attack had thus moved nearer my consulting room, from Whitehall to the Tavistock Clinic.
>
> (Ezriel 1951, p. 33)

The move is even expressed geographically in this insistence as if internal psychic space is measurable. Though there is still not a direct rebelliousness consciously, the artillery is getting nearer. A predicted change must come specifically from the interpretation. Similarly, Ezriel's vignette in the previous chapter, was a man with repressed Oedipal rivalry and castration anxiety confounded by the death of his father. He sustained an especially submissive relationship with the analyst, which the patient required in order to avoid a direct challenge to the analyst, which, on past experience, could be a fatal challenge. The interpretation of that avoided relationship leads to the specific prediction that following the interpretation there will be a move toward a more direct challenge.

The prediction is precise; a movement within the meaning of rebelliousness. Any change other than *that* precise movement would be a negative result, so, responses following the extraneous factors listed by Schafer at the end of the last chapter (p. 134), would be discernibly different. We may observe any change, but only the precise one predicted on the basis of the interpretation of required and avoided relationships, will count as confirmation.

Wallerstein (1964) noted Ezriel's (1956) three-part structure of prediction, but chose a longer timescale for the Menninger research (Wallerstein 1986). But his team did place prediction at the centre of their method: 'the entire predictive complex of conditions, prediction proper, and assumptions clause is set down in advance as is also the predetermined evidence' (Wallerstein 1964, p. 686). Prediction was captured by the three enquiries – 'if', 'then', and 'because' (Sargent *et al.* 1968). Ezriel's precision has not been seriously followed up; the Menninger work merely noted it, and it has subsequently been more or less relegated to footnote status. Nevertheless it has great power. Whatever the theory chosen for interpretation (a Type 2, metapsychological theory), the predicted change is quite specific within that Type 2 theory.

False positives: an example

In Ezriel's vignette above, the move was very concrete; the patient moved his complaint to one against the authorities in the Tavistock Clinic (where Ezriel was working) instead of complaining of the government in Whitehall. That response to interpretation represented a move, expressed in geographical terms, towards a much nearer direct challenge to Ezriel himself. Any other change, after the interpretation, could have been claimed as significant confirmation of the interpretation, but it would in fact have been a false positive. *Only* a move towards the avoided relationship given in the interpretation will confirm that interpretation

An example of a failure of prediction is a 45-year-old professional man, Mr X, who came for a second analysis because of feelings of depression, and an awareness that he did not always follow good sense, including, for instance, resorting to cocaine. He was quite omnipotent in many respects, which led him to be unreliable, sometimes alarmingly. He was diabetic, but his lifestyle led to his taking insulin irregularly, and from time to time he had hypoglycaemic spells when he did not eat regularly. He told me this often happened unexpectedly, and he was somewhat casual about it, leaving me far from casual and wondering what I would do if it happened in a session. In addition, he frequently went to sleep in his session, with loud snoring and, more alarmingly, sleep apnoea. This also worried me. I was often beset by the sense that I did not have the capacity to help make an impact on his problems with the resources that I had.

In one mid-week session, Mr X told me of a meeting he had with a friend with whom he was working on a project. The friend did very little towards the project, rarely contributed what he had agreed to do, and was in fact a very unreliable man. My patient was extraordinarily fond of and loyal to this friend. I found myself thinking what an unreliable patient *I* had, who sometimes even went to sleep on the project I was conducting with him. I felt a mixture of irritation that I was struggling to make headway with his analysis; at the same time I thought a patient has a right to use his analysis to express his problems in his own way – and he was certainly doing that, I thought.

This material is a story about an unreliable friend, causing frustration in a loyal relationship; and I said something about unreliable friends, comparing how we both struggled to keep a project going, him with his friend, and I with him. I said the frustration of his work with his friend demanded a loyalty and tolerance, and he may be anxious about my tolerance of how he made use of the analysis.

My interpretation articulates a supposed (and repressed) anxiety that my tolerance may be limited. There is an avoided relationship, in which he oversteps that limit. This implies a *prediction* – that his concern at my intolerance will become clearer and less repressed. Did it? Continuing, he was characteristically silent, and then he started snoring until he woke with his apnoea and a nasty gasping intake of breathe. He remembered what he had been talking about, and the interpretation, and he courteously acknowledged the link I had made. I felt he was reassuring me, even patronising me a little. He continued to tell me how he had worked with his friend all evening and well into the night. He explained how the friend needed a lot of encouragement and reassurance, and his own role was to be very tolerant while doing most of the work.

This does not confirm the prediction. In other words, he did *not* express more directly a concern about *my* tolerating his unreliability. In fact, rather the opposite – he went off to sleep! I felt him soothing me and he was not more anxious, as predicted.

Actually, there was some change (going to sleep, and a courtesy and reassurance), but it was not the predicted change – towards a greater anxiety that I may be intolerant. So, the interpretation, as made, was wrong. To be sure sleep could be a response to the anxiety, maybe greater anxiety, and it might have been a greater repression. But it was not the *predicted* change, which would have been a more manifest anxiety, a *less* repressed one.

We can be precise about this. It is quite possible to theoretically re-interpret going to sleep as confirmation – on the grounds that he was so challenged by the interpretation he had to *increase* his repression, and thus confirm the interpretation. However such a construction is surely a wishful contrivance to reassure the interpreter, rather than genuinely to assess the interpretation. If the change were regarded as a significant therapeutic effect of the interpretation, it would be a false positive. Instead, we can see that when the change does *not* follow the course of the predicted one, we should instead be concerned that something was wrong here.

Unpredicted changes: If there is a change but it is *not* in the direction of the predicted move, then we have several possible conclusions we can draw:

- the interpretation is likely to have been wrong, and the Type 2 theory is not valid – at least in this instance; and
- the patient may be reacting to some extraneous aspect of the interpretation, the analyst or the setting (for instance the sheer satisfaction of being listened to, or any of Schafer's factors).

Negative therapeutic reaction: In addition, there is the case of a negative therapeutic reaction. This is a paradoxical reaction which confounds the interpretation, and tends towards dismissing a correct one. It is in effect a *false negative*. It may be the result of various causes, due to repetition-compulsion, secondary gain, primary envy, and so on; different schools will tend to see the NTR in their own ways.

If the state of mind of the patient at that point is potentially a negative attitude to the psychoanalyst or to interpretations then one could say the negativity needs to be a part of the interpretation. If the interpretation does not include an inference about a negativity resulting in the NTR, then it is effectively 'incorrect' – incorrect, at least, in the sense of incomplete. In other words, a negative therapeutic reaction to an interpretation, requires an interpretation of that negative reaction. The NTR is, according to the operational rules sketched out above, a required relationship. Then the avoided one would be some more co-operative relationship, and the predicted move would be from the required negativity to a degree more accepting of the psychoanalyst's thinking and work. In other words such an interpretation is potentially a test of the nature, and motives, of an NTR.

Conclusion

Prediction is a powerful tool for separating out false positives, that is, those changes that can be claimed as confirmation, but are not. A rigorous use of prediction can go a long way to identify and rule them out, including the effects of Schafer's factors. Claiming the success of an interpretation on the basis of a simple change, without the specifics of a prediction, and a consistency of theory before and after in the interpretive sequence, amounts in effect to a false positive result. And any positive result claimed in case reports should be assessed against these conditions.

So, any old change will not do. Ezriel's operational rules – comprising the three-part interpretation of required and avoided relationships, and the catastrophe to be avoided – do give a means of formulating predictions which are effective as a kind of litmus paper test to decide for or against an interpretation, and thus for (or against) the metapsychological theory on which the interpretation is based. But a strict reporting formulated in terms of predictions is rarely used in clinical case histories – which is surprising, considering the extensive claims to scientificity over the years.

Chapter 20

Causes *and* meanings: again

In conclusion to Part III, we will summarise the main steps in the argument in this book. Various parts of the logical model have now been described – the design, binary questions, prediction, data collection, meaning occurrences and the change sequence. The aim is that one theory may be compared with another, between groups or schools of psychoanalysts. This may be done with as little as one single case, even a single clinical interpretation.

1   If a particular theory informs the selection of the material (an occurrence) then that theory will be the basis for, first of all, an interpretation, and then a specific prediction of change in response to that interpretation. A theory (at risk from testing) must be used consistently for all three elements: (a) the selection of a meaning occurrence; (b) the interpretation of the occurrence; and (c) the prediction of change. In addition, a fourth element (d) must rely on that same theory, the selection of the post-interpretive occurrence.

2   The elements are arranged in a sequence from (a) to (d) which is a causal sequence comparable to a scientific experiment, and involves a change that is to be observed (partly by the subjective instrument of the psychoanalyst's experience) by using the clinical theory of transference-countertransference.

3   Observation in this way produces data of two kinds, called sequences and occurrences in this book.

4   Psychoanalytic theories are of two different kinds, performing two different functions:

   (a) clinical theory applied to the understanding of the sequence (process) of change in the transference from pre-interpretive material to post-interpretive material; as distinct from

   (b) metapsychological theories from which interpretations are formulated and by which meaning is inferred from the two segments of material (before and after the interpretation).

5   The two sets of material pre- and post-interpretive must acquire meaning via the *same* metapsychological theory.
6   The shift post-interpretively must be precisely as predicted, towards the emergence of that which is unconscious according to the theory, and no other shift, however promising, will do.
7   The selection of the sets of material, before and after the interpretation, has to be exactly identified by a protocol which should preferably conform to the method of triangulation.

Occurrences are those segments of clinical material that have meaning according to a metapsychological theory (a theory under test), and are best identified according to a protocol I have called a 'triangulation' – two perspectives, the actual material and the countertransference, yielding similar inferences that can be checked against each other.

This model successfully fulfils a number of conditions set for it by the various problems and criticisms reviewed in Chapter 1. The outcome of the change sequence is a comparison of the post-interpretive occurrence with the pre-interpretive one, with the following possibilities:

- a shift in the post-interpretive material in line with the prediction, as indicated by the theory, will give a confirmation of the interpretation, and thus the validity of the theory in this instance;
- some other shift, after an interpretation, however apparently productive, will *not* confirm the interpretation;
- no shift at all, or the need for different theories to understand the two different sets of material, will be a disconfirmation of the prediction, the interpretation, and the theory.

Hermeneutics

Despite the claim of this argument to relate psychoanalysis to science and to derive a precise research model out of the scientific one, it does diverge from the scientific model; and it diverges exactly where the hermeneutic approach becomes important. Meaning is the nature of the *field* of study, while, in science, meaning is the end aimed for. Theories about meaning and narrative are psychoanalytic metapsychology, the theories psychoanalysts dispute among ourselves, and therefore the focus of this research model.

Separating the means of observation from the results of observation (clinical theory from metapsychology) is an important accomplishment conceptually. As a result, meaning and cause come into the logical model from different directions, contribute in quite different ways, but are both integral to the whole complex. Visually, we can represent it as two dimensions at right angles (orthogonal):

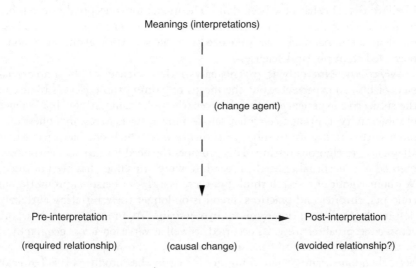

Meanings (interpretations)

(change agent)

Pre-interpretation   -------------------------------->   Post-interpretation

(required relationship)   (causal change)   (avoided relationship?)

Figure 20.1 Meaning and causality aligned

Geometrically these are orthogonal co-ordinates, at right-angles to each other, and therefore not correlated. We can evaluate the *effect* of an interpretation independently of its *content*. And it is that independence of the test from the theoretical allegiances of the tester for which we have journeyed so long. Moreover, separating the meaningful content of interpretation from the causal effect of an interpretation has achieved a reconciliation of science and hermeneutics, and put them in an ordered relationship with each other. There is also a sense in which the artificial separation of 'research in psychoanalysis and research on psychoanalysis' (Kächele *et al.* 2009, p. 6) is healed by this model – or at least the two researches become differentiated and related.

The question of turning *meanings*, the working material of hermeneutics, into *data*, the working material of science, has proved challenging. Nevertheless, occurrences in the flow of meaningful associations do appear to be entirely possible, given (a) a consistency in the process of inference of the different elements; (b) the possibility of checking countertransference against the actual associations, and vice versa; and (c) the precise use of prediction.

Core problems of psychoanalysis

In Chapter 1, we established that the core problems to be addressed here were:

*   subjectivity
*   single-case studies
*   science as testing, and
*   data collection.

I believe that this has now been done. The model for conceptual research has been evolved with these problems in mind. In the course of tackling these problems a number of changes were needed in the standard, off-the-shelf model borrowed from physical science.

Subjectivity: Not only is psychoanalysis the 'science' of the immaterial facts of human experience, but the means of gaining those facts is by use of the subjective experience of the observer (the psychoanalyst). Such a 'science of subjectivity' is prone to circular, self-seeking answers to research questions, often with a resistance to subjecting theories, to which one has a particular allegiance, to rigorous testing. This prompts the need for just such a rigorous method of conceptual research, a search to which this book has been devoted. Without rigour of research thinking, there is a risk of personal promotion of concepts, theories and practices. Freud is no longer the arbitrating authority despite the loyal attention to his body of writing. As a result, a wide diaspora across conceptual territory has occurred, as well as variation across geographical territory. And theoretical consistency among psychoanalysts appears to have been abandoned, and an 'anything goes' attitude has produced the Tower of Babel which needs calling to order.

The fierce loyalty that defends the various metapsychological schools of thought is unfortunately a part of the research instrument itself, and drives the dispersal of psychoanalysis into schools as much as into research thinking. Only the most rigorous methods of research investigation can tackle this problem, in order to reach greater consensus. However, considerable personal and emotional work no doubt needs to be achieved before that destination can be arrived at. Clearly metapsychology cannot be used as a basis for founding a psychoanalytic research method; indeed it is exactly what we need the methodology for.

The separation of clinical and metapsychological theories: In this book it has been argued that there is, in fact, a way out, as a number of researchers (including George Klein and Robert Wallerstein) believe that there are some psychoanalytic theories which most schools accept. These are the clinical theories, indeed happily those with which we make observations. And therefore there is a real possibility of separating off those accepted theories we use to make observations, from those contentious theories which need the rigorous comparative research and testing.

Causes and meanings: Interestingly, a spin-off from the arguments developed in this book is that the fetish for the scientific status of psychoanalysis, and the reactive hermeneutic turn, can surprisingly be both encompassed. The theories and data required for observation are in the realm of clinical theories, while the research comparisons can then be made between schools of metapsychological concepts.

Single-case studies: Much heartache has come from the problem that psychoanalysis is particularly unsuited to the large sample methodologies of medicine and psychology. However, it has been argued here that if psychoanalysts truly wish to be scientists they might respect the fact that the best scientific experiments are in effect single-case designs. This still does not make psychoanalysis into science, but it does release us from the trance-like reverence for RCTs and drug trials. The research designs of natural science might be considered rather than those of medicine. In fact it can be shown (and has here been shown) that single cases can be definitive, even in psychoanalytic debate. However, there are conditions for single-case designs to be effective.

Binary questions: For a single case to decide an issue there has to be a question that is answerable in a yes/no way. Such questions are posed so that a single case is the one that demolishes a theory. A case that does not show an Oedipus complex, destroys the theory that all human beings have Oedipus complexes. The outcome is the need to either abandon the theory, or to adapt it with some kind of protective 'conventionalist strategem', as Popper called it (Chapter 7).

Generalisation: Theories are derived from noting the multiple common occurrences. These accumulate by an intuitive recognition of their common features and by induction a generalisation results, so that a prediction can be made on the basis that those common features of multiple instances will apply across the board to all the instances of the entire class. Such a generalisation is however risky, and this places psychoanalytic generalisations – theories – in a similar place to natural science. Theories are risky, and can be definitively falsified by a single counter-instance.

Science as testing: Freud's heavy dependence on inductive thinking was quite normal for scientists of the nineteenth century. They evolved theories from collecting samples (or facts). However the catastrophic impact from Newton's physics having been shown to be defective, has led to increased scepticism about scientific theories. The 'evidence base' of most sciences is now on testing theories, testing to destruction, rather than bolstering with increasing numbers of supporting instances. Testing now requires not only more rigour, but also a different kind of justification. Despite many claims, that psychoanalysis is beyond the pale of hypothetico-deductive testing is not in fact the case, as I hope this book has shown. Psychoanalysts are potentially able to test their knowledge. However a testing protocol is not easy. Part III of this book has been devoted to working out what that valid protocol for subjective data would be.

Change sequence: Central to psychoanalysis as testable knowledge is the dramatic fact that the interpretation drops into process with an observable effect, in much the way that a scientific experiment drops into the flow of time in the laboratory to have an observable effect. A change happens in the field of vision of the observer (the psychoanalyst).

Prediction: As we have noted, many changes may happen for all sorts of reasons, and it is important to know what are the significant changes, and what the 'false positives'. This discrimination is best performed by making predictions about the effect of the interpretation. This then entails developing precise rules about making predictions. The *form* of a prediction and not its content will be observed on the basis of clinical theories – and those tend to be more accepted across the schools of psychoanalysis. These theories give rise to a set of 'operational rules', for identifying change and for specifying the specific change.

Operational rules: The theory of a transference neurosis is that the patient sets up a specific relationship, and requires it for unconscious reasons. This relationship can then be specifically connected with another, avoided relationship, and the prediction can be made that the transference will move towards the avoided relationship. In effect, a degree of lifting of repression. This is the basis of the prediction to be expected with a particular transference, and the effect of an interpretation of that transference.

Data collection: Perhaps the most difficult problem of all has been to understand the nature of psychoanalytic data, and how to identify it.

Subjectivity is an issue that cannot be underestimated as a problem – nor also as an opportunity. Highly personal 'immaterial facts' do not have physical properties. They are human experience, meaning, usually shaped in the form of a narrative. The argument developed here is that this is only one kind of data, the meanings on which interpretations are formulated, and then assessed by the response. But then there is the process of the interpretation and its effects, that is, the change sequence, which yields process data much as an experiment in a laboratory. This book has attempted to identify the main ingredients of a protocol that is sufficiently rigorous to provide data – called occurrences – that will comprise the sequence around the interpretation.

Inference and meanings: Segments of free association are normally selected, which offer themselves as conforming to the demands of a particular metapsychological theory. These will be elements of experience that have meaning for the patient. They also have meaning for the psychoanalyst in both the human terms the patient expresses, and also in terms of his more general theories (implicit as well as explicit) about the nature of human experience. The analyst uses his theories to infer particular significance in certain of the patient's expressions.

Countertransference and meaning occurrences: At the same time as the psychoanalyst identifies these meaningful segments of free association, he will experience the impact of the relationship with the person he is working with. His own experience may not always be relevant, but the telling occurrence is when the countertransference expresses something of the same meaning/ relationship as the contents of the free associations. This I have called a triangulation – a convergence of meaning from two perspectives, the contents of the free associations produced by the patient, and the relationship as experienced by the psychoanalyst. This kind of triangulating form of observation is often pointed out by psychoanalysts, though not usually raised to the level of a formal protocol. The recommendation here is that it should be a part of a protocol. This does not mean that other forms of identifying segments of material are not, or should not, be in use, but it does mean that other forms of intervention are deemed non-psychoanalytic. It is only that for the purpose of testing metapsychologies, that the psychoanalytic interpretation is the key action.

Consistency of inferences: Inferences based on a metapsychological theory provide the basic ingredient for constructing an interpretation. It is important however that the *same* theory is used to infer the subsequent data indicating a change following the interpretation. In fact the post-interpretation occurrences must conform to the prediction, which is based on the theory employed to select the pre-interpretative occurrence in the first place which was responsible for the interpretation. Only inferences based on that same theory can be used for the second, the post-interpretive of the occurrences in the change sequence.

It is claimed that operating the model and respecting these various rules and conditions will greatly enhance the rigour of psychoanalytic research and testing. Though it may never be perfect – is there perfection in natural science either? – we stand a chance of being significantly tougher and more rigorous than at present with our laissez-faire pluralism.

Conclusions

Although this book started with a curiosity about what sort of knowledge psychoanalytic knowledge is, the answer may not have emerged very satisfactorily. It is clearly not scientific, though not completely unlike science, at least in this model. Nor is it properly hermeneutics. It may be felt unsatisfactory that it is neither; but at the same time it could also be quite uplifting that it is its very own kind of knowledge.

Such are the results of the investigation of this book. It remains to take a look at the way the research model might play out in practice with a variety of kinds of material.

Part IV

Testing the test

Can research emerge from the ordinary work of the clinical psychoanalyst? It seems unhappily true that 'Researchers note unhappily that practising analysts show little interest in empirical psychoanalytic research' (Schachter and Luborsky 1998, p. 965). But they could be at the centre of it. This book has attempted to describe in as clear and logical a way as possible one model of how *clinical* research might be formulated.

In Part IV, we will set about testing the model with session material from the published literature. If research data from case reports published for clinical purposes reveals occurrences and sequences as described above, then Freud's dictum that therapy and research are inseparable would be greatly strengthened, and dedicated (and expensive) out-of-session research projects become less necessary. Clinical material is reported most often for two reasons; one because the clinical moment (or case) is a difficult one, and the second for the purpose of introducing, or supporting some theoretical development. Sometimes it is for both purposes, the claim for a favourite theory *because* it resolves an especially difficult moment.

To use clinical material for research purposes, the model described here depends on two reporting conditions:

1 that the published material should have verbatim (or near-verbatim) accounts of within-session *process*, and not just generalised description; and
2 that the author should be sufficiently in touch emotionally with the encounter that he/she gives some idea of his own reactions (counter-transference).

These are not big demands for clinicians.

There follow a number of illustrations, only the last of which is original clinical material selected for a research question. In Chapter 21, I shall choose some material intended to demonstrate aspects of the model; single cases showing a change sequence, with occurrences identified by a triangulation process of content plus countertransference, and selected on the basis of a

Type 2 metapsychological theory. Prediction of change based on that theory can be clearly confirmed – or not. Thus the various elements of the model – a binary question, the separation of metapsychological theory from clinical theory (causation from meaning), the operational rules of the required and avoided relationships, and the selection of occurrences according to a process of triangulating content and countertransference – appear to be usable in practice. In consequence I shall claim that the model could in principle function as intended.

In the instances in Chapter 21 a change sequence in line with the prediction merely supports the theory. Thus it adds to the verifying instances, and contributes to a process of enumerative induction (see Chapter 6). Where the interpretation does not work, we cannot tell if the theory is wrong or if the interpretation is incorrect on that occasion.

These first demonstrations do not actually test a metapsychological theory; they only test the working of the model. It will be a bit like revving the car in neutral, before going somewhere. In Chapter 22, I will endeavour to go somewhere!

To test a theory (rather than the interpretation) requires the special conditions of a binary question, and Chapter 22 addresses that functioning of the model. Since innovative new theories like self-psychology, or Weiss's new theory of higher mental functioning in the unconscious (see Chapters 2 and 14) need to be tested, and not just proposed, we shall consider how the model could be used to test these two theories. In fact, clinical accounts by Kohut and by Weiss do not provide material that satisfies the two reporting conditions specified above. And so after a brief consideration of both theories and what would be necessary, to test a theory, the last example considers a different and contentious metapsychological disagreement. The research design requires an appropriate research question, and some fresh clinical material ('The angry lad') is offered to demonstrate the model in its full research capacity.

In short we must examine if it is possible to adequately specify the elements of the model, and then its functioning as a potential research tool. In Chapter 21, I shall specify the main elements:

- the (metapsychology – Type 2) theory under test;
- research question;
- the pre-interpretive occurrence, the required relationship (preferably a triangulation, though this is not always possible);
- the prediction based on the avoided relationship, hypothesised on the basis of the (Type 2) theory under test;
- the interpretation indicating both the required and avoided relationships, and why it is avoided (the three-part interpretation);
- the post-interpretation occurrence using the same theory as the pre-interpretive occurrence – and again preferably a triangulation occurrence;

- the causal change sequence (Type 1) shown by the change from pre- to post-interpretive occurrence, i.e. the impact of the interpretation on the transference-countertransference relationship;
- the test result of the theory.

So, the final example of Chapter 22 puts the model in gear, as it were, to answer a conceptual research question.

Chapter 21

What you can do with clinical material: some case illustrations

The first step is to demonstrate the possibility of following the sequences with all the ingredients of the occurrences in a single case. Although an example was presented in Chapter 19 (an example of a false positive), the following has a more fruitful result, albeit in a difficult case.

A moment of repression

The following vignette, reported by Robert S. White (1996, p. 708–9) for ordinary purposes, was selected more or less at random The report satisfies the two reporting criteria – a verbatim process record, and a transparency to the analyst's reactions. It demonstrates a particularly obvious process taking place where a change can be predicted and then gauged, using the recommended method of selecting occurrences by triangulation of content and countertransference.

I shall give the vignette as reported in White's published paper and comment as the various parts of the model appear:

> A male patient, in the beginning phase of an analysis, opened an hour by talking about his weekend. I started to notice that I felt bored and detached but was unable to pinpoint what I might be feeling. He then started to complain about his lack of creativity and feeling blocked. Without any reflection on my part, I said to him, 'What do you think stops you from doing these things?' I knew as soon as I spoke that this was an inflammatory statement. He said quickly, 'I hate people asking me that,' but went on to reassure me that it didn't bother him when I asked. I asked him how he felt when I asked him and he said, 'Nothing.'

Here is an opening sequence of a session in which we get a vivid account of the interaction. In this case the analyst identifies his countertransference very quickly – he felt bored and detached. Though the analyst knew that boredom meant he was angry, he had not thought about it, with that knowledge repressed, the psychoanalyst asked, without reflection, 'What do you think stops you from doing these things?' He also described how the patient could then feel inflamed by the thoughtless enquiry but in fact claimed to be unaffected. There is quite a bit of enactment which the psychoanalyst eventually became aware of. There is a fairly obvious process in which a non-aggressive pact was established between them.

- The psychoanalyst made a polite enquiry about how the patient felt when he was denying hatred the patient said 'nothing', indicating the politeness and denial of aggression and hate. With the content of bland denial and the countertransference of boredom two perspectives can be triangulated. This is the pre-interpretive occurrence.
- Let us designate that as the required relationship.
- It prompts then a prediction. There is a hidden potential, and even actuality, for considerable aggression. This would be the avoided relationship, a move towards it in the transference is the prediction.
- In turn, we can see that this presupposes a theory of a catastrophe which could unfold and both parties aim to avoid with their collaborative enactment of detachment and and boredom.

Let us make a prediction that there is a castration phantasy in which the patient believes his potency is seriously at risk (coupled with the analyst's repudiation of the image of himself as dangerous). Thus there is in my construction a Type 2 metapsychological theory of castration anxiety.

Continuing with the record:

> I then wondered if he wasn't being polite when he said it didn't bother him. He said, 'Trying to protect you?' I said, 'Yes.'

This intervention is not the standard three-part interpretation, but it is in fact sufficient for our purposes. The interpretation referred to the required politeness, as if it was suspect. It is clear to the patient that the comment meant to point out a protection against something, and that is what an interpretation should be aiming to do, to bring insight about something avoided (protected against).

We then get a rich piece of material which can be regarded as the response:

> He then asked me if he had ever told me about his broken finger. He had been visiting his father for the weekend after his parents had separated. Trying to please his father, he was carrying objects too heavy for his age, fell and hit his hand. His hand continued to hurt and began to swell. His father refused to seek medical attention, then got angry and told him he was a sissy when he cried and continued to complain. It later turned out that he had a serious compound fracture that required months of treatment.

There is very explicit content about the anger and damage – and an indication of why, in the session, the politeness is preferred.

This is the immediate post-interpretive occurrence. However, the story contains a very clear catastrophe. And in fact the broken finger is not a bad substitute idea for the repressed castration phantasy, the same Type 2 meta-psychological theory.

The analyst describes a very different palpable emotional atmosphere in the session:

> As he was telling the story, he became visibly angry at his father. Only at this point could he say spontaneously to me, 'I hated you when you said that.'

We can say that this is the psychoanalyst's intuitive sensing of the relationship. There is not an enactment now, as the analyst is much more fully aware of his experience with the patient in the post-interpretive occurrence. Thus we can note the *triangulation* of two perspectives – the *content*, that is, the story of the complicated relationship with the father, and the *countertransference* recognition of a radical change in the emotionality of the session, changing from boredom/detachment to explicit hatred, first of the father and then to the analyst of a moment ago – 'I hated you' – though not to the analyst now, perhaps.

The record continues with the psychoanalyst's reflections on the session, and the degree of self-analysis he did in spotting the anger behind his boredom which almost certainly put a stop to the enactment. These are his reflections:

> At the beginning of the hour, what was evident was his resistance and my counterresistance. I knew from my own analysis and previous clinical experience that boredom for me is often a signal of defense against aggression. I only became aware of my aggression after my first statement to him that contained obvious critical and aggressive elements, an eruption of my transference and countertransference (a mixture of my own activated anger and being drawn into his projected image of his father). He responded with activated anger, which he then tried to repress. I was now back on track and interpreted his resistance to transference. This allowed his activated transference to be gradually and fully expressed, first in the memory and then directly at me.

This account by the analyst is not too distant from the one I have given. However it is written in a very different manner. There are assertions about what is going on which are claimed, perhaps with the authority of the person there. White does not 'evidence' his assertions in the way I have tried to do. And he therefore opens himself easily to the possibility of contention and dispute.

First, with his material as recorded, the analyst could have described a change sequence, which unfolded from before to after the interpretation. He could have shown the consistency of the metapsychology before and after the intervention.

So, the vignette has, in short, a result: it confirms the intervention/ interpretation about the need for protection. And moreover, there is evidence of therapeutic advance into territory that has been repressed.

But there is another result; our result. It is that for which we turned to this vignette. That result is that the examination of this case confirms that the various elements of the model are observable and usable in practice. We may note that the intervention was not given as fully as it might have been. It was nevertheless good enough.

Sexual hyperactivity disorder

In the next example, the intervention is less clear, and it leaves an ambiguity about the significance of the vignette. Of course it needs acknowledging that the analyst was put under a great deal of emotional stress in the session he records for us.

Wayne Myers tells us of a 22-year-old, attractive, promiscuous woman with a poor relationship with her mother (Myers 1994, pp. 1166–8). She had been diagnosed with ADHD, as a child, and remained on Ritalin. His formulation of the dynamics was that her intense athleticism and physicality during sex worked with the Ritalin to alleviate anxiety and inner frenzy. In turn, it then served to reinforce her sexual behaviour.

The process record was sufficiently verbatim and transparent to provide sufficient details for the purposes of the model. I will give the material as recorded in the published paper, following the steps of the model.

Pre-interpretive occurrence:

> [S]he occasionally dreamed of me as a comforting maternal figure.
>
> After one such dream, near the end of the second year of the treatment, Danielle appeared for a session the next day without any undergarments beneath the outer clothes which she was wearing. The short skirt she had on rode high up on her thighs, and her pubic hair was exposed. The top buttons on her blouse were open, and it was apparent that she had nothing on underneath. She kept quiet for a while and only licked her lips in a lascivious manner. When I asked her what she was thinking about, she walked slowly over to the couch and motioned to me to join her there.
>
> 'Why don't we talk about your thoughts,' I said, remaining where I was seated. 'They ought to be pretty obvious to you,' she replied. 'I'm not so sure they are,' I commented. 'Yesterday you had a dream in which you wanted me to be the sort of mother you never had, and now you

want me to join the ranks of your lovers. It doesn't sound all that clear to me.' 'Don't be so fucking analytic about it, doctor,' she responded, 'I'm just horny, that's all. I didn't have anybody yesterday. It's one of the first times I've missed all year.'

Both of us were silent for a short while, as she unbuttoned the few remaining buttons on her blouse and exposed her bare breasts to me. 'Like them, doc?' She asked, as she shook her breasts provocatively.

I was puzzled as to how to reply. Besides, the experience was proving to be unsettling. I knew that part of my discomfort was related to my feeling sexually aroused by the provocative actions of a young woman not much older than my daughter. In addition, I was in a quandary as to just who Danielle perceived me to be in this transference enactment. On one hand, I was a man the age of her father, and she had often mentioned that the older men she slept with had more 'staying power' sexually than the younger ones. By this she meant that they were capable of remaining intravaginally erect for long periods of time so that she might feel 'filled up'. I had the feeling that with them, she could pretend to have a penis of her own so that she would be the boy-man she believed her mother would find lovable.

As I thought about these ideas, I regained some modicum of composure.

This is a powerful experience. The analyst was puzzled, disconcerted and perhaps a little ashamed. He was at a loss and and uncertain what to do. But he did recover himself, and would go on to make an intervention.

The required relationship: The *content* appears to be a powerful demandingness, which connects with and complements the psychoanalyst's *countertransference* experience of helplessness. In short, there is a possible triangulation: the powerful woman and the helplessly aroused man in both perspectives.

The prediction and avoided relationship: Given the required relationship as described, we might suppose that the patient needs to avoid some quite different relationship. The obvious hypothesis is that she fears the power-lessness of being needy (needing to be filled up), and looking to someone else all the time to ease her pain, as the analyst put it. She avoided that by a powerful assertiveness of her sexuality. This relies on a *Type 2 metapsychological theory* about need and omnipotence. In fact, pre-empting the interpretation made, it is a theory about a confusion between breast and penis, and an ensuing transgressive acting out.

A prediction will therefore be that an interpretation based on this theory will be deemed correct if the patient moves towards a more needy and helpless transference, acknowledging the patient's more oral wishes.

The interpretation:

[The analyst] said: 'What you mentioned a little while ago, about not having anyone yesterday, I think that's very hard for you to tolerate. Men have always been there to ease the pain you felt within yourself. So it's only natural to ask me to perform that function for you now. But if I were to do that, I'd just be another modularly replaceable man in your life. And that would not help you very much. Besides, I have the feeling that the breasts you're offering to me this moment are really emblematic of what you'd like me to offer you. Maybe, in some way, breasts and penises have gotten confused in your mind, since they seem to perform the same function for you.

'I also have the feeling that sitting on the couch right now, is a specific way of testing me out to see what will happen if you actually begin to use it for your treatment. Will I sleep with you and immediately gratify you the way that every other man in your life has, if you lay down on it, or will I sit back and be different and help you to become different than you've ever been before?'

This is quite a long interpretation, and given the helplessness the psychoanalyst had to overcome, he can be allowed a bit of assertiveness of his own position, perhaps. The psychoanalyst does describe clearly the required relationship which the patient has of men, and then interprets the choice that is available to her for using him.

It is not always the best technique to offer alternatives in this way, as so often the patient may believe that it is an instruction in disguise – that the patient ought to choose one of them. In this case, she ought to settle down to using him as a psychoanalyst and not as a man to ease her pain. Possibly, the psychoanalyst *did* wish to give such an instruction; it would not be at all unnatural if he did. However the strength of the emotional and erotic situation may have left it difficult to stress the understandingness about why she was making the 'wrong' choice.

The post-interpretive occurrence:

Danielle stared at me for a while, as if she were undecided how to respond. Then she began to rock back and forth and to cry. She took one of the Moroccan carpets I have thrown across my couch and wrapped herself in it, as in a swaddling blanket. The transformation from seductress one moment to wounded child the next was quite startling.

The next day, she began to use the couch. The change of treatment venue did not immediately presage a change in her driven sexual behavior. If anything, she seemed even more frantic in her pursuit of men.

There is clearly a change, a startling change. And there is a move towards a baby-like posture, needing physical comfort. One gets the hint not just of the psychoanalyst's relief, but a degree of sympathetic response to her abject unhappiness. He regained a comfortable position. We presume he no longer felt the pressure of her sexual power, and felt again his own analytic potency.

The swaddling blanket would suggest the need for a maternal role rather than a seduced male. Indeed it does look as though both of them, patient and analyst, are involved in realising a scene from the patient's dream. This move is in line with the prediction and the theory inspiring the interpretation.

The change sequence: The patient changed abruptly and completely from a powerful sexual predator, playing on men's sexual needs, to becoming a tearful child wrapping herself in a swaddling blanket. The triangulated occurrence before the interpretation is based on the confused or contradictory demands of a breast relationship and a penis relationship. And after the interpretation this was reversed.

However, there is potentially a dispute here. When the analyst wrote, 'Danielle stared at me for a while, as if she were undecided how to respond' is it that she was stunned by the insight? Or was she affected by the implicit instruction about which choice she should be making – or rather the implication that she should be making the opposite choice to the one she was making? We cannot really be sure, and it is possible that this is what, in Chapter 19, I referred to as a Schafer effect, a change not due to the correctness of a metapsychological theory on which an interpretation had been based.

There are several indications that we should be cautious:

- First of all the interpretation does not follow the pattern as closely as it might. There is not a clear re-presentation back to the patient of the defensiveness of her powerful position, though it is implied. Instead the analyst appears to be a little challenging and, in fact, to be including in what he says a slightly urgent wish to protect the psychoanalytic setting.
- Then, second, although the change is very striking, the analyst confided that he found it necessary to reserve judgement on the full and immediate character of the change, since her *external* relations with men did not change, and even seemed to get more desperate!

These indications might lead us to doubt the change as reported. Indeed because the logical model is precise, we are alerted more readily to questions about the accuracy of the work.

This indicates how important it is to establish the structure of an interpretation. Whatever the other interventions which might be appropriate and used in a psychoanalytic treatment, an interpretation is the most clear and overt expression of the concept brought into use. Without the clarity and accuracy of the three-part interpretation we cannot be sure of the nature of the effect and change, and therefore the accuracy of the interpretation.

Though the change was very striking, it was hardly a move into dangerous territory. There was a complete reversal. At one moment a power struggle over being in need, and the next an abject acceptance of neediness and a kind of babyhood. It suggests an ego instability in which such diverse states of mind seem to have equipotentiality. In other words interpretation may not have given a push towards some resolution of the inner dynamic between predatory seducer and regressed baby, but rather a provocation to alternate between them. This is a speculative idea, and it indicates the way in which psychoanalytic debate can tail off into vague possibilities without a precision in the way the 'experimentation' is conceived and practised.

No doubt the striking outcome was the reason the psychoanalyst wished to report this case, but we may be exploring the possibility of a false positive again. Precision in formulating interpretations and observing the subsequent occurrences is necessary to avoid the inconclusive and speculative debates that characterise psychoanalysis. It is always possible that interventions may provoke change, and, in the view of the clinician, achieve useful therapeutic results, but there often is no clear argument as to why the change happened.

Clinical archaeology: the Ratman

I have chosen a third illustration from one of Freud's case histories. If we use published material, then how far back can we go? Freud was working on this case long before there was debate about the scientificity of psychoanalysis, or the validity of its knowledge. Disputes with his colleagues – Jung and Adler – were only at the very earliest stages in 1909. The notions of the Popperian hypothetico-deductive logic were still half a century in the future. And the complex variety of different psychoanalytic schools was undreamed of. Can a model designed for the present conditions work with material reported in the very different conditions prior to 1909? If we found it possible to work with that material, it does suggest that there is still a consistent core to the clinical process which has endured to today, which makes it serviceable data still.

Freud published the therapeutic treatment of the Ratman case for its research results (Freud 1909b). It contributed new knowledge. Freud claimed that shameful repressed anal-sadistic impulses underlie obsessional neurosis. We now have not only Freud's paper, but also the clinical notes he made during the treatment, session by session (published by Strachey in the *Standard Edition*, in 1955, pp. 259–318). The notes augment Freud's texts by giving a more discursive account.

Ernst Lanzer (the Ratman) complained that his mind was intruded upon by alarming and cruel phantasy rituals, and also by word-insertion into ritualistic sentences, prayers, and so on, turning benign thoughts into malign ones. Freud's process notes describe the patient's free associations as a 'confession' (Freud 1909b, p. 282). In his second session, the patient had a 'violent struggle' (p. 260) to explain why he had come to analysis. Freud conveyed how tortured the patient was in his unavailing attempts to control his macabre sadistic phantasies. In the paper, Freud recalls

> [I] went on to say that I would do all I could, nevertheless, to guess the full meaning of any hints he gave me. Was he perhaps thinking of

impalement? – 'No, not that; . . . the criminal was tied up . . .' – he expressed himself so indistinctly that I could not immediately guess in what position – '. . . a pot was turned upside down on his buttocks . . . some rats were put into it . . . and they. . .' – he had again got up, and was showing every sign of horror and resistance – '. . . bored their way in . . .' – Into his anus, I helped him out.

At all the more important moments while he was telling his story his face took on a very strange, composite expression. I could only interpret it as one of horror at pleasure of his own of which he himself was unaware. He proceeded with the greatest difficulty: 'At that moment the idea flashed through my mind that this was happening to a person who was very dear to me.'

(Freud 1909b, pp. 166–7)

The Ratman was tortured by his own shameful thoughts, and he appeared to need help to confess this painful guilt. The case verified Freud's hypothesis about obsessional compulsive disorder. However, our model allows more than that inductive support of Freud's theory. We could *test* the theory as well. There is at least a *possibility* of falsification if the material is sufficient to show effectively the change sequence in relation to a key interpretation.

The metapsychology (Type 2) theory under test: Freud's theory is that obsessional states result from the repression of infantile anal–sadistic impulses. This is a hermeneutic (Type 2) metapsychology theory which captures the *meaning* in the Ratman's obsessional symptoms.

Research question: The theory is a risky one; it is a generalisation that all obsessional states have roots in anal erotism. In principle this could be falsified, as a generalisation, by one case that does not show the relics of anal erotism. Therefore the binary question is: does the Ratman show elements of anal erotism? It can be answered in only two ways; 'yes' or 'no'. A 'no' destroys the generalisation.

The clinical notes: I propose to take a single instance from the notes:

He was very cheerful and has had a relapse into masturbation, which has hardly disturbed him at all. When he first masturbated he had an idea it would result in an injury to someone he was fond of (his cousin). He therefore pronounced a protective formula constructed as we already know from extracts from various short prayers and fitted with an isolated 'amen'. We examined it . . .

Next day he came in a state of deep depression, and wanted to talk about indifferent subjects; but he soon admitted he was in a crisis. The most frightful thing had occurred to his mind while he was in a tram yesterday. It was quite impossible to say it. His cure would not be worth such a sacrifice. I should turn him out, for it concerned the transference. Why should I put up with such a thing? None of the explanations about the transference (which did not sound at all strange to him) had any effect. It was only after a forty minute struggle – as it seemed to me – and after I had revealed the element of revenge against me and had shown him that by refusing to tell me and by giving up the treatment he would be taking a more outright revenge on me than by telling me – only after this did he give me to understand that it concerned my daughter. With this, the session came to an end.

It was still hard enough. After a struggle and assertions by him that my undertaking to show that all the material concerned only himself looked like anxiety on my part, he surrendered the first of his ideas.

(Freud 1909b, pp. 280–81)

Pre-interpretative occurrence (Type 2): This is some six weeks after starting the treatment, when in one session, he was very cheerful, and though he had resorted to masturbation, he had used a 'protective formula'. But 'next day he came in a state of deep depression', and struggled to tell Freud. Freud, as we saw, had a strong reaction to the struggling, a sympathy with the patient's horror and need to confess. We can therefore designate the benign collaborative confessional as the *required* relationship, in which confessor and penitent both took their parts. Here is an enactment to which, as before, both sides contributed.

Prediction – the avoided relationship: The prediction then is that the *avoided* relationship is not benign, so that if interpreted, the transference-countertransference should become more of a relationship in which the Ratman intended sadistic harm to the psychoanalyst. We might even say that the analytic relationship may come to resemble a rat-like gnawing intrusion into Freud.

Interpretation: Freud described his intervention. He speculated on a kind of harmful revenge towards him personally; there was a 40-minute struggle that implied 'a more outright revenge' against Freud himself. Freud was describing a rather cruel effect that the patient intended. This is as precise a description of the avoided relationship, as we could expect.

Post-interpretative occurrence: We hear from Freud that *after* the interpretation new associations did occur: 'only after this did he give me to understand that it concerned my daughter. With this, the session came to an end.' As Freud put it, it was only after a struggle that he surrendered his ideas (the first idea apparently was a naked bottom with nits).

This was clearly a change, and the reference to a bottom, to an infestation and to a violation of Freud's daughter does imply anal-intrusive phantasies. This is precisely the predicted change, moving towards the avoided relationship, explicit and conscious. It is no longer implicit in the intruding transference, but an explicit *content* of an intruding violation. In addition, the Ratman's precise sexual fantasies had moved nearer to the psychoanalyst (if not all the way to Freud's actual person). The apparent threat to Freud's daughter is similar to Ezriel's example of a man whose rebelliousness moved nearer to the psychoanalyst (Chapter 19).

So much for the post-interpretive content, but what of the counter-transference, as we would understand it today? Freud did not explicitly refer to it of course, but the notes say that as part of the struggle, there were 'assertions by him that my undertaking to show that all the material concerned only himself looked like anxiety on my part'. There is an awareness by the Ratman that Freud was anxious, a perception picked up by Freud. And indeed why would Freud not have been anxious, given the potential threat to his daughter? So, whereas previously there had been a benign relationship, now the patient indicated Freud's anxiety. The notes do not tell us if Freud *did* feel anxious. Certainly it was the Ratman's construction that Freud's peace of mind had been imposed on 'harmfully', by the Ratman. However, Freud did convey he had to work desperately hard to get his point across, indicating perhaps he had been anxious, consciously, that the treatment might collapse. But, more to the point, there was a threat to Freud's daughter, from a sexual sadist! Freud might (should) have been anxious.

So, if we take the *content* about violating Freud's daughter, and the *countertransference*, a harmful invasion into Freud's peace of mind about the treatment, there is an overlap in the meanings of both perspectives. This is again a triangulation occurrence; the converging perspectives were (a) the content of the associations which contained a violating act against Freud's daughter, and (b) a probable countertransference enactment of an invasion of anxiety into Freud's mind.

The causal change sequence (Type 1): So the post-interpretation occurrence indicates a change away from the benign state of mind of a confessional. And indeed the change did seem to be a good match for the prediction. Freud's theory of obsessional neurosis would predict that some cruel, invasive element would emerge more directly into the relationship with Freud. And that predicted change did seem to happen after the interpretation, and is precise evidence of the correctness of the interpretation. This result – a change sequence – could be observed according to the clinical theory (Type 1 theory) of the transference and countertransference, with the same Type 2 theory (about obsessional states) both before and after.

Test result: The predicted change seemed to occur precisely according to the operational rules. The transference–countertransference relationship moved towards the avoided one. The result is that Freud's metapsychological theory of the aetiological link between sadism and obsessional neurosis passed the test.

The binary question – whether the interpretation based on this theory resulted in a change precisely towards the avoided relationship – was answered decisively. The sequence from pre- to post-interpretive occur-rences was a change demonstrating something like a causal effect on the transference–countertransference relationship. It is not any old change, but the precise one predicted on the basis of the metapsychological Type 2 theory.

This result is striking given that, at the time the case was conducted and written up, the countertransference and the three-part interpretation had not been conceptually worked out.

The analysis of this piece of process could be contested of course. Freud's hard work, 'struggling' to impose his interpretation on the patient, might instead be regarded as having an intrusive quality, intruding *his* interpretation into the patient's mind against resistance. So, one objection is that the relationship at that point characterised by mutual intrusiveness may hypothetically have been provoked from either side, and did not necessarily conform to the prediction about the Ratman's intrusion into Freud's mind.

In addition, another potential, and potent, criticism is that I have simply selected particular comments (asides, even) in Freud's record, which suit my argument. These objections could be valid, but it would need support from other material in the record, demonstrating an alternative structure of required/ avoided/catastrophe, and a move, following an appropriate interpretation, towards a different avoided relationship. Others may find such material in Freud's notes.

Despite the possibility of debate – always a possibility in any science – there are results from the use of the logical model. A new theory can be put at risk by testing. It appears this is possible however far back we go. The caveat is that the record must satisfy the two conditions of verbatim reporting and transparency of personal reactions.

This illustration, conveying possible change sequences in clinical work, may date from long ago before the critiques of psychoanalysis as science, and before the concerns about a purely inductive generalisation that needs supplementing with a form of deductive testing. In the period when Freud was making his discoveries, it was standard in medical science to generalise from a few carefully observed particulars to generalities. However, Freud's account gives us sufficient detail of the work, and indeed sufficient transparency, to do more than follow the generalisation – using the logical model, we can test it.

Conclusions

The three illustrations in the chapter are varied and demonstrate the elements of the model, including the importance of interpretation, of the interactive transference–countertransference activity, the binary question research design, the operational rules, prediction, and the usable data from triangulated perspectives. All these appear to be thoroughly practical.

It does not mean that there cannot be dispute, as in any discipline that develops its body of knowledge empirically. Nor does it close down the possibility of new developments and variations. It means that new developments and the comparisons with conventional theories could now be more rigorously assessed. New generalisations can (must) still be pondered, supported and debated, but they cannot be simply claimed as knowledge on the basis of generalising a few cases with some common feature. So we do not have to tolerate the anything-goes pluralism, without a means to put some order into the variation.

This specific kind of comparative research we will turn to in the next chapter.

Chapter 22

Comparative research: illustrative examples of the model at work

In this final chapter, I shall discuss more focused comparative research. The final illustration in this chapter uses the model to produce data – sequences and occurrences – for a specific conceptual question. In this instance, it will involve following the process through two interpretations, and thus two change sequences.

However, before that I want to touch briefly on two illustrative examples of new theoretical concepts growing out of clinical practice. These will be Heinz Kohut's key paper on his 'discovery' of self-psychology with Mr Z, and Joseph Weiss's higher functioning theory, referred to in Chapter 2 of this book. In both cases, clinicians substituted new ideas for classical theories. In each case, however, the researchers do not report material adequate enough to *test* the research claims as required by the model. The status of the authors views therefore remains opinion. Nevertheless they have both gathered followings of others, who have accepted the claims for the new concepts, and the practices. They have gained currency therefore through methods other than empirical testing. In terms of the processes of conviction described in Chapter 4, the new ideas have become established on the basis of the impact of making good sense (a narrative), and the power of authoritative assertions.

There is nothing bad about making sense, and Edelson (1985), for instance, makes this the criterion for comparing two theories – the one that makes sense of the most data wins, as discussed in Chapter 14. This is the criterion of plausibility (or coherence for hermeneuticists). It is still an appeal to the inductive (intuitive) recognition of a pattern that satisfies good sense. It therefore fails to deliver the categorical punchline of falsification. My intention in including these two illustrations here is partly to point to the continual practice, down to the present day, of Freud's use of generalisation from a few cases to a general category; and partly to ask what would be needed to supplement the generalisation with the precision of the logical model based on deduction.

The two analyses of Dr Kohut

The first project is a very curious incident in comparative work. Kohut's attempt to compare self-psychology with classical psychoanalysis was the interesting comparison of Mr Z's two analyses, one before Kohut developed his new theories and one after. The latter, based on self-psychology principles, gave 'access to certain sectors of his personality that had not been reached in the first part of his treatment' (Kohut 1979, p. 3). Thus one psychoanalyst could work with new sectors of the same patient when using different theories. Kohut's account of this two-part psychoanalysis was published to demonstrate a comparative evaluation of two key concepts in the different metapsychology frameworks – narcissism as a defence (classical psychoanalysis), and primary narcissism as re-aroused in the idealised transference (self-psychology). Despite being marred by the fact that Mr Z's analyses seem to have been Kohut's own, his first classical analysis followed by his later self-analysis (Giovacchini 2000), there is, in addition, no in-session process record, apart from one significant moment. At one point in the first 'analysis', Kohut introduces an interpretation with the innocent phrase, 'Of course, it hurts when one is not given what one assumes to be one's due' (Kohut 1979, p. 5), and this changed the patient from a state of rage into a more compliant patient. Kohut rests a great deal on that change, on that new kind of interpretation and the response to it. The interpretation introduced an *understanding* of that primitive narcissistic experience, and it was not an interpretation of a defence against some pain.

The quite dramatic change – from rage to compliance – is clear enough, though not predicted. In fact, that is the point: it was unexpected, a stumbling upon something new. Kohut is making the case that something new is a valid reason for reconstructing theory, in this case the development of self-psychology. However, we know that it is dangerous to put much weight on *any* change. Any change is not enough, since it may be one of those extraneous effects (a false positive, due to the Schafer effect, and not directly to do with theory). To rely on the change being genuinely due to the interpretation, and the theory it is based on, it is necessary to have a more telling argument. That needed to be based empirically on a process and on thinking which actually Kohut did not give us. One confirming process could be the design, the operational rules, and the precise data collection laid out in this book.

A possible test: What prediction would test Kohut's claim that his new theory is superior? We need to have enough information to be able to judge the status of the change from rage to compliance. If rage had been a *required* transference, and it was kept in place to avoid a compliant relationship, which had to be *avoided*, then we want to know what catastrophe (the 'because clause') made compliance so dangerous. This could be in self-psychology terms, a hypothesis about primary narcissism, and a catastrophic de-idealisation. But to use the response as given we would need to be satisfied that the interpretation specified the problem of narcissism, and the avoidance of its dissolution, and a prediction of a move towards the avoided. Kohut's argument gave us a post hoc justification; and no 'rational account' supported his opinion. Strictly speaking we would have to say, with Plato, this remains an opinion and not professional knowledge. That does not make the opinion wrong just that, as it stands, there are no grounds for claiming self-psychology has survived a careful testing.

Moreover, we are able to say that there *could* be grounds if we knew of the rest of the actual interpretation which was referred to, but not given. Had we been able to see the meanings before the interpretation, then the predictions the interpretation implies, and the eventual outcome in terms of the emergence of the avoided relationship, there may have been grounds for Kohut's claims as knowledge rather than opinion.

An entitlement to what one believes is due, is a common enough human experience. The considerable theoretical superstructure of self-psychology has been built on that observation, involving a number of new technical ideas such as 'self-object', 'mirror transference', and so on. However, Kohut's primary distinction was the difference between a defensive secondary regression to narcissism as described in classical psychoanalysis (Freud 1914), and a primary narcissism where the original developmental journey has not been fully accomplished in earlier life. He postulated that in narcissistic personality disorders, a 'split-off' part of the ego sustained a persistent primary narcissism by means of an undifferentiated identification (merger or enmeshment) with an idealised mother. Secondary narcissism has a defensive function in the formulations of classical psychoanalysis; it is Oedipal and genital, and clearly contrasts with the more primitive states of idealisation and merger arising from pre-Oedipal relations with primary objects.

That distinction between primary and secondary narcissism is the feature necessary to test the new idea. We can make the hypothesis, characteristic of self-psychology, that in a narcissistic personality, interpretations of defensive narcissism will be inadequate, and those concerning merger and idealisation will result in change. This leads to a hypothesis:

> Narcissistic personalities will *not* show a significant change as a response to interpretations of defensive narcissism.

In other words, interpretation needs to be at a level of primary narcissism. Then we can ask the binary question: does a particular narcissistic personality demonstrate a predicted change immediately after an interpretation of defensive narcissism? The question can have two answers and two only. If the answer is 'yes', such a narcissistic person did change after the interpretation of his defence, then the case *against* the self-psychology hypothesis as stated has succeeded.

Weiss's Miss P

Turning to another new theory, we met Joseph Weiss's Miss P in Chapters 2 and 14. An occurrence in her analysis provoked Weiss to launch a new theory, the 'higher mental functioning theory', and to compare it with the existing and classical 'automatic functioning hypothesis'. In Chapter 2 we described the development of Weiss's research strategy, starting with the new theory:

> Higher functioning (secondary process) occurs at the unconscious level.

This differed from classical theory in that beyond an unconscious threshold, unpleasure *automatically* triggers a primary process repression mechanistically (Weiss and Sampson 1986, pp. 23–6). Miss P subsequently produced a long-forgotten memory indicating the opposite, indicating the lifting of repression. And this single test case, Weiss and his co-workers claimed, showed *unconscious* higher functioning. The research thinking stressed the emergence of a memory somewhat akin to the emergence of the avoided relationship in the present model. However, there is not an exactitude in the observations of the change sequence. The researchers merely saw the emergence of the memory as closely in line with the new theory. It was, in effect, an instance which was elaborated inductively into a generalisation, and not tested. Moreover the agent of change here was not an interpretation. So the result they achieved has to be classed as a Schafer effect, until tested and proved otherwise.

Comparative psychoanalysis: the angry lad

Because of the prevalent method for proposing and promulgating a new school of psychoanalysis, formal testing of concepts is unusual and difficult to exemplify from the published literature. Therefore I shall now demonstrate the detailed use of the model with some clinical material of my own to compare two theories.

Research design: It is first of all necessary to establish the exact conceptual comparison to be made. This requires us to define a key distinctive feature which differentiates the two concepts, and this may be articulated as a binary question, necessary for the single-case research that psychoanalysis relies on. There are four steps for implementing the model in this comparative research:

1   Identify the two concepts about which a *dispute* can be clearly laid out.
2   Pinpoint the *key element* that differentiates them.
3   Question whether this key element is present or absent (the binary research question).
4   Select the necessary *clinical material* from which the existence (or not) of the key element can be determined through the change sequence around the interpretation.

The conceptual dispute: I propose to take a *central dispute* within current psychoanalysis. More than 50 years ago Melanie Klein (1957) described early or primary envy (see also Spillius 1993; Etchegoyen, *et al.* 1987; Spillius *et al.* 2011). This has not been generally accepted, and there has been challenge, to the point of scorn sometimes, to this conceptual development (Joffe 1969; Yorke 1971; Zetzel 1956). Klein's paper proved the climax to the dispute between British object-relations and Austrian–American ego-psychology dating back 30 years before that. It remains a stumbling block to the relations between certain psychoanalytic schools, and continues to serve as a rallying point for adherence to different camps that stifles the possibility of useful debate.

What are the issues? This is not the place for an extensive theoretical debate (see Hinshelwood 1991; Roth and Lemma 2008; Spillius *et al.* 2011); but a brief summary of the controversy includes:

* whether the early ego is capable of such complex phantasies;
* whether there is an *innate* awareness of separation between self and object as the concept of Kleinian envy depends on it;
* whether the destructiveness of envy comes from all levels of development, not just oral; or
* whether it is secondary to frustration and possessiveness;
* whether envy arises from problems of narcissism;
* whether people in general are averse to such malignant destruction in innocent infants;
* whether it is innate and impossible to alter by interpretation; and
* if the envy concept is clinically unnecessary.

There are therefore many possible issues that could be decided by an interpretation and its response. The fundamental difference however can be captured in two incompatible positions, either:

1   it is necessary to interpret envy in severe disorders; or
2   what Kleinians interpret as envy can be understood as simply deriving from other negative emotions, notably frustration and jealousy.

This provides us therefore with a *key distinctive element*; as the two theoretical statements are mutually exclusive, the data must support either one or the other. From the second position we can construct the hypothesis:

Envy is an unnecessary concept and no change will occur after interpreting it.

This hypothesis allows a logical certainty that if one case of envy can be shown by a *predicted* change after its interpretation, then position (2) is not tenable, and new questions need to be asked – such as when does envy apply, and when not?[1] So, in the clinical setting we can develop a *binary question* from this dispute. The question can be put as:

Does this case demonstrate resistance due to envy?

This question is answerable with the protocol of the logical model. I propose in fact to test this with *case material* of a persisting aggressive transference.

The following is clinical material to show how the model can answer this discriminating question. The material here covers two interpretations, and is thus more complex than earlier examples. First an interpretation was given of the patient's aggression as frustration and fear of intrusion. And then, with the striking lack of success after that interpretation, a new prediction was made followed by an interpretation based on envy as a destructiveness towards learning and constructiveness for its own sake. So, there were *two* change sequences, involving two key interpretations based on separate metapsychological theories.

Record of the clinical process: I will give the material as recorded (it was previously used for presentations of Kleinian technique).

This man in his mid-30s came to analysis with the problem that he had had a number of good relationships with women but that they had ultimately failed after 2–3 years. Outwardly they were successful relationships. However, for my patient, the women neglected him and he felt they exploited him for their own neurotic reasons, whilst seeing him as the problem. He believed strongly in his ability to understand them, and the relationship. Although, at times he feared he might be quite paranoid.

In the early part of the analysis, he did indeed get very angry, and he could have described himself justifiably as paranoid. His particular complaint of me was that I did not understand him properly. I was often driven to making interventions which were little more than repeating back what he said. In so doing I was trying to change my position in relation to him, rather than to interpret it. At about a year into the analysis, there was a persisting antipathy about my contributions. One could say that an impasse had occurred at even this early stage of analysis. A great deal of the material was devoted to his efforts to teach me how to understand properly – to understand him, and also more generally to understand my patients as an analyst.

This patient was very alert to my mind and how it operates, and watchful of possible intrusions. He was interpreting me rather than listening to me.

Pre-interpretive occurrence: The required relationship was clearly a hostile one:

On one occasion he was telling me how bullish and overbearing his father was. He was clearly hurt by his father's manner of speaking. I said, 'Your father sounds boorish and overbearing,' and added that, 'I think you felt very small when your father paid little attention to what you thought.' That seemed completely correct, as far as it went; but he was cross with me. He was silent for a while. By now I was very familiar with the quality of the silence – I was to be chastised for something wrong. Over about five minutes he conveyed what it was; clearly even to communicate his hurt, did also hurt him. He believed the way I spoke my comment suggested that I was sceptical, that I must believe his father was not so bad. He was sure that I was saying his hurt was more to do with his sensitivity than with his father's boorishness. Therefore, I had introduced my own point of view. I had therefore not listened properly to his point of view before jumping in with mine.

My countertransference at this time was complicated and indicates the stress of this particular analysis.

At this point I was quite disconcerted and unsure. On the one hand, I had really tried to listen carefully and to say no more than what was in his account – the facts and the feelings. His anger with my effort seemed unfair.

On the other hand, I have from time to time, as a Kleinian, been confronted by other analysts with the criticism that I must make deep and intrusive interpretations which leave the patient feeling violated. At the time, all this came to mind and I had to seriously wonder if I had been responsible for a psychological penetration and violation.

I was aware I seemed to be criticised for exactly what his father did to him. There had been some material some weeks before about a memory of being a toddler and bathed by his father, who also being naked had cuddled the patient in a way that sounded rather sensuous. So I wondered about a fear of homosexual penetration. However, I thought he was conveying some sense of violation that was not as coherent as a libidinal homosexual fantasy. It seemed rather that his whole sense of being was in jeopardy rather than his sexual orientation.

In the early part of this material the *content* was about his bullish and overbearing father who clearly hurt him by this manner of speaking. I seemed also to be explicitly chastised for talking as his father does and forcing my views onto him.

His driven state of mind had an impact on me, which appeared to click with this content he was actually saying. This countertransference I felt to be unfair, and a distortion of my words, and of my intentions. What

I actually did was to attempt to avoid being intrusive, on the grounds that he genuinely experienced me like that, and I wished very much to avoid playing that role. I wished to be judged fairly, and I seemed to be fitting in with a requirement that we both veer away from analytic work, and attend to justice and fairness.

The prediction (the avoided relationship): The prediction is that the aggression and unfairness prevented an avoided relationship in which analytic work did take place, but led to my concentrating on my thoughts, and leaving him to feel left out as a participant. A form of primal scene enacted at the level of abstract thinking. Thus the theory used to construct the meaning of this pre-interpretive occurrence is an Oedipal one, concerning the exclusion from the primal scene of my thinking mind.

The prediction arising would be a move from the aggression to something more fearful – a real involvement in the Oedipal scene with the fear of murder, castration, and so forth.

Interpretation 1: I could on the particular occasion I report, make an attempt at an interpretation of this structure, and his fear of obliteration:

> I said: 'You are cross with me for not listening properly, and for paying too much attention to my own thoughts. Then you feel not just misunderstood but it demolishes your whole sense of existence, your sense of being a person is threatened.'

This interpretation conveys, in its own way, the avoided relationship in which my thoughts, taken in by him, threaten his own sense of self and having his own mind.

Post-interpretive occurrence: In fact there was not much change.

> However, this compounded my error, because from his point of view I was just constructing my own narrative out of my thoughts, not his. 'No', he said, 'that's not it.' He began to remonstrate about what he had actually been trying to say, 'I was saying, my father is overbearing, he just talked, and went on and on about how he is going to distribute his money amongst his children . . .' At the end of the session, which came soon, he stormed out of the room. His father, it seemed, was omnipotent and narcissistic, and the patient wanted me to know about that pathology, and how he is a victim of it.

So, the content of the associations remained the same. My thoughts continued to be experienced as no more than a threat, like his self-preoccupied father, and thus rejected. That is, one could not say that the primal scene theory was relevant to this situation and this analysis. My countertransference, too, remained the same.

Change sequence: The sequence could be said to be quite unchanging, very familiar.

> I continued to feel I could do little other than acknowledge what an impossible position he occupied. And eventually, I became attentive to the material and whether there was material that could show a primary envy behind this state of affairs. After many weeks of talking about *my* problems, he came to a Tuesday session in his usual intimidating way. But on this occasion, I suddenly had a new thought. It was about his mother, who had divorced his father many years ago when the patient was 10 or so. At this point, I thought for the first time really that I could see something behind my patient's 'paranoia'. I could really feel it first in an empathy he was conveying for certain members of his family. I could see the needy side of these objects that he was presenting to me, and not just their intrusiveness that took him over.

The lack of change indicates we should drop this way of looking at it, and the metapsychology theory on which it is based. The primal scene theory is simply not relevant. The next is the initial material for the second sequence

Further pre-interpretive occurrence: There was considerable detailed material, about the family of his partner (Margaret) who would be visiting London.

> He confided, 'When Margaret's parents come they want to be looked after, taken around London to see the sights. They want us to cook for them, but Margaret and I are busy full-time so it is difficult.' He paused. Although he was presenting his usual misfortune in being captured by someone else's needs, I could see the *needy* side of these objects that he was presenting, not just their intrusiveness that took him and his house over for their purposes. He changed the subject as if trying to fill me in on all the significant things that had happened since yesterday's session. 'At work yesterday, this other bloke I've talked about, sat in the seat I normally use. He says he uses it more so he has a right to it. I tried to explain that I normally sit in that one. But he took no notice. I could have gone to the supervisor, but . . .' He seemed hopeless, vulnerable and angry.

This is the same story – about the injustice of his exclusion from his rightful place. But this is where a new thought occurred to me. Though the *content* appears as usual, here is a hint of his vulnerability in this displaced position. But the *countertransference* is of interest, too. I felt much more sympathetic, sympathetic to both the child-like family 'lost' in London, and also to his sense of invasion and intrusion. In other words the two perspectives, content and countertransference, overlapped now on the vulnerability to being displaced, as the common feature, and it was not just the hostile outrage that was common.

Prediction, and alternative avoided relationship: There was the appearance, by implication, of a need to be looked after in the strange city, and indeed a need for a concerned supervisor at work. Could this be the avoided relationship? I tried a new interpretation.

Interpretation 2: I made an attempt to address the relation between his anger and this vulnerability.

> I said, 'I think you want to tell me, like your supervisor, about how easily you feel displaced, but then feel hopeless about getting a response to the pain it causes you. I think you have found it easier then to get angry, and perhaps it is the case that being angry is a way of shielding how vulnerable you feel.' He did not respond immediately, and I was sure on past experience that he was reacting to my having expressed my own ideas on his problem. So, before he spoke, I said, 'Right now, I think you are torn between being angry with me for forcing my ideas on to you, on one hand, and on the other, responding more appreciatively to my attempt to understand how pushed out and vulnerable you feel.'

Though the interpretation as given was in two parts and therefore a little ragged, it conveys the use of a relationship (the angry one) to shield another one from sight. And this fared better!

Post-interpretive occurrence: Despite the usual angry response, he admitted to a much more complex conflict going on as well. The record includes how he could begin to have his own 'new thought', too. At least it was new to the analysis – he could seem to regret his anger and make attempts to control it. Here is the record:

> Then he did acknowledge his anger. He said, tight-lipped, 'You're right. I feel angry.' However, unusually there was a little distance, as if talking about himself. And he added, 'I don't want to agree with you about feeling vulnerable. But . . . I was. There was nothing I could do about that bloke.' He was silent for a while, and I could sense he was seething, about my description of him and his conflict. But also, I thought it was much more apparent that he was struggling to recognise I had understood him a bit.
> After some time, he said, 'I suppose, I want to avoid being vulnerable.' In that moment, he was taking an idea from me, as if it was his own. I did not challenge his possessiveness, as I thought he could only take the small step in his own way. The session was at an end, and he seemed to be taken by surprise. He left as if tense and without looking at me.

This change was certainly heartening, but it also had an equally heartening echo in a dream during the night which he reported the next day:

The next day, an early morning session, he came with a dream. He was a little late for the session, was customarily silent in a familiar frozen manner, and then started off a bit hesitant as usual. He told the dream with a puzzled air. In the dream, he was walking in some local woods, but there was a school in the middle of the woods. He had mixed feelings about the school.

He implied he did not understand the dream, but said no more. As I waited, it seemed to me the puzzlement in the dream about the school suggested his wish to consider how he related to a learning institution; and that implied his mixed feelings about learning from the analytic institution, that is, his analysis with me. I knew that this was my interpretation and not his, but as the session seemed to have frozen again, I said just that: 'I think you are very quiet because you are afraid I might have my own ideas about the dream, and might expect you to learn from me. Then you would have very mixed feelings and negative ones, if this session became like a school, when you would prefer to have a familiar walk in a local wood by yourself.'

I had wondered how to approach this new material,

I could have said more about seeing the wood for the trees, and the 'wood' in my name, but I thought this too provocative. As it was, he shifted uncomfortably as if he did indeed have a negative reaction to my ideas. He sighed as if it was tedious to have to cope with me, but with an effort at genuine co-operation, he told me something about his schooling. He had been to a very authoritarian school that taught through rote-learning. He had been so distressed as a boy that he had been sent to another school where the teachers encouraged the children to discover things for themselves. He was then silent again.

We can understand this occurrence as having a *content* – about learning. In addition the content made a specific reference to a 'wood' that implied a reference to myself. He was so averse to being led in his learning by an authority that the school situation broke down for him. From the countertransference perspective, there was the familiar hesitancy about being overbearing, but now it was much more clearly connected with the learning situation, and his aversion to learning by guidance from others. We have therefore a triangulation which demonstrates the overlap between the experiences in the content, with the visiting family needing to be looked after, and my countertransference experience of needing to avoid being a learning guide. The overlap appeared to be a story about the aversion to being helped.

Change sequence: The significant change after the second interpretation concerned with the pain of being looked after and 'given' a place (as opposed to rightful ownership of it) suggest that it is indeed a problem of a destructive relationship with help, guidance, and the teacher from whom he can learn – that amounts to the standard view of envy as the destruction of goodness and truth.

Test result: This material was chosen, of course, because of the striking change after the second interpretation. The change was such a contrast with the earlier interpretive sequence when no change whatsoever occurred. What's more, the change did not seem to be 'any old change' but one in line with the prediction. Being in need – in this case the need to learn something – was an extraordinary vulnerability for him, laying him open to the relentless rage against the one who made him feel in need. I should claim this conflict as a move considerably nearer to the avoided learning relationship which aroused his envy rather than his primal scene phantasies of frustration and exclusion.

Clearly the two interpretations fared very differently. Hence the two theories – aggression due to (Oedipal) fears, or aggression due to envy – are distinguished. One cannot be subsumed by the other. One appeared to be right in this case, judging by the fulfilled prediction.

Conclusion: This is a single case which enters the debate decisively, showing that hatred of learning *can* exist. And this bears decisively upon the hypothesis that in certain cases, at least, envy can occur.

Of course the standard response of those opposed to the concept of primary envy is that really the envy only looks like it, but is in fact an ordinary resistance if only the analyst had not jumped to the conclusion, and it is merely a case of finding what he was already looking for. However that argument falls, in this case, because different interpretations based on *both* concepts were made at different times with this patient. With radically different effects. Thus it is not possible to argue that this is just another case in support of an inductive generalisation, merely adding to the stock of supporting cases. This case pits the two rival concepts against each other. And one had an effect; and the other did not.

In fact in this case the psychoanalyst was at first persuaded to think that the patient looked more like a case of avoidance of pain.[2] In fact, I did actually go on rather a long time with that view (frustration as opposed to primary envy). Only in the face of repeated failures of interpretations, and of the interpretations of failure, did the analyst take recourse to another point of view – that there was a primary destructiveness aimed at the vulnerability of learning, and the learning institution.

It is not simply that a change sequence supported envy of learning, but that another interpretation (of resistance due to repressed fear) did not show the change sequence predicted. Hence it may be concluded that the hypothesis as stated is false: it is not valid that *envy is an unnecessary concept and no change will occur after interpreting it*. At the least in this one case it *is* necessary. The two concepts must be allowed to co-exist, and more precise work needs to be done by both sides of the dispute to determine when each is appropriate.

The conclusion is that envy as a motive underlying resistance in the transference-countertransference relationship has to be included, and it cannot always be reduced to resistance arising from repressed conflict, fear, and jealousy.

The example has demonstrated that clinical data can decide between two theoretical positions. And this has been accomplished by a single case.

Conclusion

Though single-case studies are the frequent rule in natural science, such as Eddington's observations of the magnetic pull on light during the eclipse of 1919, not to mention Columbus's geographical 'experiment', it can be just as valid in psychoanalytic research. However, the definitive nature of a single case depends in psychoanalysis on a carefully thought out design just as in science.

We have tried out the logical model with various kinds of material. My examples do not cover all the necessary uses of such a logical model. None of the material was presented originally for the present purposes, so it is surprising that we find it not so difficult to find usable pre- and post-interpretive occurrences. Yet, it has been possible to put clinical material into a research format *after* its publication. Thus clinical material from therapeutic work, if reported completely enough, can be fed into the protocol. My test of the test does give results that suggest a usable model, provided certain conditions are met, including predictions based on required/avoided relationships, and above all the precise generation of research data as occurrences which allow the use of two separate kinds of theory – causal (Type 1) theory and hermeneutic (Type 2) theory (especially the triangulation occurrences).

This protocol is the culmination of an enquiry about using clinical material for research. We have evolved a mould, a protocol, within which one can work in a manner comparable to the logical model of natural science. Being logical, the end result has a degree of certainty about it which is transparent enough to be critiqued by others. The point of the protocol is to keep the intuitive inspiration of the psychoanalyst (and the patient) focused into one area of work, and to give space for a logical appreciation and testing of that, essentially human, intuition.

Transparency: Clinical material can be sufficiently transparent to other researchers, who are not present in the research setting. This is surprising since it is usually assumed that the privacy of the psychoanalytic consulting room cannot be genuinely transparent to the critical scrutiny of third parties. In fact, it is not different from subsequent reporting of a laboratory experiment by a physical scientist to those who are not present in his laboratory.

Such a logical model can therefore go some way to reduce the anything-goes Babel state of psychoanalytic theory, and to give some protection to the work of making comparisons which can remain undamaged by the inevitably painful conflicts of interests that will arise.

In conclusion

This model has given its acceptance to the hermeneutic stress on meanings as well as to the scientific notion of causality. It has moved away from instincts/drives, and towards subjective experience, intersubjectivity and object-relations proper. This may not be acceptable to everyone. However, those movements are, in my view, trends that are going on within the psychoanalytic world anyway at the present time. That trend may be enhanced if we have a means of evaluating better the comparative effects of the different theories.

The acceptance of the model is therefore only likely to increase as time goes on – provided, of course, the model produces results. The required results are the clearer discrimination between concepts and schools, and will not always be acceptable to those for whom the verdict goes against their particular theories. What happens to such schools of thought depends on their ability to meet the challenge of added theoretical work. Unfortunately this may be true in any discipline that seeks to establish a rigorous claim for its knowledge against rivals and counter-claims.

What are the options for a psychoanalyst, or a school of psychoanalysts, who find their cherished ideas disconfirmed. This is the same question that can be asked of scientists, it was Einstein's question when he found his disapproval of quantum theory was constantly undercut by new evidence and formal mathematical proofs. As we saw in Chapter 8, there are various strategies. One is a modification of the theory, so that instead of general application – e.g. all narcissistic patients exhibit a primary narcissism – a conditional theory may be substituted – some narcissistic patients, those of category 'X' exhibit a primary narcissism. The theory then survives, less strongly, but the onus is then to discover the qualifying conditions – which of the narcissistic patients (the category X ones) exhibit primary narcissism, and when.

Another strategy we saw is that a theory does not have to be given up if there is no alternative theory that can be used however imperfect. A poor theory is better than no theory. When anthropologists in the 1920s dismissed the universality of the Oedipus complex, psychoanalysts were still compelled to use the theory as if universal, even though it may have restricted psychoanalytic effectiveness to a particular set of cultures. There was no usable alternative at the time.

Another strategy would be to question the input and output of the logical model. For instance, self-psychologists might dispute that the seductive patient treated by Wayne Myers (described in Chapter 22) was not of the variety that they meant when Kohut evolved his theory. It could be argued possibly that she did not have the correct 'vertical split', or some other parameters did not fit her for the category self-psychologists intended.

Taking issue with the specific configuration of required and avoided relationships is another potential dispute, but it is to some extent taken care of by the requirement that both the required and the predicted move to the avoided relationship is governed by one, and only one, metapsychological theory for selection of content and for countertransference.

However, a more potent source of questioning to discredit the conclusions of this model might be the gathering of the data. While the model has gone a very long way to eliminate the circularity in data collection, there is still potential for some degree of dispute over a bias in the selection of occurrences before and after. Even when those occurrences have theoretical consistency by being inferred on the basis of a single metapsychological theory, it is always possible to claim that some other piece of metapsychology should have been used, for both, and therefore become the theory under test, rather than the theory cherished by the psychoanalytic group.

I present these various arguments that may dispute the model because I am not trying to purvey perfection. Once again, referring to the analogy with science, findings are always under challenge which is the process that keeps scientific knowledge alive and energetic. That our knowledge should be under constant challenge, too, merely means we need such a model to keep working at the task of testing. Not only that, but there is no reason why this particular model is the most perfect that can be devised, and its own potential for modification may be no less than those of the theories it tests. In other words the model will not be without imperfections of various kinds and will need improvement, so that *some* imperfections are no grounds for disposing of it altogether. There is no attempt to claim this is the only usable research model. For instance a previous study was published to compare 'repression' and 'splitting' (Hinshelwood 2008). There a different and more complex research design was tried. It employed a number of binary questions to be answered by a single-case study. In that case numerous questions were generated from a study of definitions of both terms gained from classical and Kleinian texts. Criteria for each term were derived from descriptions in those texts, and used to identify the phenomena in clinical material. That was essentially a different research design, using a different kind of data, and not employing the exact logical model generated here.

Causes and intentions: One of the results of the investigation in this book which seems important is that there is an inherent relationship between causes (as a physical scientist understands them) and meaningful intentions as a psychoanalyst understands them. The intention of the psychoanalyst is to 'make a difference' to have an effect of some kind on the patient's mental functioning and the way he lives his life. But he has a particular strategy for making a difference. That strategy is the interpretation, using his ability to distil an unconscious meaning. The interpretation is intended as the cause of an effect, an effect which the analyst will intend to create. As described earlier, intentions and causes join forces, they integrate together in a model of thinking, such that both causal effects and meaningful intentions co-operate.

The development of such a model that straddles causes and meanings, science and hermeneutics, takes it out of the strict purview of the natural sciences. But this does not in fact mean a lessening of rigour, and if the answer to the question of whether psychoanalysis is a science turns out to be 'no', then the argument of this book is that it is something pretty much like science, a para-science, so to speak.

What to recall: As many readers who have reached this point may not have diligently read every page, I shall reiterate the main steps to which they might return in order to recall the model for use. First of all be aware of the different logical processes – induction which moves from a restricted number of particular cases to generalised patterns, theories and narratives; and deduction which tests the generalisations to support their claims to be knowledge (Chapters 6 and 7). Both processes are essential, and in the last 50 years natural science has come increasingly to be formulated in terms of both theory-building and theory-testing. Psychoanalysis must move into the business of testing, and not just generalising to more and more theoretical novelties.

It is the testing that is the most contentious – partly because subjectivity has to be specially treated – both the subjectivity of the material observed, and the subjectivity of the observer. Both are of the same class of thing (Chapter 12). And it is contentious also because of the tenacious loyalty psychoanalysts have to their theories. It is necessary to divide psychoanalytic theory into two classes, each used for a different job (Chapter 12). Clinical theories are about the observing instrument and its ability to spot changes *due to* interpretations; and metapsychological theories – those under investigation – are to be tested *by* interpretation.

Subjectivity for all its apparent waywardness, can be tamed. The protocol developed here requires a set of operational rules (the required and avoided relationships that structure the material and the interpretations) to determine the change sequences occurring as a result of interpretations (Chapter 18). These structures importantly allow *prediction* which determines what is a significant change and what is not (Chapter 19). But these sequences can only be spotted, selected and used as data if they are rigorously inferred using the hermeneutic (that is, metapsychology) theories (Chapter 16). Data collection – that is, the process of identifying the significant meaningful occurrences before and after an interpretation – requires considerable ingenuity, and the observance of a precise method of observation. This form of observation requires the ability ideally to look from two perspectives – the content and the countertransference. Such a dual perspective is called a triangulation (Chapter 17).

Curiously this model does not just pit one concept against another, one school against another; it places intimately together psychoanalysts committed to scientific causality with those committed to a hermeneutic approach. In this way, we might claim a particular realisation of Caper's pertinent characterisation, 'Psychoanalysis works not only by being compassionate about human passions . . . but also by being dispassionate about them as well' (Caper 2009, p. 95).

There may well be flaws in the argument, and in its use, which result from my own limitations. The consequence is to hone the dubious aspects of the model to smooth out its failings, and to extend its range of use, not to dismiss it. Threatening though the testing of our theory may be for individual psychoanalysts and for groups and schools of psychoanalytic thought, nevertheless the capacity to give a more rigorous account to justify our beliefs can in the long-run only benefit all psychoanalysts *and all our patients*.

My own wish is that the development of a model such as this one is a contribution to the future of psychoanalysis, however troubling the task of comparing our theories with each other's is going to be – and that, in the long run, both psychoanalysts and the public might have more confidence in psychoanalysis being a body of coherent knowledge.

Notes

1 Holding the centre

1 Incidentally, and prophetically for some perhaps, Burt was an associate member of the British Psychoanalytical Society in the 1920s.
2 For examples of the work of these writers, see Popper 1959; Cioffi 1970; Grunbaum 1984; Roazen, 1971; Ellenberger 1970; Sulloway 1979; Millett 1970; Timpanaro 1974; Szasz 1969; Rycroft 1985; Sutherland 1976; Sands 2000; Webster 1995; Crews 1998; and Masson 1984.

2 Research off the couch

1 This hypothesis gradually evolved into 'control/mastery theory'; see Weiss *et al.* 1995; Siberschatz, *et al.* 1988.

7 The scientific model of knowledge-production

1 Interestingly, Freud did know of a distant relative of Karl Popper's in Vienna (Freud 1923, 1932; see also Renik 1978). This was Josef Popper-Lynkeus, a physicist and contemporary of Ernst Mach. He was responsible for the well-known saying, 'Every time a man dies, a whole world dies with him.' Popper-Lynkeus developed a theory that was somewhat parallel with Freud's idea of distortion in dreams, which was also published in 1899, exactly the year of writing *The Interpretation of Dreams*. He was also known personally to Fritz Wittels, one of Freud's early circle. Wittels left Vienna to settle in New York in 1928 and was less likely to have noticed Karl Popper's book in 1935. There is no evidence of Karl Popper's philosophical views in the earlier work of Popper-Lynkeus. It is most unlikely Freud ever had to test his ideas of natural science against the emerging ideas of science that Karl Popper developed.

22 Comparative research: illustrative examples of the model at work

1 Of course, one could take a hypothesis from the first position. So, if one severe disorder improves *without* interpreting envy, then again that demands new thinking.
2 The problem of disentangling envy from frustration is well described as follows: '[The patient] showed an increasing intensity of emotions . . . This originated in what he felt was my refusal to accept parts of his personality. Consequently he strove to force them into me with increased and violence. His behaviour, isolated from the context of the analysis, might have appeared to be an expression of primary aggression' (Bion 1959, p. 312).

References

Ablon, S.J. and Jones, E.E. 2005 On analytic process. *Journal of the American Psychoanalytic Association* 53: 541–68.

Abraham, Karl 1921 Contribution to a discussion on tic. In Abraham, Karl 1927 *Selected Papers on Psychoanalysis*. pp. 323–5. London: Hogarth.

Ahumada, Jorge 2006 The analytic mind at work. In Canestri, Jorge 2006 (ed.) *Psychosis: from Practice to Theory*. pp. 127–46. Chichester: Whurr Publications (Wiley).

Arlow, Jacob 1982 Psychoanalytic education. *Annals of Psychoanalysis* 10: 5–20.

Asch, Solomon 1952 *Social Psychology*. Englewood Cliffs, NJ: Prentice-Hall.

Aslan, Carlos Mario 1989 Common ground in psychoanalysis: Aims and clinical process. As I see it. *International Journal of Psychoanalysis* 70: 12–16.

Auden, W.H. 1939 Memory of Sigmund Freud. In *Another Time*. New York: Random House.

Ayer, A.J. 1936 *Language, Truth and Logic*. London: Gollancz.

Bateman, Anthony and Fonagy, Peter 2001 Treatment of Borderline Personality Disorder with a psychoanalytically oriented partial hospitalization: An 18 month follow up. *American Journal of Psychiatry* 158: 36–42.

Bell, David 2009 Is truth an illusion? Psychoanalysis and postmodernism. *International Journal of Psychoanalysis* 90: 331–45.

Berger, P. and Luckman, T. 1967 *The Social Construction of Reality*. Harmondsworth: Penguin.

Bibring, E. 1937 Contribution to the Symposium on the theory of the therapeutic results of psycho-analysis. *International Journal of Psychoanalysis* 18: 125–89.

Bion, W.R. 1954 Notes on the theory of schizophrenic. *International Journal of Psychoanalysis* 35: 113–18. Expanded as 'Language and the schizophrenic', in Klein, Melanie, Heimann, Paula and Money-Kyrle, Roger 1955 (eds) *New Directions in Psychoanalysis*. pp. 220–39. London: Tavistock. Republished (1967) in Bion, W.R. *Second Thoughts*. pp. 23–35. London: Heinemann.

Bion, W.R. 1959 Attacks on linking. *International Journal of Psychoanalysis* 40: 308–15. Republished in Bion, W.R. 1967 *Second Thoughts*. London: Heinemann; and in Spillius, Elizabeth Bott 1988 *Melanie Klein, Today, Volume 1*. London: Routledge.

Bion, W.R. 1970 *Attention and Interpretation*. London: Tavistock.

Blass, Rachel and Carmeli, Zvi 2007 The case against neuropsychoanalysis: On fallacies underlying psychoanalysis' latest scientific trend and its negative impact on psycho-analytic discourse. *International Journal of Psychoanalysis* 88: 19–40.

Bleuler, Eugen 1919 *Das autistisch-unddizplinierte Denken in der Medizin und seine Überwindung.* Berlin: Springer.

BMJ 1907 Freud and hysteria. *British Medical Journal* 1: 103–4.

Boesky, Dale 2002 Why don't our institutes teach the methodology of clinical psychoanalytic evidence? *Psychoanalytic Quarterly* 71: 445–75.

Brabant, Eva, Falzeder, Ernst and Giamperi-Deutsch, Patrizia 1993 *The Correspondence of Sigmund Freud and Sandor Ferenczi, Volume 1.* Cambridge, MA: Harvard University Press.

Brenner, Charles 1955 Presentation to panel on 'Validation of psychoanalytic techniques'. Reported in Marmor, Judd 1955 Validation of psychoanalytic techniques. *Journal of the American Psychoanalytic Association* 3: 496–505.

Breuer, Josef and Freud, Sigmund 1895 *Studies on Hysteria. Standard Edition of the Complete Psychological Works of Sigmund Freud, Volume 2.* London: Hogarth.

Britton, Ron and Steiner, John 1994 Interpretation: Selected fact or overvalued idea? *International Journal of Psychoanalysis* 75: 1069–78.

Brook, Andrew 1995 Explanation in the hermeneutic science. *International Journal of Psychoanalysis* 76: 519–32.

Bucci, W. and Maskit, B. 2007 Beneath the surface of the therapeutic interaction: The psychoanalytic method in modern dress. *Journal of the American Psychoanalytic Association* 55: 1355–97.

Busch, F. and Schmidt-Hellerau, Cordelia 2004 How can we know what we need to know? Reflections on clinical judgment formation. *Journal of the American Psychoanalytic Association* 52: 689–707.

Campbell, D.T. 1956 *Leadership and its Effects upon the Group.* Columbus, OH: Ohio State University Press.

Canestri, Jorge 2003 The logic of psychoanalytic research. In Leuzinger-Bohleber, Marianne, Dreher, Anna Ursula and Canestri, Jorge 2003 (eds) *Pluralism and Unity? Methods of Research in Psychoanalysis.* London: International Psychoanalytical Association.

Canestri, Jorge 2006 (ed.) *Psychosis: From Practice to Theory.* Chichester: Whurr Publications (Wiley).

Caper, Robert 1988 *Immaterial Facts.* New York: Jason Aronson.

Caper, Robert 2009 *Building out into the Dark.* London: Routledge.

Cavell, M. 1998a In response to Owen Renik's 'The analyst's subjectivity and the analyst's objectivity'. *International Journal of Psychoanalysis* 79: 1195–202.

Cavell, M. 1998b Triangulation, one's own mind and objectivity. *International Journal of Psychoanalysis* 79: 449–67.

Cavell, M. 1999 Response to Owen Renik. *International Journal of Psychoanalysis* 80: 1014–16.

Chiesa, Marco 2009 Research and psychoanalysis: A 'controversial' relationship revisited. *Annual Research Lecture of the British Psychoanalytical Society*, 4 February.

Chiesa, Marco and Fonagy, Peter 2000 Cassel personality disorder study. *British Journal of Psychiatry* 176: 485–91.

Chiesa, M., Fonagy, P., Holmes, J., Drahorad, C. and Harrison-Hall, A. 2002 Health service user costs by personality disorder following specialist and non-specialist treatment: A comparative study. *Journal of Personality Disorders* 16: 160–73.

Cioffi, F. 1970 Freud and the idea of a pseudo-science. In Berger and Cioffi (eds) *Explanation in the Behavioural Sciences.* Cambridge: Cambridge University Press.

Clinical Commentary 1987 Clinical Commentaries VII. *British Journal of Psychotherapy* 3: 370–83.

Cohen, D.J. 1991 Tourette's syndrome: A model disorder for integrating psychoanalysis and biological perspectives. *International Review of Psychoanalysis* 18: 195–208.

Crews, Frederick 1993 The unknown Freud. *New York Review of Books* November 18: 55–65.

Crews, Frederick 1998 *The Unauthorized Freud*. London: Penguin.

Crombie, Alistair 1953 *Augustine to Galileo: The History of Science*. London: Heinemann.

Dahl, Hartvig 1983 On the definition and measurement of wishes. In Masling J. (ed.) *Empirical Studies of Psychoanalytical Theories*. pp. 39–68. Hillsdale, NJ: The Analytic Press.

Dahl, Hartvig, Kächele, Horst, Thomä, Helmut (eds) 1988 *Psychoanalytic Process Research Strategies*. Berlin: Springer.

Davidson, Donald 1963 Actions, reasons and causes. *Journal of Philosophy* 60: 685–700. Reprinted 1980 in Davidson, Donald *Essays on Actions and Events*. Oxford: Oxford University Press.

Denzin, N.K. 1978 The logic of naturalistic enquiry. In Denzin, N.K. (ed.) *Sociological Methods: A Sourcebook*. New York: McGraw-Hill.

Dreher, Anna Ursula 2000 *Foundations for Conceptual Research in Psychoanalysis*. London: Karnac.

Eagle, Morris 1980 A critical examination of motivational explanation in psychoanalysis. *Psychoanalysis and Contemporary Thought* 3: 329–80.

Eagle, M. 1997 Contributions of Erik Erikson. *Psychoanalytic Review* 84: 337–47.

Edelson, Marshall 1983 Is testing psychoanalytic hypotheses in the pychoanalytic situation really impossible? *Psychoanalytic Study of the Child* 38: 61–109.

Edelson, Marshall 1984 *Hypothesis and Evidence in Psychoanalysis*. Chicago, IL: Chicago University Press.

Edelson, Marshall 1985 The hermeneutic turn and the single case study in psychoanalysis. *Psychoanalysis and Contemporary Thought* 8: 567–614.

Edelson, Marshall 1986 Causal explanation in science and in psychoanalysis – implications for writing a case study. *Psychoanalytic Study of the Child* 41: 89–127.

Eisold, Kenneth 1994 The intolerance of diversity in psychoanalytic institutes. *International Journal of Psychoanalysis* 75: 785–800.

Ellenberger, Henri F. 1970 *The Discovery of the Unconscious: The History and Evolution of Dynamic Psychiatry*. New York: Basic Books.

Erikson, Eric. 1958 The nature of clinical evidence. *Daedalus* 87: 65–87.

Etchegoyen, Horatio, Lopez, Benitez and Rabih, Moses 1987 On envy and how to interpret it. *International Journal of Psychoanalysis* 68: 49–60.

Evans, G. 1982 *The Varieties of Reference*. Oxford: Oxford University Press.

Eysenck, Hans and Rachman, Jack. 1965 *The Causes and Cures of Neurosis*. London: Routledge and Kegan Paul.

Ezriel, Henry 1951 The scientific testing of psycho-analytic findings and theory. *British Journal of Medical Psychology* 24: 30–34.

Ezriel, Henry 1956 Experimentation within the psychoanalytic session. *British Journal for the Philosophy of Science* 7: 29–48.

Ferenczi, Sandor 1921 Psycho-analytical observations on tic. *International Journal of Psychoanalysis* 2: 1–30.

Feyerabend, Paul 1975 *Against Method*. London: Verso.

Fish, Stanley 1989 Withholding the missing portion: Psychoanalysis and rhetoric. In *Doing What Comes Naturally: Change, Rhetoric and the Practice in Literary and Legal Studies*. pp. 525–54. Oxford: Oxford University Press.

Flugel, J.C. 1954 Review: *The Hixon Lectures on the Scientific Status of Psycho-analysis.* By Hilgard, Ernest R., Kubie, Lawrence, Pumpian-Mindlin, E. Edited by Pumpian-Mindlin, E. (Stanford, California: Stanford University Press. London: Geoffrey Cumberlege). *International Journal of Psychoanalysis* 35: 71–4.

Fonagy, P. 1982 The integration of psychoanalysis and experimental science: a review. *International Review of Psycho-Analysis* 9: 125–45.

Fonagy, Peter 1989 On tolerating mental states: theory of mind in borderline personality. *Bulletin of the Anna Freud Centre* 12: 91–115.

Forrester, John 1997 *Dispatches from the Freud Wars.* Cambridge, MA: Harvard University Press.

Franke, Christine 2006 'Living on the edge of possibility': a study of autistic object relations. Ph.D. University of Essex, Colchester, UK.

Frazer, James 1890 *Golden Bough.* London: Macmillan.

Freeman, Thomas 1998 *But Facts Exist.* London: Karnac.

Freud, Anna 1936 *The Ego and the Mechanisms of Defence.* London: Hogarth.

Freud, Sigmund 1896 The aetiology of hysteria. *Standard Edition of the Complete Psychological Works of Sigmund Freud, Volume 3.* pp. 189–221. London: Hogarth.

Freud, Sigmund 1900 *The Interpretation of Dreams. Standard Edition of the Complete Psychological Works of Sigmund Freud, Volumes 4–5.* London: Hogarth.

Freud, Sigmund 1901 On dreams. *Standard Edition of the Complete Psychological Works of Sigmund Freud, Volume 5.* pp. 633–85. London: Hogarth.

Freud, Sigmund 1905 Three essays on the theory of sexuality. *Standard Edition of the Complete Psychological Works of Sigmund Freud, Volume 7.* pp. 125–245. London: Hogarth.

Freud, Sigmund 1907 Obsessive actions and religious practices. *Standard Edition of the Complete Psychological Works of Sigmund Freud, Volume 9.* pp. 117–27. London: Hogarth.

Freud, Sigmund 1909a Analysis of a phobia in a five-year-old boy. *Standard Edition of the Complete Psychological Works of Sigmund Freud, Volume 10.* pp. 3–149. London: Hogarth.

Freud, Sigmund 1909b Notes upon a case of obsessional neurosis. *Standard Edition of the Complete Psychological Works of Sigmund Freud, Volume 10.* pp. 153–249. London: Hogarth.

Freud, Sigmund 1911 Psycho-analytic notes on an autobiographical account of a case of paranoia dementia paranoides. *Standard Edition of the Complete Psychological Works of Sigmund Freud, Volume 12.* pp. 3–82. London: Hogarth.

Freud, Sigmund 1912 Recommendations to physicians practising psychoanalysis. *Standard Edition of the Complete Psychological Works of Sigmund Freud, Volume 12.* pp. 3–82. London: Hogarth.

Freud, Sigmund 1913 *Totem and Taboo. Standard Edition of the Complete Psychological Works of Sigmund Freud, Volume 13.* pp. 1–162. London: Hogarth

Freud, Sigmund 1914 Remembering, repeating and working-through. *Standard Edition of the Complete Psychological Works of Sigmund Freud, Volume 12.* pp. 145–56. London: Hogarth.

Freud, Sigmund 1915 *Instincts and their Vicissitudes. Standard Edition of the Complete Psychological Works of Sigmund Freud, Volume 14.* pp. 111–40. London: Hogarth.

Freud, Sigmund 1916–17 *Introductory Lectures on Psycho-Analysis: 1916–1917. Standard Edition of the Complete Psychological Works of Sigmund Freud, Volume 15–16.* London: Hogarth.

Freud, Sigmund 1918 From the history of an infantile neurosis. *Standard Edition of the Complete Psychological Works of Sigmund Freud, Volume 17,* 7-123. London: Hogarth.

Freud, Sigmund 1920 Beyond the pleasure principle. *Standard Edition of the Complete Psychological Works of Sigmund Freud, Volume 18.* pp. 7–64. London: Hogarth.

Freud, Sigmund 1921 Group psychology and the analysis of the ego. *Standard Edition of the Complete Psychological Works of Sigmund Freud, Volume 18*. pp. 67–143. London: Hogarth.

Freud, Sigmund 1923 Josef Popper-Lynkeus and the theory of dreams. *Standard Edition of the Complete Psychological Works of Sigmund Freud, Volume 19*. pp. 261–63. London: Hogarth.

Freud, Sigmund 1925 The resistances to psycho-analysis. *The Standard Edition of the Complete Psychological Works of Sigmund Freud, Volume 19*, pp. 211–24. London: Hogarth.

Freud, Sigmund 1926 Inhibitions, symptoms and anxiety. *Standard Edition of the Complete Psychological Works of Sigmund Freud, Volume 20*. pp. 77–174. London: Hogarth.

Freud, Sigmund 1930 Civilization and its discontents. *Standard Edition of the Complete Psychological Works of Sigmund Freud, Volume 21*. pp. 59–145. London: Hogarth.

Freud, Sigmund 1932 My Contact with Josef Popper–Lynkeus. *Standard Edition of the Complete Psychological Works of Sigmund Freud, Volume 22*. pp. 219–24. London: Hogarth.

Freud, Sigmund 1938a Some elementary lessons in psycho-analysis. *The Standard Edition of the Complete Psychological Works of Sigmund Freud, Volume 23*. pp. 281–86. London: Hogarth.

Freud, Sigmund 1938b An outline of psycho-analysis. *The Standard Edition of the Complete Psychological Works of Sigmund Freud, Volume 23*. pp. 139–208. London: Hogarth.

Freud, Sigmund 1938c *Constructions in Analysis. Standard Edition of the Complete Psychological works of Sigmund Freud, Volume 23*. pp. 257–69. London: Hogarth.

Fromm, Erich [1970] 1973 *The Crisis of Psychoanalysis*. London: Penguin.

Fuller, Steve 2003 *Kuhn versus Popper*. Cambridge: Icon.

Fürstenau, P. 1977 Praxeologische Grundlagen der Psychoanalyse. In Pongratz, L.J. (ed.) *Handbuch der Psychologie: Vol. 8. Klinische Psychologie*. Göttingen: Hogrefe.

Gabbard, Glen 1996 The analyst's contribution to the erotic transference. *Contemporary Psychoanalysis* 32: 249–73.

Gabbard, Glen 1997 A reconsideration of objectivity in the analyst. *International Journal of Psychoanalysis* 78: 15–26.

Gabbard, Glen and Williams, Paul 2002 New initiatives. *International Journal of Psychoanalysis* 83: 1–2.

Gadamer, Hans-Georg 1975 *Truth and Method*. London: Sheed & Ward.

Gardner, Sebastian 1993 *Irrationality and the Philosophy of Psychoanalysis*. Cambridge: Cambridge University Press.

Gergely, György and Watson, John 1996 The social biofeedback theory of parental affect-mirroring: The development of emotional self-awareness and self-control in infancy. *International Journal of Psychoanalysis* 77: 1181–1212.

Gill, Merton 1979 The analysis of the transference. *Journal of the American Psychoanalytic Association* 27: 263–88.

Gill, Merton 1982 *Analysis of Transference, vol. I: Theory and Technique*. New York: International Universities Press.

Gill, Merton and Hoffman, Irwin 1982 *Analysis of Transference, vol. II: Studies of Nine Audio-Recorded Psychoanalytic Sessions*. New York: International Universities Press.

Giovacchini, Peter 2000 *Impact of Narcissism: The Errant Therapist in a Chaotic Quest*. New York: Jason Aronson.

Glaser, Barney and Strauss, Anselm 1967 *The Discovery of Grounded Theory: Strategies for Qualitative Research*. London: Weidenfeld and Nicolson.

Glover, Edward 1952 Research methods in psycho-analysis. *International Journal of Psychoanalysis* 33: 403–9.

Goldberg, Arnold 1976 A discussion of the paper by C. Hanly and J. Masson on 'A critical examination of the new narcissism'. *International Journal of Psychoanalysis* 57: 67–70.

Goldberg, Arnold 2001 Postmodern psychoanalysis. *International Journal of Psychoanalysis* 82: 123–8.

Gomez, Lavinia 2005 *Freud Wars: An Introduction to the Philosophy of Psychoanalysis*. London: Routledge.

Grunbaum, Adolph 1959 Remarks on Dr Kubie's views. In Hook, Sydney (ed.) *Psychoanalysis, Scientific Method, and Philosophy*. p. 225. New York: New York University Press.

Grunbaum, Adolph 1984 *Foundations of Psychoanalysis*. Berkeley/Los Angeles, CA: University of California Press.

Grunbaum, Adolph 1993 *Validation in the Clinical Theory of Psychoanalysis: A Study in the Philosophy of Psychoanalysis*. Madison, CT: International Universities Press.

Habermas, Jurgen 1968 *Knowledge and Human Interest*. Boston, MA: Beacon Press.

Hackett, Jeremiah 1997 Roger Bacon: His life, career, and works. In Hackett, Jeremiah, *Roger Bacon and the Sciences*. pp. 9–24. New York: Brill.

Hacking, Ian 1999 *The Social Construction of What?* Cambridge, MA: Harvard University Press.

Hampe, Michael (2003) Plurality of sciences and the unity of reason. In: Leuzinger-Bohleber, M., Dreher, A.U., Canestri, J.(eds) *Pluralism and Unity? Methods of research in psychoanalysis*. London: International Psychoanalysis Library.

Hanly, Charles 1983 A problem of theory testing. *International Review of Psycho-Analysis* 10: 393–405.

Hanly, Charles 1990 The concept of truth in psychoanalysis. *International Journal of Psychoanalysis* 71: 375–83.

Hanly, Charles 1992 Inductive reasoning in clinical psychoanalysis. *International Journal of Psychoanalysis* 73: 293–301.

Hanly, Charles 1999 On subjectivity and objectivity in psychoanalysis. *Journal of the American Psychoanalytic Association* 47: 427–44.

Hansell, James 2000 Modern defense analysis. *Journal of the American Psychoanalytic Association* 48: 929–40.

Hargreaves, Edith and Varchevker, Arturo 2004 *In Pursuit of Psychic Change*. London: Routledge.

Harris, R.P., Helfand, M., Woolf, S.H., Lohr, K.N., Mulrow, C.D., Teutsch, S.M. and Atkins, D. 2001 Current methods of the U.S. Preventive Services Task Force: A review of the process. *American Journal of Preventive Medicine* 20(3, Supplement 1): 21–35.

Hartmann, Heinz 1958 Comments on the scientific aspects of psychoanalysis. *Psychoanalytic Study of the Child* 13: 127–46.

Hartmann, Heinz 1959 Psychoanalysis as a scientific theory. In Hook, Sydney (ed.) *Psychoanalysis, Scientific Method, and Philosophy*. New York: New York University Press.

Haynal, André 1993 *Psychoanalysis and the Sciences*. London: Karnac.

Heimann, Paula 1943 Some aspects of the role of introjection and projection in early development. In King, Pearl and Steiner, Riccardo (eds) 1991 *The Freud-Klein Controversies 1941–1945*. pp. 501–30. London: Routledge.

Heimann, Paula 1950 On counter-transference. *International Journal of Psychoanalysis 31*: 81–4. Republished in Heimann, Paula 1989 *About Children and Children-No-Longer*. pp. 73–9. London: Routledge.

Heimann, Paula 1960 Counter-transference. *British Journal of Medical Psychology* 33: 9–15. Republished in Heimann, Paula 1989 *About Children and Children-No-Longer*. pp. 151–60. London: Routledge.

Hinshelwood, R.D. 1991 *The Dictionary of Kleinian Thought*. London: Free Association Books.

Hinshelwood, R.D. 1995 Psycho-analysis in Britain: points of cultural access 1893–1918, *International Journal of Psychoanalysis* 76: 135–51.

Hinshelwood, R.D. 2002 Symptoms or relationships (Comment on Jeremy Holmes's, 'All you need is CBT'). *British Medical Journal* 324: 288–94.

Hinshelwood, R.D. 2008 Repression and splitting: Towards a method of conceptual comparison *International Journal of Psychoanalysis*: 89: 503–21.

Hinshelwood, R.D. 2009 Ideology and identity: A psychoanalytic investigation of a social phenomenon. *Psychoanalysis, Culture and Society* 14: 131–48.

Hinshelwood, R.D. 2012 Being objective about the subjective. *International Forum of Psychoanalysis* 21: 136–45.

Hoffman, Irwin 1983 The patient as interpreter of the analyst's experience. *Contemporary Psychoanalysis* 19: 389–422.

Hoffman, Irwin and Gill, Merton 1988a Critical reflections on a coding scheme. *International Journal of Psychoanalysis* 69: 55–64.

Hoffman, Irwin and Gill, Merton 1988b A scheme for coding the patient's experience of the relationship with the therapist (PERT): Some applications, extensions, and comparisons. In Dahl, Hartvig, Kächele, Horst and Thomä, Hans (eds) *Psychoanalytic Process Research Strategies*. pp. 67–98. Berlin: Springer-Verlag.

Home, H.J. 1966 The concept of mind. *International Journal of Psychoanalysis* 47: 42–9.

Hook, Sydney 1959 (ed.) *Psychoanalysis, Scientific Method, and Philosophy*. New York: New York University Press.

Hopkins, James 1982 Introduction: Philosophy and psychoanalysis. In Wollheim, Richard and Hopkins, James (eds) *Philosophical Essays on Freud*. pp. vii–xlv. Cambridge: Cambridge University Press.

Horowitz, Milton 1979 *States of Mind*. New York: Plenum.

Horowitz, Milton 1987 Some notes on insight and its failures. *Psychoanalytic Quarterly* 56: 177–96.

Hume, David [1748] 1999 *An Enquiry Concerning Human Understanding*. Oxford: Oxford University Press.

Isaacs, Susan 1939 Criteria for interpretation. *International Journal of Psychoanalysis* 20: 148–60.

Isaacs, Susan 1948 The nature and function of phantasy. *International Journal of Psychoanalysis* 29: 73–97. Republished 1952 in Klein, Melanie, Heimann, Paula, Isaacs, Susan and Riviere, Joan *Developments in Psychoanalysis*. pp. 67–121. London: Hogarth,

Jamison, Kay Redfield 1993 *Touched with Fire: Manic-Depressive Illness and the Artistic Temperament*. New York, The Free Press.

Joffe, Walter 1969 A critical review of the status of the envy concept. *International Journal of Psychoanalysis* 50: 533–45.

Johnson, Allen and Price-Williams, Douglass 1996 *Oedipus Ubiquitous*. Stanford, CA: Stanford University Press.

Jones, Ernest 1925 Mother-right and the sexual ignorance of savages. *International Journal Psycho-Analysis* 6: 109–30.

Jones, Ernest 1953 *Sigmund Freud: Life and Work, Volume I, Years of Maturity*. London: Hogarth.

Jones, Ernest 1955 *Sigmund Freud: Life and Work, Volume II, Years of Maturity*. London: Hogarth.

Jones, Enrico 1993 How will psychoanalysis study itself? *Journal of the American Psychoanalytic Association* 41: 91–108.

Jones, Enrico 2000 *Therapeutic Action: A Guide to Psychoanalytic Therapy.* Northvale, NJ: Aronson.

Joseph, Betty 1989, *Psychic Equilibrium and Psychic Change.* London: Routledge.

Joynson, Robert 1989 *The Burt Affair.* London: Routledge.

Kächele, Horst 1988 Clinical and scientific aspects of the Ulm process model of psychoanalysis. *International Journal of Psychoanalysis* 69: 65–73.

Kächele, Horst and Thomä, Helmut 1993 Psychoanalytic process research: Methods and achievements. *Journal of the American Psychoanalytic Association* 41 (Supp.): 109–29.

Kächele, Horst, Schachter, Joseph and Thomä, Helmut 2009 *From Psychoanalytic Narrative to Empirical Single Case Research.* New York: Routledge.

Kernberg, Otto 1993 Convergences and divergences in contemporary psychoanalytic technique. *International Journal of Psychoanalysis* 74: 659–73.

King, Pearl and Steiner, Riccardo (eds) 1991 *The Freud-Klein Controversies: 1941–1945.* London: Routledge.

Klein, George 1969–70 The emergence of ego psychology the ego in psychoanalysis: A concept in search of identity. *Psychoanalytic Review* 56: 511–25.

Klein, George 1973 Is psychoanalysis relevant? *Psychoanalysis and Contemporary Science* 2: 3–21.

Klein Melanie 1923 Zur Früh Analyse. *Imago* 9: 222–59; English translation 1926. Infant Analysis, *International Journal of Psychoanalysis* 7: 31–63. Early analysis. *In The Writings of Melanie Klein, Volume 1*: pp. 77–105. London: Hogarth.

Klein Melanie 1925 Zur Genese des Tics, *Internationale Zeitschrift for Psycho-Analyse* 11: 332–49; English translation 1948. A contribution to the psychogenesis of tics. In *Contributions to Psycho–Analysis.* pp. 117–39. London: Hogarth. Republished in *The Writings of Melanie Klein, Volume 1*: pp. 101–27. London: Hogarth.

Klein, Melanie 1957 *Envy and Gratitude.* London: Hogarth.

Klein, H. and Horwitz, W.A. 1949 Psycho-sexual factors in the paranoid phenomena. *American Journal of Psychiatry* 105: 697–701.

Klein, M.H., Mathieu-Coughlan, P.L., Gendlin, E.T. and Kiesler, D.J. 1969 *The Experiencing Scale: A Research and Training Manual Volume I.* Madison, WI: Wisconsin Psychiatric Institute.

Knapp, P.H., Greenberg, R., Pearlman, C., Cohen, M., Kantrowitz, J. and Sashin, J. 1975 Clinical measurement in psychoanalysis: An approach. *Psycho-Analytic Quarterly* 44: 404–30.

Kohut, Heinz 1979 The two analyses of Mr Z. *International Journal of Psychoanalysis* 60: 3–27

Kubie, Lawrence 1952 Problems and techniques of psychoanalytic validation and progress. In: Pumpian–Mindlin, E. (ed.) *Psychoanalysis as Science.* pp. 46–124. Stanford, CA: Stanford University Press.

Kuhn, Thomas 1962 *The Structure of Scientific Revolutions.* Chicago, IL: University of Chicago Press.

Lakatos, Imre 1976 *Proofs and Refutations.* Cambridge: Cambridge University Press.

Lear, Jonathan 1993 An interpretation of transference. *International Journal of Psychoanalysis* 74: 739–55.

Leuzinger-Bohleber, Marianne (2010) "Psychoanalysis as "specific" science of the unconscious." Paper given at the centenary anniversary celebration of the IPA, March 2010, London.

Leuzinger-Bohleber, Marianne and Target, Mary (eds) 2002 *Outcomes of Psychoanalytic Treatment.* London: Whurr.

Leuzinger-Bohleber, Marianne, Dreher, Anna Ursula, and Canestri, Jorge 2003 (eds) *Pluralism and Unity? Methods of Research in Psychoanalysis*. London: International Psychoanalytical Association.

Lingiardi, Vittorio and Capozzi, Paola 2004 Psychoanalytic attitudes towards homosexuality. *International Journal of Psychoanalysis* 85: 137–58.

Luborsky, Lester 1976 Helping alliances in psychotherapy. In Cleghorm, J. (ed.) *Successful Psychotherapy*. pp. 92–118. New York: Bruner-Mazel.

Luborsky, Lester 2000 Psychoanalysis and empirical research: A reconciliation. In Sandler, Joseph, Michels, Robert and Fonagy, Peter (eds) *Changing Ideas In A Changing World: The Revolution in Psychoanalysis: Essays in Honour of Arnold Cooper*. pp. 149–54. London: Karnac.

Luborsky, Lester 2001 The meaning of empirically supported treatment research for psychoanalytic and other long-term therapies. *Psychoanalytic Dialogues* 11: 583–604.

Luborsky, Lester and Crits-Christoph, Paul 1988 Measures of psychoanalytic concepts – the last decade of research from 'The Penn Studies'. *International Journal of Psychoanalysis* 69: 75–86.

Luborsky, Lester and Luborsky, Ellen 1993 The era of measures of transference: The CCRT and other measures. *Journal of the American Psychoanalytic Association* 41S: 329–51.

Luborsky, Lester and Spence, Donald 1971 Quantitative research on psychoanalytic therapy. In Bergin, A. and Garfield, S. (eds) *Handbook of Psychotherapy and Behavioral Change: An Empirical Analysis*. pp. 408–38. New York: John Wiley.

Lukacs Georg [1923] 1974 *History and Class Consciousness*. London: Merlin Press.

Mace, Chris, Moorey, Stirling and Roberts, Bernard 2001 *Evidence in the Psychological Therapies*. London: Routledge.

Mahler, Margaret 1949 A psychoanalytic evaluation of tic in psychopathology of children. *Psychoanalytic Study of the Child*, 4: 279–310.

Mahler, Margaret, Pine, Fred and Bergman, Annie 1975 *The Psychological Birth of the Human Infant*. London: Hutchison.

Masson, Jeffrey 1984 *Freud: The Assault on Truth: Freud's Suppression of the Seduction Theory*. London: Faber and Faber.

McPherson, Susan, Richardson, Phil and Leroux, Penny (eds) 2003 *Clinical Effectiveness in Psychotherapy and Mental Health*. London: Karnac.

Medawar, Peter 1969 *Induction and Intuition in Scientific Thought*. London: Methuen.

Medawar, Peter 1982 *Plato's Republic*. London: Methuen.

Meissner, W.W. 1999 The self-as-subject in psychoanalysis. *Psychoanalysis and Contemporary Thought* 22: 155–201.

Menninger, Karl 1946 Editorial *Bulletin of the Menninger Clinic* 10: 65–6.

Mergenthaler E. 1985 *Textbank Systems*. Berlin: Springer.

Michelson, Albert 1881 The relative motion of the Earth and the luminiferous ether. *American Journal of Science* 22: 120–29.

Michelson, Albert and Morley, Edward 1887 On the relative motion of the Earth and the luminiferous ether. *American Journal of Science* 34: 333–345.

Milgram, Stanley 1963 Behavioral study of obedience. *Journal of Abnormal and Social Psychology* 67: 371–78.

Millett, Kate 1970 *Sexual Politics*. New York: Doubleday.

Milton, Jane, Polmear, Caroline and Fabricius, Julia 2004 *A Short Introduction to Psychoanalysis*. London: Sage

Mitrani, Judith 1992 On the survival function of autistic manoeuvres in adult patients. *International Journal of Psychoanalysis* 73: 549–59.

Money-Kyrle, Roger 1958 On the process of psycho-analytical inference. *International Journal of Psychoanalysis* 39: 129–33.

Myers, F.W.H. 1904 *Human Personality and its Survival of Bodily Death*. London: Longmans.

Myers, Wayne 1994 Addictive sexual behavior. *Journal of the American Psychoanalytic Association* 42: 1159–82.

Nagel, Ernest 1959 Methodological issues in scientific theory. In Hook, Sydney (ed.) *Psychoanalysis, Scientific Method, and Philosophy*. New York: New York University Press.

Nagel, Thomas 1974 What is it like to be a bat? *Philosophical Review* 83: 435–50.

Nasar, Sylvia 1998 *A Beautiful Mind*. New York: Simon and Schuster.

Obholzer, Karin 1982 *The Wolfman Sixty Years Later: Conversations with Freud's Controversial Patient*. London: Routledge and Kegan Paul.

Ogden, Thomas 1992 *The Matrix of the Mind: Object Relations and the Psychoanalytic Dialogue*. London: Karnac.

Oppenheim, J. 1985 *The Other World: Spiritualism and Psychical Research in England, 1850–1914*. Cambridge: Cambridge University Press.

Paul, L. 1963 *Psychoanalytic Clinical Interpretation*. New York: Free Press of Glencoe.

Popper, Karl 1959 *The Logic of Scientific Discovery*. London: Hutchinson.

Popper, Karl 1963 *Conjectures and Refutations*. London: Routledge and Kegan Paul.

Popper, Karl 1976 *Unended Quest: An Intellectual Autobiography*. London: Fontana.

Pumpian-Mindlin, E. 1953 (ed.) *The Hixon Lectures on the Scientific Status of Psycho-analysis, by Ernest R. Hilgard, Lawrence S. Kubie, E. Pumpian-Mindlin, M.D.* Stanford, CA: Stanford University Press.

Putnam, Hilary 1981 *Reason, Truth and History*. Cambridge: Cambridge University Press.

Quinidoz, Jean-Michel 2009 *Listening to Hanna Segal: Her Contribution to Psychoanalysis*. London: Routledge.

Rahman, M.M. 1977 The Freudian paradigm. In Rahman, M.M. (ed.) *The Freudian Paradigm: Psychoanalysis and Scientific Thought*. Chicago, IL: Nelson.

Renik, Owen 1978 Neurotic and narcissistic transferences in Freud's relationship with Josef Popper. *Psychoanalytic Quarterly* 47: 398–418.

Renik, Owen 1993 Analytic interaction: Conceptualizing technique in light of the analyst's irreducible subjectivity. *Psychoanalytic Quarterly* 62: 553–71.

Renik, Owen 1997 Reactions to 'Observing-participation, mutual enactment, and the new classical models' by Irwin Hirsch, Ph.D. *Contemporary Psychoanalysis* 33: 279–84.

Renik, Owen 1998a Who's afraid of post-modernism?: Commentary on paper by Michael J. Bader. *Psychoanalytic Dialogues* 8: 55–9.

Renik, Owen 1998b The analyst's subjectivity and the analyst's objectivity. *International Journal of Psychoanalysis* 79: 487–97.

Renik, Owen 1999 Renik replies to Cavell. *International Journal of Psychoanalysis* 80: 382–3.

Richardson, Phil 2001 Evidence-based practice and the psychodynamic psychotherapies. In Mace, Chris, Moorey, Stirling and Roberts, Bernard (eds) *Evidence in the Psychological Therapies*. pp. 46–69. London: Routledge.

Richardson, Phil, Kächele, Horst and Redlund, Camilla 2004 *Research on Psychoanalytic Psychotherapy with Adults*. London: Karnac.

Ricoeur, Paul 1970 *Freud and Philosophy*. New Haven, CT: Yale University Press.

Roazen, Paul 1971 *Freud and his Followers*. London: Penguin.

Rorty, Richard 2000 Pragmatism. *International Journal of Psychoanalysis* 81: 819–23.

Ross, David 1995 *Aristotle*. 6th edition. London: Routledge.

Roth, Anthony and Fonagy, Peter 1996 *What Works for Whom?* New York: Guilford.

Roth, Priscilla and Lemma, Alessandra 2008 *Envy and Gratitude Revisited*. London: Routledge.

Rubenstein, Ben 1976 On the possibility of a strictly clinical psychoanalysis. In Gill, Merton and Holtzman, Philip (eds) *Psychology Versus Metapsychology: Psychoanalytic Essays in Memory of George S. Klein*. pp. 229–64. New York: International Universities Press.

Rubovits-Seitz, Phillip 1995 Research in psychoanalysis: An historical note. *Journal of the American Psychoanalytic Association*, 43: 651–2.

Rustin, Michael 1987 Psychoanalysis, philosophical realism, and the new sociology of science. *Free Associations* 1J: 102–36.

Rustin, Michael 1989 Observing infants: Reflections on methods. In Miller, Lisa, Rustin, Margaret, Rustin, Michael and Shuttleworth, Judy, *Closely Observed Infants*. London: Duckworth.

Sampson, Harold 1992 The role of 'real' experience in psychopathology and treatment. *Psychoanalytic Dialogues* 2: 509–28.

Sandler, Joseph 1983 Reflections on some relations between psychoanalytic concepts and psychoanalytic practice. *International Journal of Psychoanalysis* 64: 35–45.

Sandler, Joseph 1990 On internal object relations. *Journal of the American Psychoanalytic Association* 38: 859–79.

Sandler, Joseph and Sandler, Annmarie 1987 The past unconscious, the present unconscious and the vicissitudes of guilt. *International Journal of Psychoanalysis* 68: 331–41.

Sandler, Joseph and Sandler, Annmarie 1994 Phantasy and its transformations: A contemporary Freudian view. *International Journal of Psychoanalysis* 75: 387–94.

Sandler, Joseph, Dreher, Anna Ursula, and Drews, Sibylle 1991 An approach to conceptual research in psychoanalysis illustrated by a consideration of psychic trauma. *International Review of Psycho-Analysis* 18: 133–41.

Sands, Anna 2000 *Falling for Therapy*. London: Macmillan.

Sargent, Helen D., Horwitz, Leonard, Wallerstein, Robert S. and Appelbaum, Ann 1968 *Prediction in Psychotherapy Research: A Method for the Transformation of Clinical Judgments into Testable Hypotheses*. New York: International Universities Press.

Sartre, Jean-Paul 1943 *L'Etre et le Neant*. Paris: Gallimard.

Sayer, Andrew 2000 *Realism and Social Science*. London: Sage.

Schacht, Henry and Binder, Jeffrey 1982 Focusing: A manual for identifying a circumscribed area of work for time-limited dynamic psychotherapy (TLDP). Unpublished manuscript, Vanderbilt University.

Schachter, Joseph and Luborsky, Lester 1998 Who's afraid of psychoanalytic research? Analysts' attitudes towards reading clinical versus empirical research. *International Journal of Psychoanalysis* 79: 965–9.

Schafer, Roy 1976 *A New Language for Psychoanalysis*. New Haven, CT: Yale University Press.

Schafer, Roy 1992 *Retelling a Life*. New York: Basic Books.

Schafer, Roy 1999 Interpreting sex. *Psychoanalytic Psychology* 16: 502–13.

Scharff, Jill 2001 Case presentation. *Psychoanalytic Inquiry* 21: 469–82.

Schlesinger, Herbert 1984 Research in dynamic psychotherapy. *Psychoanalytic Psychology* 1: 83–4.

Shedler, Jonathan 2010 The efficacy of psychodynamic psychotherapy. *American Psychologist* 65: 98–109.

Sherif, M. and Sherif, C.W. 1956 *An Outline of Social Psychology*. New York: Harper.

Shevrin, Howard 1995. Is psychoanalysis one science, two sciences, or no science at all? A discourse among friendly antagonists. *Journal of the American Psychoanalytic Association* 43: 963–86.

Solms, Mark and Turnbull, Oliver 2002 *The Brain and the Inner World*. London: Karnac.

Spence, Donald 1983 Narrative persuasion. *Psychoanalysis and Contemporary Thought* 6: 457–81.

Spence, Donald 1993 The hermeneutic turn: Soft science or loyal opposition? *Psychoanalytic Dialogues* 3: 1–10.

Spence, Donald 1994 The special nature of psychoanalytic facts. *International Journal of Psychoanalysis* 75: 915–25.

Spillius, Elizabeth 1993 Varieties of envious experience. *International Journal of Psychoanalysis* 74: 1199–212.

Spillius, Elizabeth, Milton, Jane, Garvey, Penelope, Couve, Cyril and Steiner, Debbie 2011 *The New Dictionary of Kleinian Thought*. London: Routledge.

Steele, Robert 1979 Psychoanalysis and hermeneutics. *International Review of Psycho-Analysis* 6: 389–411.

Steiner, John 1993 *Psychic Retreats*. London: Routledge.

Steiner, R. 1994 'The Tower of Babel' or 'After Babel in contemporary psychoanalysis'? – Some historical and theoretical notes on the linguistic and cultural strategies implied by the foundation of the *International Journal of Psychoanalysis*, and on its relevance today. *International Journal of Psychoanalysis* 75: 883–901.

Stengel, Erwin 1951 The scientific testing of psychoanalytic findings. *British Journal of Medical Psychology* 24: 26–9.

Stern, Daniel 1985 *The Interpersonal World of the Infant: A View from Psychoanalysis and Developmental Psychology*. New York: Basic Books.

Stone, Leo 1981 Some thoughts on the 'here and now' in psychoanalytic technique and process. *Psychoanalytic Quarterly* 50: 709–33.

Stove, David 1986 *The Rationality of Induction*. Oxford: Oxford University Press.

Strachey, James 1934 The nature of the therapeutic action of psychoanalysis. *International Journal of Psychoanalysis* 15: 127–59. Republished 1969 *International Journal of Psychoanalysis* 50: 275–192.

Strawson, P.F. 1963 *Individuals: An Essay in Descriptive Metaphysics*. New York: Anchor Books.

Strenger, Carlo 1991 *Between Hermeneutics and Science*. Madison, CT: International Universities Press.

Strupp, Hans, Schacht, Thomas, and Henry, W. 1988 Problem – treatment – outcome complex: A principle whose time has come. In Dahl, Hartvig, Kächele, Horst and Thomä, Hans (eds) *Psychoanalytic Process Research Strategies*. pp. 1–14. Berlin: Springer-Verlag.

Sulloway, Frank 1979 *Freud: Biologist of the Mind*. London: Burnett.

Sutherland, S. 1976 *Breakdown*. London: Weidenfeld and Nicolson.

Szasz, Thomas 1969 *The Ethics of Psychoanalysis*. London: Routledge and Kegan Paul.

Talvitie, Vesa and Ihanus, Juhani 2011 On neuropsychoanalytic metaphysics. *International Journal of Psychoanalysis* 92: 1583–601.

Target, Mary and Fonagy, Peter 1996 Playing with reality: II. The development of psychic reality from a theoretical perspective. *International Journal of Psychoanalysis* 77: 459–79.

Teller, Virginia and Dahl, Hartvig 1993 What psychoanalysis needs is more empirical research. *Journal of the American Psychoanalytic Association* 41 (Supplement): 31–49.

Thomä, Helmut 1969 Some remarks on psychoanalysis in Germany, past and present. *International Journal of Psychoanalysis* 50: 683–92.

Timpanaro, Sebastiano 1974 *The Freudian Slip*. London: New Left Books (1976).

Toulmin, Stephen 1948 The logical status of psychoanalysis. In MacDonald, M. (ed.) *Philosophy and Analysis*. New York: Philosophical Library, 1954, pp. 132–9.

Trevarthen, C. 1977 Descriptive analysis of infant communicative behaviour. In Schafer, H.R. (ed.) *Studies in Mother-Infant Interactions*. New York: Academic Press.

Truax, Charles and Carkuff, Robert 1967 *Toward Effective Counseling and Psychotherapy*. Chicago, IL: Aldine.

Tuckett, David 1994a The conceptualisation and communication of clinical facts in psychoanalysis – Foreword. *International Journal of Psychoanalysis* 75: 865–70.

Tuckett, David 1994b Developing a grounded hypothesis to understand a clinical process: The role of conceptualisation in validation. *International Journal of Psychoanalysis* 75: 1159–80.

Tuckett, David 2000 Theoretical pluralism and the construction of psychoanalytic knowledge. In *Changing Ideas In A Changing World: The Revolution in Psychoanalysis. Essays in Honour of Arnold Cooper*. pp. 237–46. London: Karnac.

Tuckett, David 2005 Does anything go? *International Journal of Psychoanalysis* 86: 31–49.

Tuckett, David 2008a On difference, discussing differences and comparisons. In Tuckett, David, Basile, Roberto, Birkstead-Breen, Dana, Bohm, Tomas, Denis, Paul, Ferro, Antonino, Hinz, Helmut, Jemstedt, Arne, Mariotti, Paola and Chubert, Johan, *Psychoanalysis Comparable and Incomparable*. London: Routledge.

Tuckett, David 2008b Reflection and evolution: Developing the two-step method. In Tuckett, David, Basile, Roberto, Birkstead-Breen, Dana, Bohm, Tomas, Denis, Paul, Ferro, Antonino, Hinz, Helmut, Jemstedt, Arne, Mariotti, Paola and Chubert, Johan, *Psychoanalysis Comparable and Incomparable*. London: Routledge.

Tuckett, David, Basile, Roberto, Birkstead-Breen, Dana, Bohm, Tomas, Denis, Paul, Ferro, Antonino, Hinz, Helmut, Jemstedt, Arne, Mariotti, Paola, and Chubert, Johan 2008 *Psychoanalysis Comparable and Incomparable*. London: Routledge.

Wallerstein, Robert 1964 The role of prediction in theory building in psychoanalysis. *Journal of the American Psychoanalytic Association* 12: 675–91.

Wallerstein, Robert 1984 The analysis of the transference: A matter of emphasis or of theory reformulation? *Psychoanalytic Inquiry* 4: 325–54.

Wallerstein, Robert 1986 *Forty-two Lives in Treatment*. New York: Guilford Press.

Wallerstein, Robert 1988 One psychoanalysis or many? *International Journal of Psychoanalysis* 69: 5–21.

Wallerstein, Robert 1990 Psychoanalysis: The common ground. *International Journal of Psychoanalysis* 71: 3–2.

Wallerstein, Robert 2000 Psychoanalytic research: Where do we disagree? In Sandler, Joseph, Sandler, Anne-Marie and Davies Rosemary (eds) *Clinical and Observational Psychoanalytic Research*. pp. 27–31. London: Karnac.

Wallerstein, Robert 2001 The generations of psychotherapy research. *Psychoanalytical Psychology* 18: 243–67.

Wallerstein, Robert 2005 Will psychoanalytic pluralism be an enduring state of our discipline? *International Journal of Psychoanalysis* 86: 623–6.

Wallerstein, Robert 2006 The relevance of Freud's psychoanalysis in the 21st Century. *Psychoanalytic Psycholology* 23: 302–26.

Webster, Richard 1995 *Why Freud Was Wrong: Sin, Science and Psychoanalysis*. Oxford: Orwell Press.

Weiss, Joseph 1988 Testing hypotheses about unconscious mental functioning. *International Journal of Psychoanalysis* 69: 87–95.

Weiss, Joseph 1992 The role of interpretation. *Psychoanalytic Inquiry* 12: 296–313.

Weiss, Joseph and Sampson, Harold 1986 *The Psychoanalytic Process*. New York: Guilford.

Weiss, Joseph, Sampson, Harold and O'Connor, Lynn 1995 How psychotherapy works: The findings of the San Francisco Psychotherapy Research Group. *Bulletin of the Psychoanalytic Research Society* 4: 13–19.

Werman, David 1988 Freud's 'narcissism of minor differences': A review and reassessment. *Journal of the American Academy of Psychoanalysis* 16: 451–9.

White, Robert 1996 Psychoanalytic process and interactive phenomena. *Journal of the American Psychoanalytic Association* 44: 699–722.

White, Robert 2001 The interpersonal and Freudian traditions. *Journal of the American Psychoanalytic Association* 49: 427–54.

Whitebook, Joel (2010) "Sigmund Freud – A philosophical physician." Lecture at the 11th Joseph Sandler Research Conference: Persisting shadows of early and later trauma. Frankfurt a.M., 2010.

Widlocher, Daniel 2003 Foreword. In Leuzinger-Bohleber, Marianne, Dreher, Anna Ursula, and Canestri, Jorge (eds) *Pluralism and Unity? Methods of Research in Psychoanalysis*. London: International Psychoanalytical Association.

Williams, Donald 1947 *The Ground of Induction*. Cambridge, MA: Harvard University Press.

Wisdom, John 1943 *Other Minds*. Oxford: Blackwell.

Wisdom, J.O. 1949 Regarding Aubrey Lewis's 'Philosophy and psychiatry' *Philosophy* XXIV(89): 1–19.

Wisdom, J.O. 1967 Testing an interpretation within a session. *International Journal of Psychoanalysis* 48: 44–52.

Wittgenstein, Ludwig [1942] 1966 Conversations on Freud. In *Lectures and Conversations on Aesthetics, Psychology and Religious Belief*. Oxford: Blackwell.

Wollheim, Richard 1984 *The Thread of Life*. Cambridge: Cambridge University Press.

Yeats, W.B. 1921 The second coming. In *Michael Robartes and the Dancer*. Dundrum: Cuala, 1921.

Yorke, Clifford 1971 Some suggestions for a critique of Kleinian psychology. *Psychoanalytic Study of the Child* 26: 129–55.

Zachrisson A. and Zachrisson, H.D. 2005 Validation of psychoanalytic theories: Toward a conceptualization of references. *International Journal of Psychoanalysis* 86: 1353–71.

Zetzel, Elizabeth 1956 An approach to the relation between concept and content in psychoanalytic theory – (with special reference to the work of Melanie Klein and her followers). *Psychoanalytic Study of the Child* 11: 99–121.

Index